EXILES

THE TRIAL OF THE EXILES

EXILES #7-8

SALADIN AHMED
WRITER

ROD REIS
WITH LEE FERGUSON
(PENCILS & INKS, PGS. 18-20)
ARTISTS #7

JOE QUINONES (PENCILS & INKS)
& JOE RIVERA (INKS)
ARTISTS #8

JORDAN GIBSON &
CHRIS SOTOMAYOR WITH
MUNTSA VICENTE
& JOE QUINONES
COLORISTS #8

MIKE McKONE
COVER ART

EXILES #9-12

SALADIN AHMED & JAVIER RODRÍGUEZ
STORYTELLERS

ÁLVARO LÓPEZ
INKER

MUNTSA VICENTE
COLORIST

DAVID NAKAYAMA
COVER ART

VC's JOE CARAMAGNA
LETTERER

SARAH BRUNSTAD
EDITOR

WIL MOSS
SUPERVISING EDITOR

TOM BREVOORT
EXECUTIVE EDITOR

COLLECTION EDITOR: Kateri Woody
ASSISTANT EDITOR: Caitlin O'Connell
EDITOR, SPECIAL PROJECTS: Mark D. Beazley
SENIOR EDITOR, SPECIAL PROJECTS: Jennifer Grünwald
VP PRODUCTION & SPECIAL PROJECTS: Jeff Youngquist
SVP PRINT, SALES & MARKETING: David Gabriel

BOOK DESIGNER: Adam Del Re

EDITOR IN CHIEF: C.B. Cebulski
CHIEF CREATIVE OFFICER: Joe Quesada
PRESIDENT: Dan Buckley
EXECUTIVE PRODUCER: Alan Fine

EXILES VOL. 2: THE TRIAL OF THE EXILES. Contains material originally published in magazine form as EXILES #7-12. First printing 2019. ISBN 978-1-302-91166-9. Published by MARVEL WORLDWIDE, INC., a subsidiary of MARVEL ENTERTAINMENT, LLC. OFFICE OF PUBLICATION: 135 West 50th Street, New York, NY 10020. **Printed in Canada.** DAN BUCKLEY, President, Marvel Entertainment; JOHN NEE, Publisher; JOE QUESADA, Chief Creative Officer; TOM BREVOORT, SVP of Publishing; DAVID BOGART, SVP of Business Affairs & Operations, Publishing & Partnership; DAVID GABRIEL, SVP of Sales & Marketing, Publishing; JEFF YOUNGQUIST, VP of Production & Special Projects; DAN CARR, Executive Director of Publishing Technology; ALEX MORALES, Director of Publishing Operations; DAN EDINGTON, Managing Editor; SUSAN CRESPI, Production Manager; STAN LEE, Chairman Emeritus. For information regarding advertising in Marvel Comics or on Marvel.com, please contact Vit DeBellis,

A mutant refugee from the Age of Apocalypse, Blink was a member of the original EXILES, a team of heroes plucked from their respective realities and tasked with stabilizing the dangerously shifting Multiverse. After saving reality many times over, Blink set out to live her own life. But the Multiverse keeps calling her...

When an entity known as the Time-Eater began destroying the Multiverse, a dimension-hopping device called the Tallus recruited a new team of Exiles composed of Blink and the alternate-universe heroes known as Iron Lad, Valkyrie and Wolvie. With the help of the Unseen — the being formerly known as Nick Fury, who is now cursed to watch all reality pass him by — the Exiles defeated the Time-Eater and saved the Multiverse.

But during their adventures, Blink learned that her old team had gotten separated and was lost in the Multiverse. When she resolved to rescue them, the Exiles rallied around their leader's cause. Somehow sensing their collective intention, the Tallus brought the team to the Wild West, where they hoped to find Blink's lost friends. So far, all they've found is the dreaded Magnus Gang, headed by the sharpshooting Magneto! The Gang kidnapped Iron Lad, and to get him back, the Exiles will need help from a man called "King" — A.K.A. T'Challa, the Black Panther of the West!

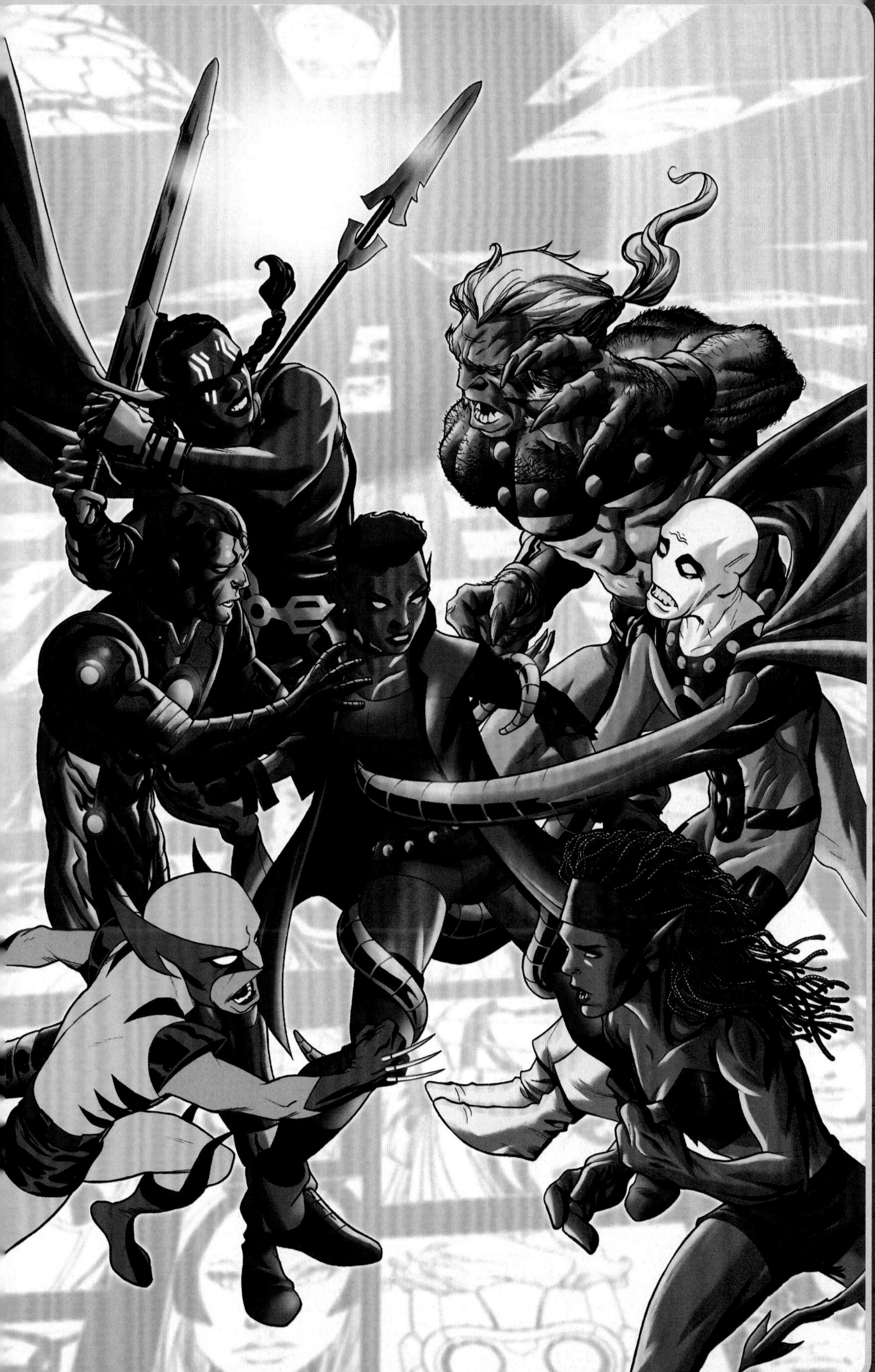

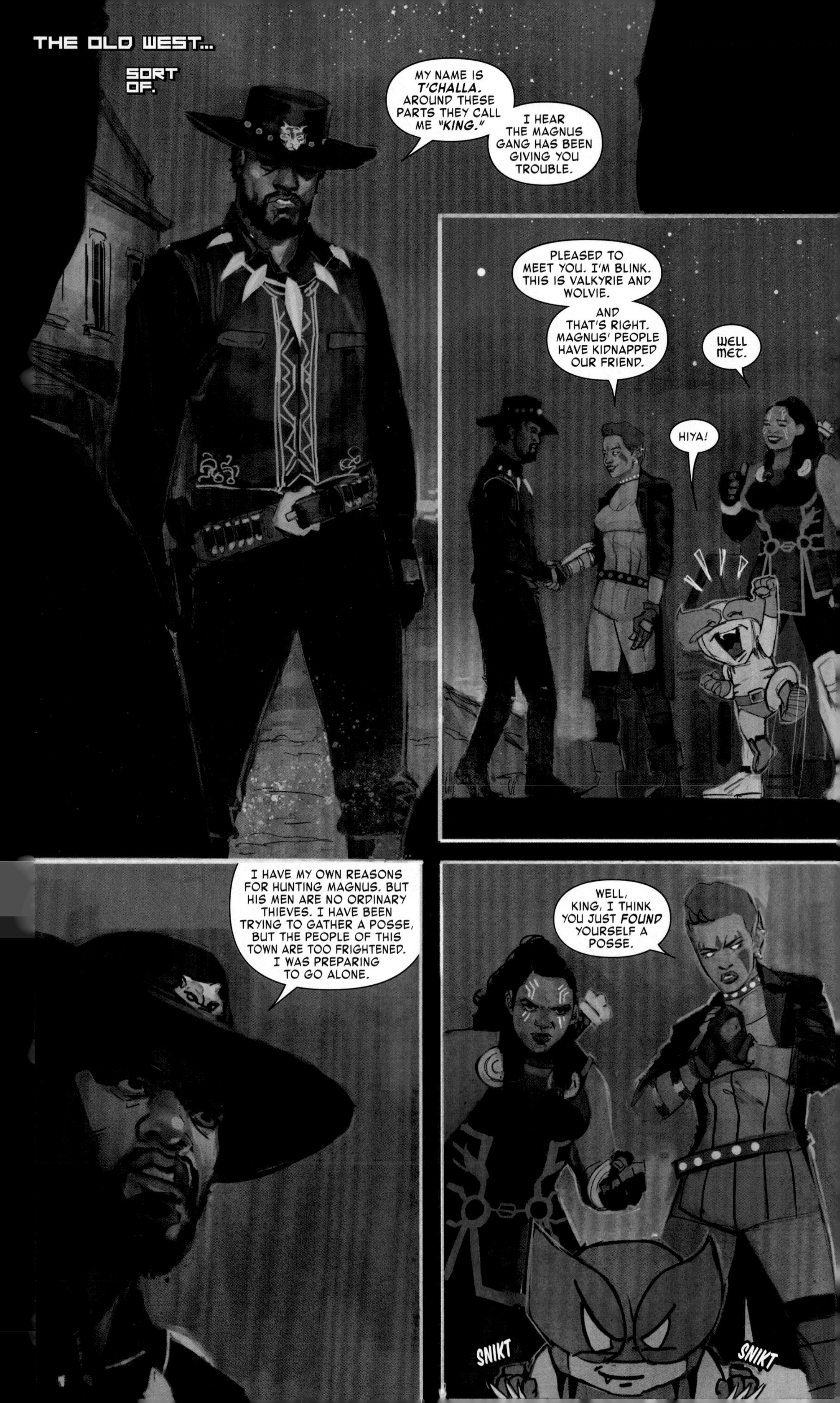
THE OLD WEST...
SORT OF.
MY NAME IS T'CHALLA. AROUND THESE PARTS THEY CALL ME "KING."
I HEAR THE MAGNUS GANG HAS BEEN GIVING YOU TROUBLE.
PLEASED TO MEET YOU. I'M BLINK. THIS IS VALKYRIE AND WOLVIE.
AND THAT'S RIGHT. MAGNUS' PEOPLE HAVE KIDNAPPED OUR FRIEND.
WELL MET.
HIYA!
I HAVE MY OWN REASONS FOR HUNTING MAGNUS. BUT HIS MEN ARE NO ORDINARY THIEVES. I HAVE BEEN TRYING TO GATHER A POSSE, BUT THE PEOPLE OF THIS TOWN ARE TOO FRIGHTENED. I WAS PREPARING TO GO ALONE.
WELL, KING, I THINK YOU JUST FOUND YOURSELF A POSSE.
SNIKT
SNIKT

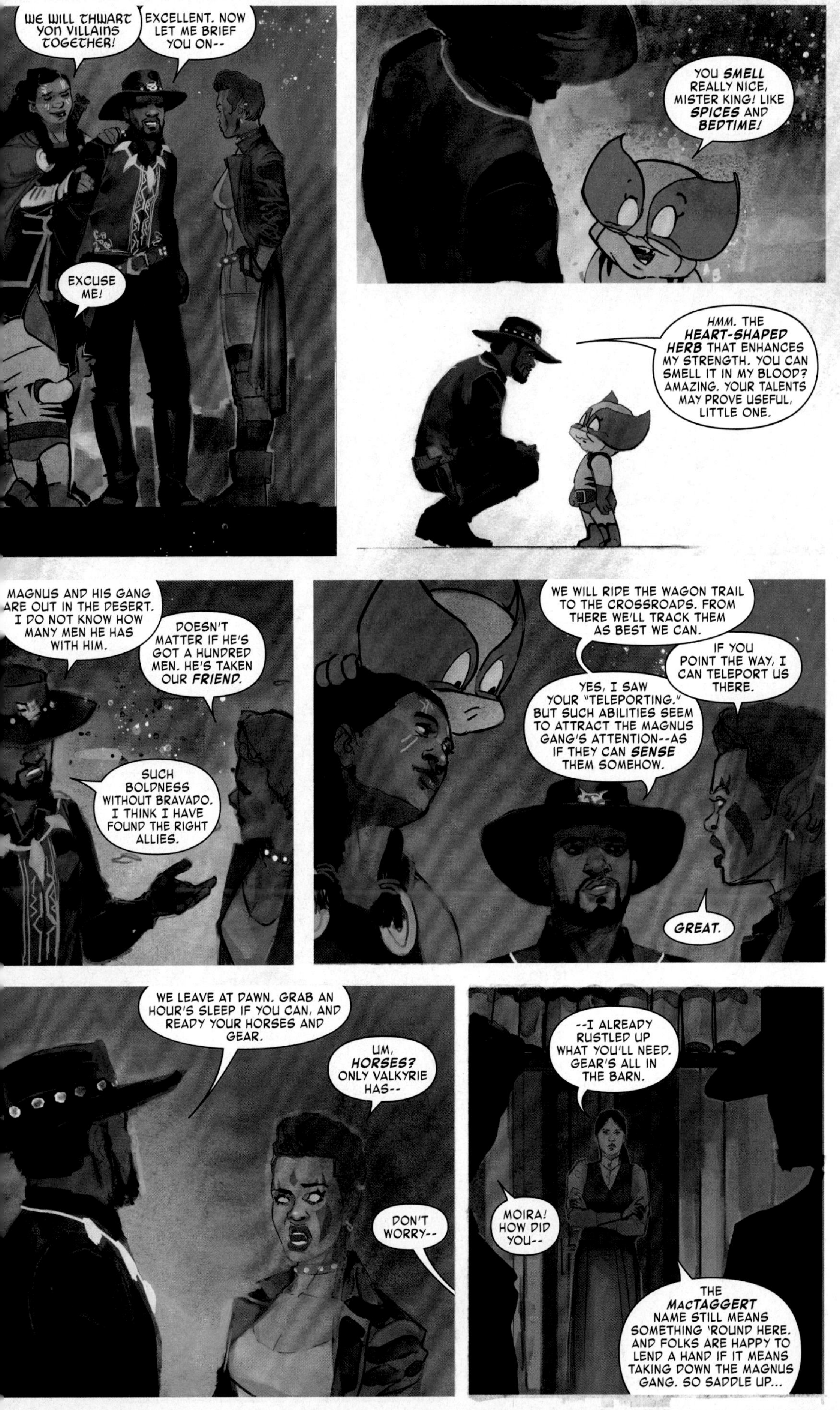
WE WILL THWART YON VILLAINS TOGETHER!
EXCELLENT. NOW LET ME BRIEF YOU ON--
EXCUSE ME!
YOU SMELL REALLY NICE, MISTER KING! LIKE SPICES AND BEDTIME!
HMM. THE HEART-SHAPED HERB THAT ENHANCES MY STRENGTH. YOU CAN SMELL IT IN MY BLOOD? AMAZING. YOUR TALENTS MAY PROVE USEFUL, LITTLE ONE.
MAGNUS AND HIS GANG ARE OUT IN THE DESERT. I DO NOT KNOW HOW MANY MEN HE HAS WITH HIM.
DOESN'T MATTER IF HE'S GOT A HUNDRED MEN. HE'S TAKEN OUR FRIEND.
SUCH BOLDNESS WITHOUT BRAVADO. I THINK I HAVE FOUND THE RIGHT ALLIES.
WE WILL RIDE THE WAGON TRAIL TO THE CROSSROADS. FROM THERE WE'LL TRACK THEM AS BEST WE CAN.
IF YOU POINT THE WAY, I CAN TELEPORT US THERE.
YES, I SAW YOUR "TELEPORTING." BUT SUCH ABILITIES SEEM TO ATTRACT THE MAGNUS GANG'S ATTENTION--AS IF THEY CAN SENSE THEM SOMEHOW.
GREAT.
WE LEAVE AT DAWN. GRAB AN HOUR'S SLEEP IF YOU CAN, AND READY YOUR HORSES AND GEAR.
UM, HORSES? ONLY VALKYRIE HAS--
DON'T WORRY--
--I ALREADY RUSTLED UP WHAT YOU'LL NEED. GEAR'S ALL IN THE BARN.
MOIRA! HOW DID YOU--
THE MacTAGGERT NAME STILL MEANS SOMETHING 'ROUND HERE. AND FOLKS ARE HAPPY TO LEND A HAND IF IT MEANS TAKING DOWN THE MAGNUS GANG. SO SADDLE UP...

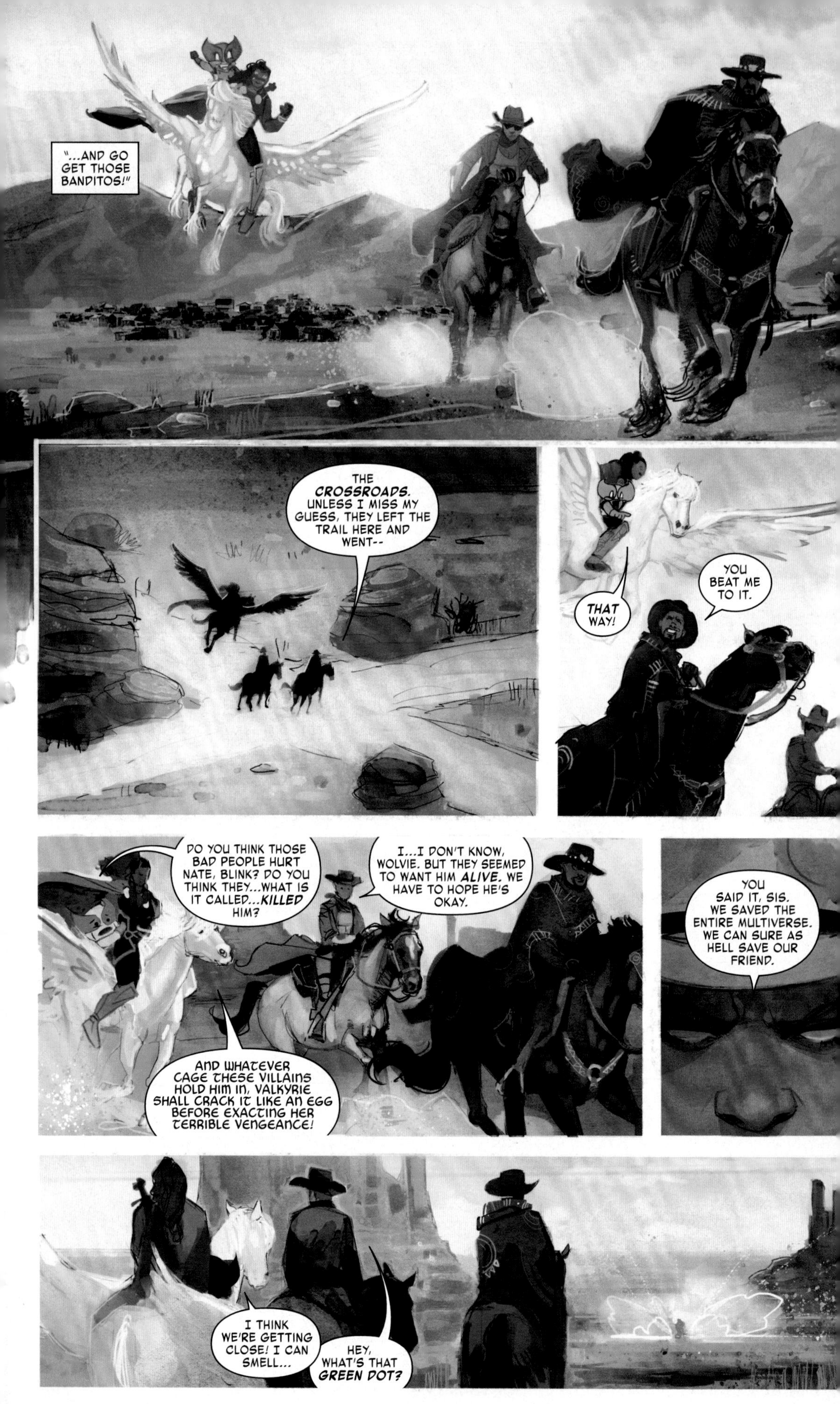
"...AND GO GET THOSE BANDITOS!"
THE *CROSSROADS.* UNLESS I MISS MY GUESS, THEY LEFT THE TRAIL HERE AND WENT--
THAT WAY!
YOU BEAT ME TO IT.
DO YOU THINK THOSE BAD PEOPLE HURT NATE, BLINK? DO YOU THINK THEY...WHAT IS IT CALLED...*KILLED* HIM?
I...I DON'T KNOW, WOLVIE. BUT THEY SEEMED TO WANT HIM *ALIVE.* WE HAVE TO HOPE HE'S OKAY.
AND WHATEVER CAGE THESE VILLAINS HOLD HIM IN, VALKYRIE SHALL CRACK IT LIKE AN EGG BEFORE EXACTING HER TERRIBLE VENGEANCE!
YOU SAID IT, SIS. WE SAVED THE ENTIRE MULTIVERSE. WE CAN SURE AS HELL SAVE OUR FRIEND.
I THINK WE'RE GETTING CLOSE! I CAN SMELL...
HEY, WHAT'S THAT *GREEN DOT?*

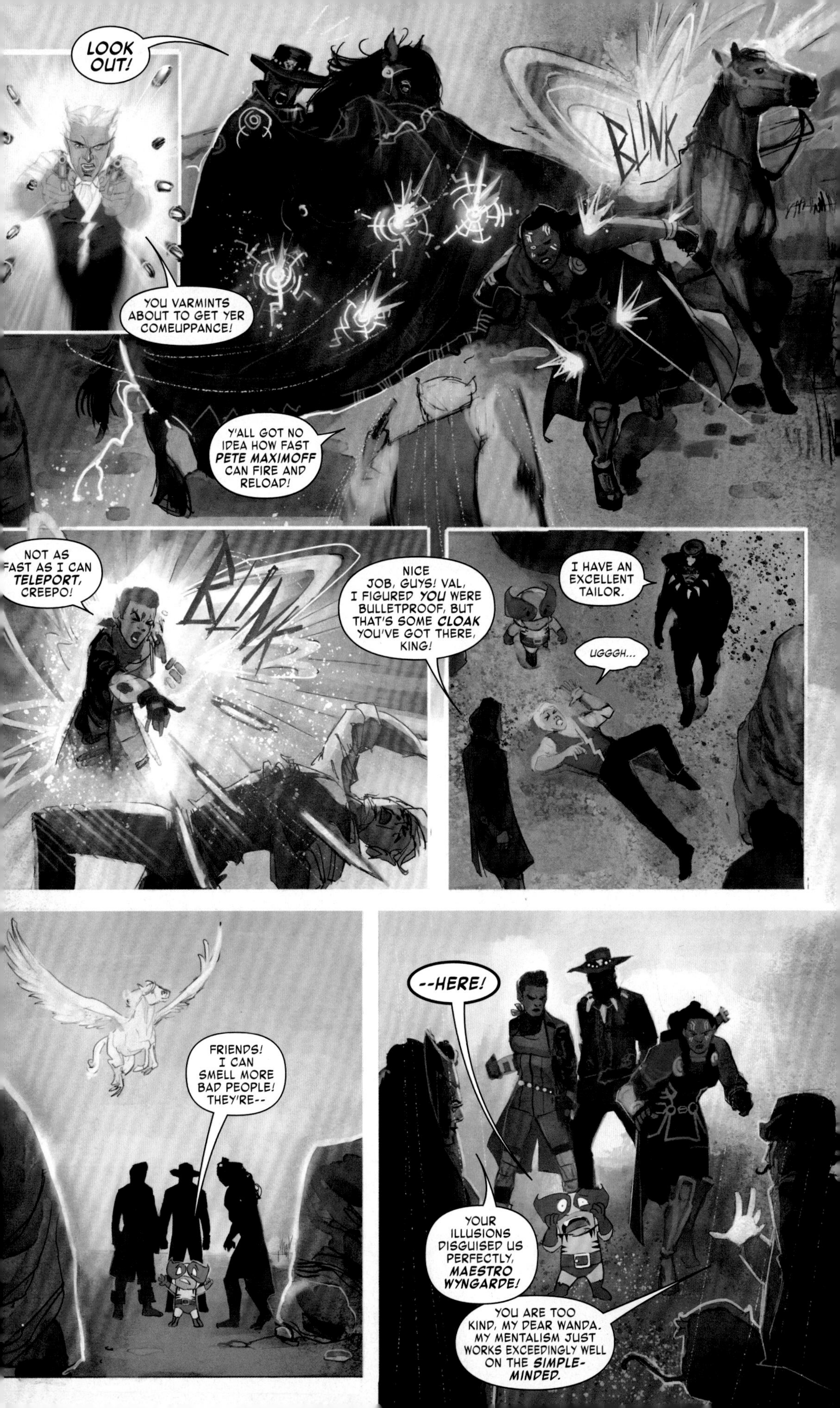
LOOK OUT!
YOU VARMINTS ABOUT TO GET YER COMEUPPANCE!
BLINK
Y'ALL GOT NO IDEA HOW FAST PETE MAXIMOFF CAN FIRE AND RELOAD!
NOT AS FAST AS I CAN TELEPORT, CREEPO!
BLINK
NICE JOB, GUYS! VAL, I FIGURED YOU WERE BULLETPROOF, BUT THAT'S SOME CLOAK YOU'VE GOT THERE, KING!
I HAVE AN EXCELLENT TAILOR.
UGGGH...
FRIENDS! I CAN SMELL MORE BAD PEOPLE! THEY'RE--
--HERE!
YOUR ILLUSIONS DISGUISED US PERFECTLY, MAESTRO WYNGARDE!
YOU ARE TOO KIND, MY DEAR WANDA. MY MENTALISM JUST WORKS EXCEEDINGLY WELL ON THE SIMPLE-MINDED.

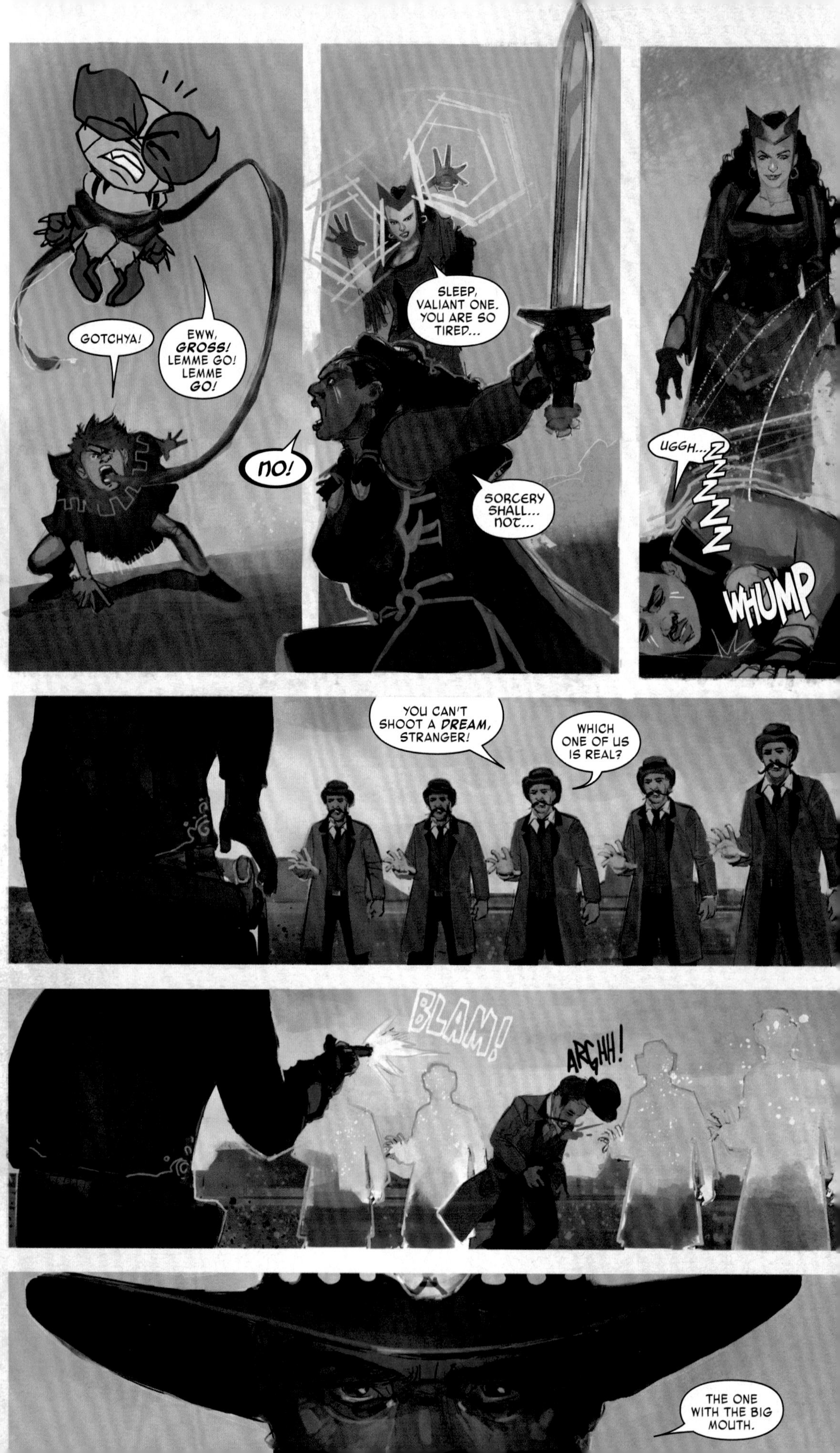
GOTCHYA!
EWW, GROSS! LEMME GO! LEMME GO!
NO!
SLEEP, VALIANT ONE. YOU ARE SO TIRED...
SORCERY SHALL... NOT...
UGGH...
ZZZZZ
WHUMP
YOU CAN'T SHOOT A DREAM, STRANGER!
WHICH ONE OF US IS REAL?
BLAM!
ARGHH!
THE ONE WITH THE BIG MOUTH.

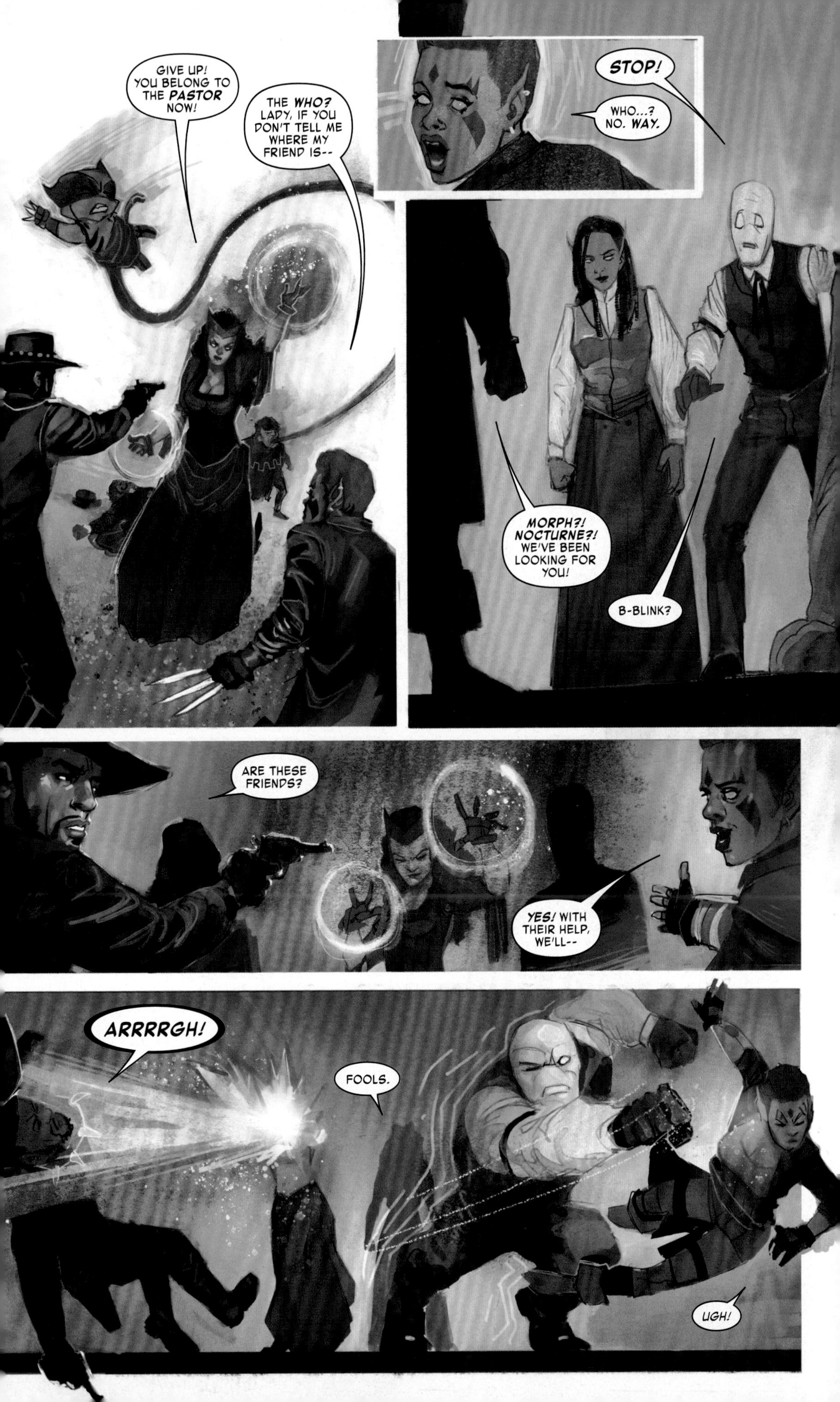
GIVE UP! YOU BELONG TO THE PASTOR NOW!
THE WHO? LADY, IF YOU DON'T TELL ME WHERE MY FRIEND IS--
STOP!
WHO...? NO. WAY.
MORPH?! NOCTURNE?! WE'VE BEEN LOOKING FOR YOU!
B-BLINK?
ARE THESE FRIENDS?
YES! WITH THEIR HELP, WE'LL--
ARRRRGH!
FOOLS.
UGH!

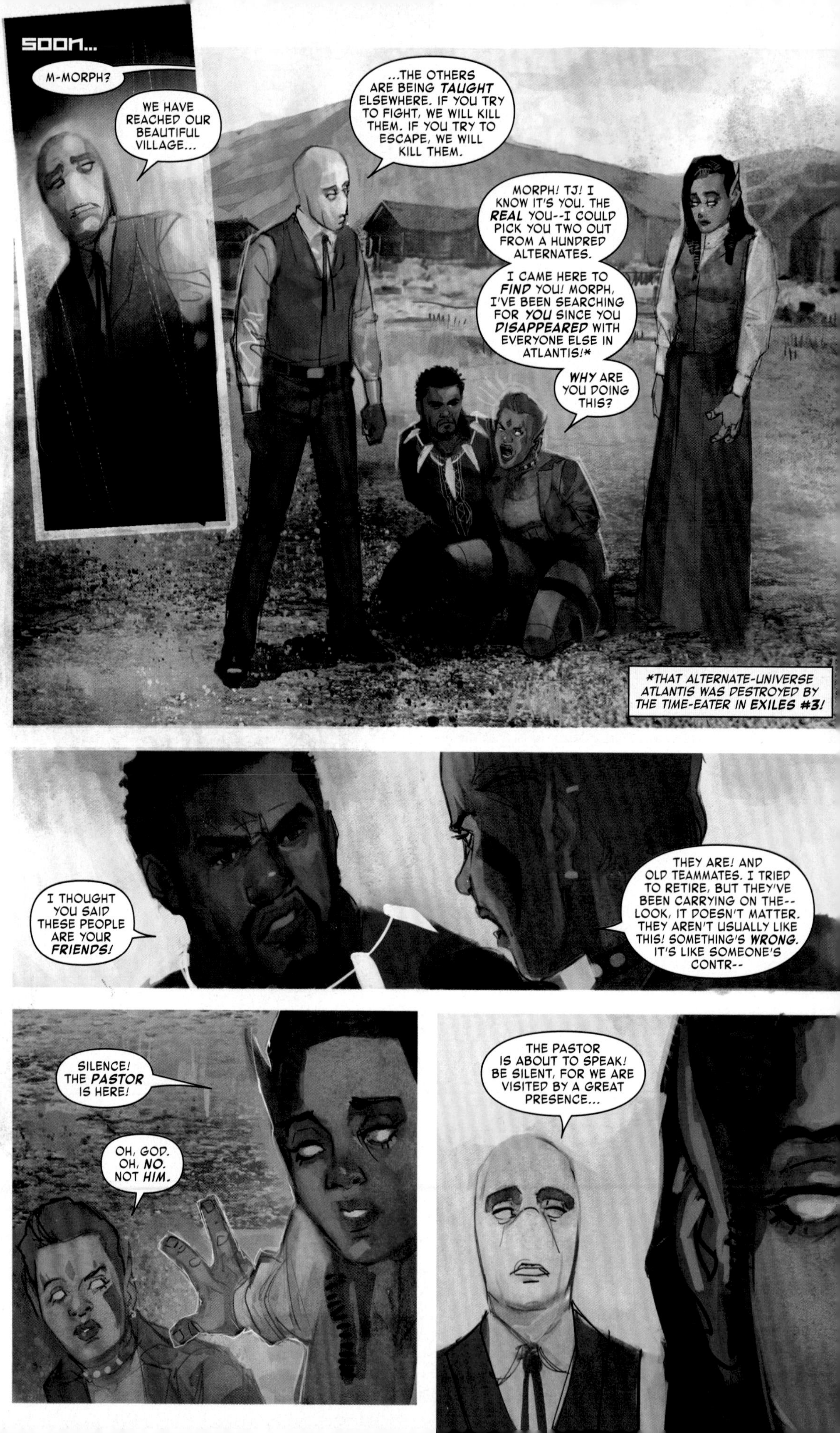
SOON...
M-MORPH?
WE HAVE REACHED OUR BEAUTIFUL VILLAGE...
...THE OTHERS ARE BEING TAUGHT ELSEWHERE. IF YOU TRY TO FIGHT, WE WILL KILL THEM. IF YOU TRY TO ESCAPE, WE WILL KILL THEM.
MORPH! TJ! I KNOW IT'S YOU. THE REAL YOU--I COULD PICK YOU TWO OUT FROM A HUNDRED ALTERNATES.
I CAME HERE TO FIND YOU! MORPH, I'VE BEEN SEARCHING FOR YOU SINCE YOU DISAPPEARED WITH EVERYONE ELSE IN ATLANTIS!*
WHY ARE YOU DOING THIS?
*THAT ALTERNATE-UNIVERSE ATLANTIS WAS DESTROYED BY THE TIME-EATER IN EXILES #3!
I THOUGHT YOU SAID THESE PEOPLE ARE YOUR FRIENDS!
THEY ARE! AND OLD TEAMMATES. I TRIED TO RETIRE, BUT THEY'VE BEEN CARRYING ON THE--LOOK, IT DOESN'T MATTER. THEY AREN'T USUALLY LIKE THIS! SOMETHING'S WRONG. IT'S LIKE SOMEONE'S CONTR--
SILENCE! THE PASTOR IS HERE!
OH, GOD. OH, NO. NOT HIM.
THE PASTOR IS ABOUT TO SPEAK! BE SILENT, FOR WE ARE VISITED BY A GREAT PRESENCE...

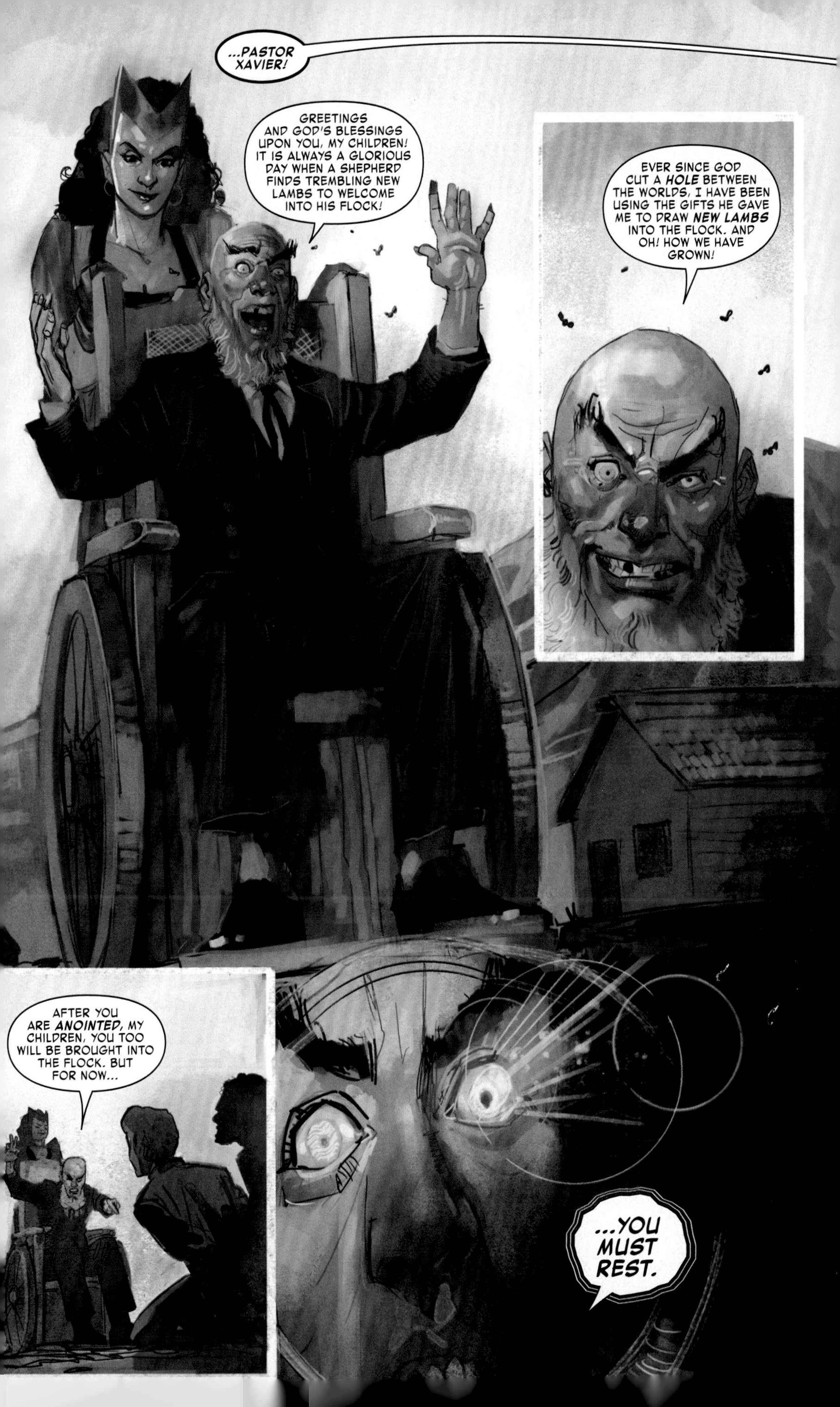
...PASTOR XAVIER!
GREETINGS AND GOD'S BLESSINGS UPON YOU, MY CHILDREN! IT IS ALWAYS A GLORIOUS DAY WHEN A SHEPHERD FINDS TREMBLING NEW LAMBS TO WELCOME INTO HIS FLOCK!
EVER SINCE GOD CUT A HOLE BETWEEN THE WORLDS, I HAVE BEEN USING THE GIFTS HE GAVE ME TO DRAW NEW LAMBS INTO THE FLOCK. AND OH! HOW WE HAVE GROWN!
AFTER YOU ARE ANOINTED, MY CHILDREN, YOU TOO WILL BE BROUGHT INTO THE FLOCK. BUT FOR NOW...
...YOU MUST REST.

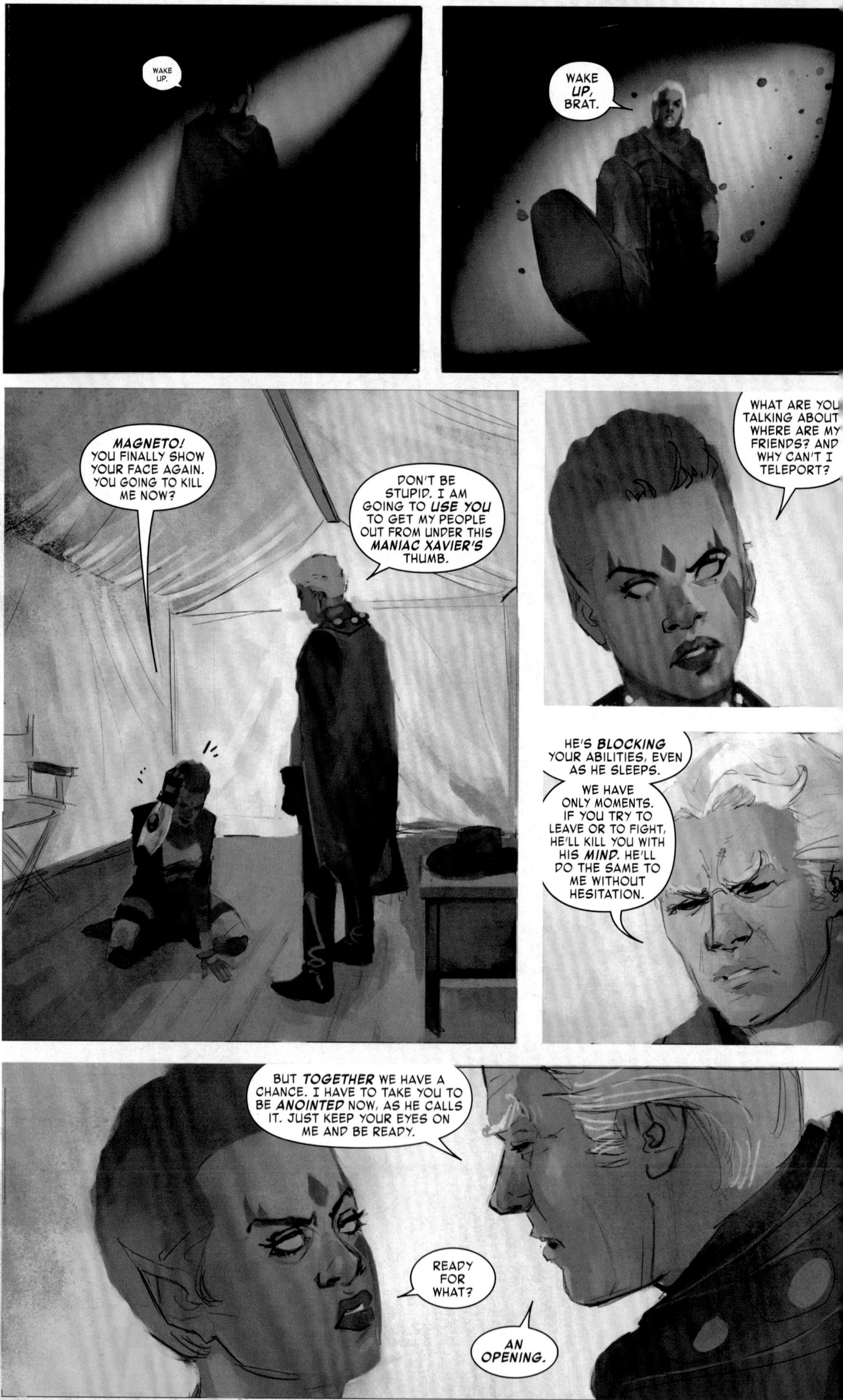
WAKE UP.
WAKE UP, BRAT.
MAGNETO! YOU FINALLY SHOW YOUR FACE AGAIN. YOU GOING TO KILL ME NOW?
DON'T BE STUPID. I AM GOING TO USE YOU TO GET MY PEOPLE OUT FROM UNDER THIS MANIAC XAVIER'S THUMB.
WHAT ARE YOU TALKING ABOUT? WHERE ARE MY FRIENDS? AND WHY CAN'T I TELEPORT?
HE'S BLOCKING YOUR ABILITIES, EVEN AS HE SLEEPS.
WE HAVE ONLY MOMENTS. IF YOU TRY TO LEAVE OR TO FIGHT, HE'LL KILL YOU WITH HIS MIND. HE'LL DO THE SAME TO ME WITHOUT HESITATION.
BUT TOGETHER WE HAVE A CHANCE. I HAVE TO TAKE YOU TO BE ANOINTED NOW, AS HE CALLS IT. JUST KEEP YOUR EYES ON ME AND BE READY.
READY FOR WHAT?
AN OPENING.

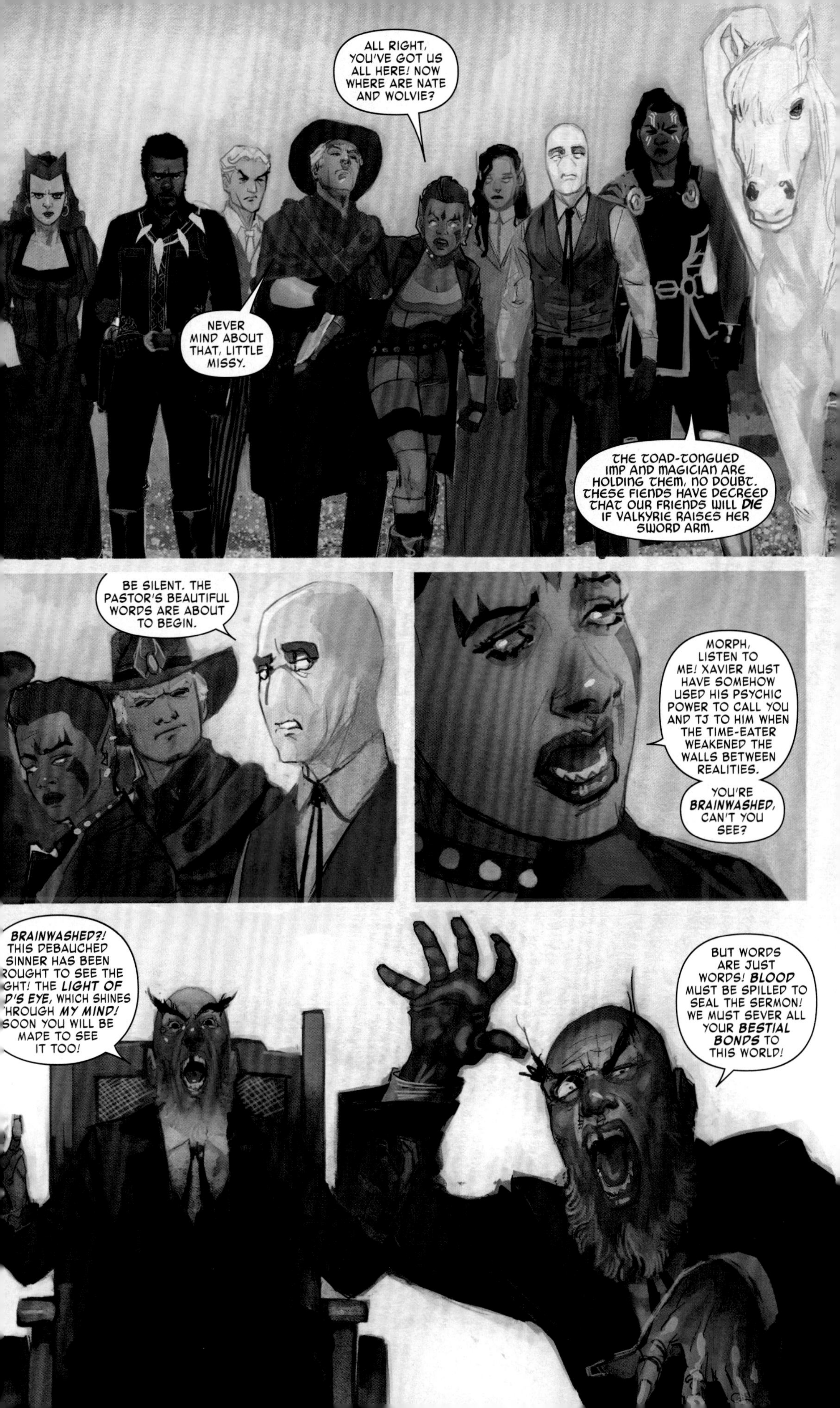

ALL RIGHT, YOU'VE GOT US ALL HERE! NOW WHERE ARE NATE AND WOLVIE?
NEVER MIND ABOUT THAT, LITTLE MISSY.
THE TOAD-TONGUED IMP AND MAGICIAN ARE HOLDING THEM, NO DOUBT. THESE FIENDS HAVE DECREED THAT OUR FRIENDS WILL DIE IF VALKYRIE RAISES HER SWORD ARM.
BE SILENT. THE PASTOR'S BEAUTIFUL WORDS ARE ABOUT TO BEGIN.
MORPH, LISTEN TO ME! XAVIER MUST HAVE SOMEHOW USED HIS PSYCHIC POWER TO CALL YOU AND TJ TO HIM WHEN THE TIME-EATER WEAKENED THE WALLS BETWEEN REALITIES.
YOU'RE BRAINWASHED, CAN'T YOU SEE?
BRAINWASHED?! THIS DEBAUCHED SINNER HAS BEEN ROUGHT TO SEE THE GHT! THE LIGHT OF D'S EYE, WHICH SHINES THROUGH MY MIND! SOON YOU WILL BE MADE TO SEE IT TOO!
BUT WORDS ARE JUST WORDS! BLOOD MUST BE SPILLED TO SEAL THE SERMON! WE MUST SEVER ALL YOUR BESTIAL BONDS TO THIS WORLD!

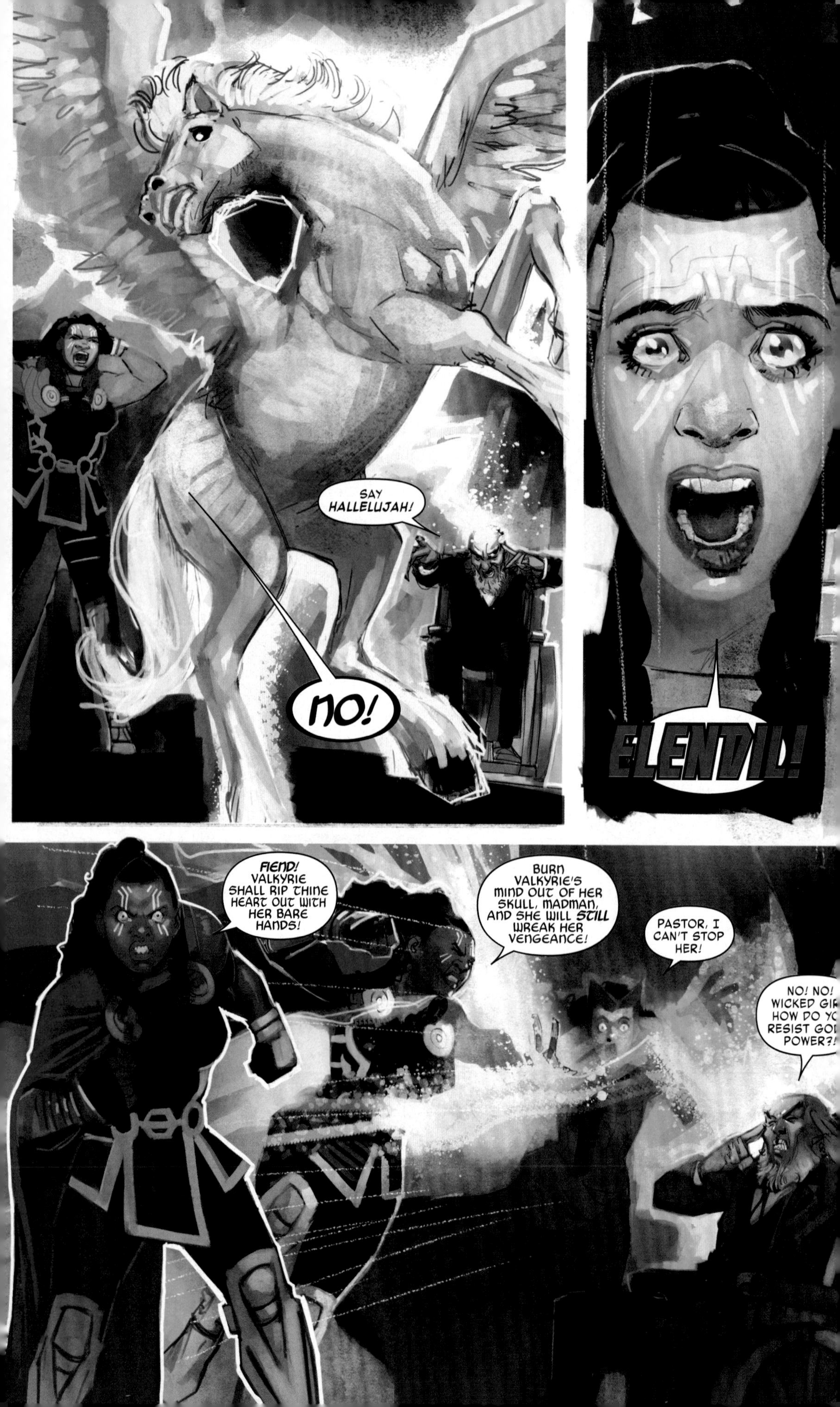

SAY HALLELUJAH!
NO!
ELENDIL!
FIEND! VALKYRIE SHALL RIP THINE HEART OUT WITH HER BARE HANDS!
BURN VALKYRIE'S MIND OUT OF HER SKULL, MADMAN, AND SHE WILL STILL WREAK HER VENGEANCE!
PASTOR, I CAN'T STOP HER!
NO! NO! WICKED GI HOW DO Y RESIST GO POWER?!

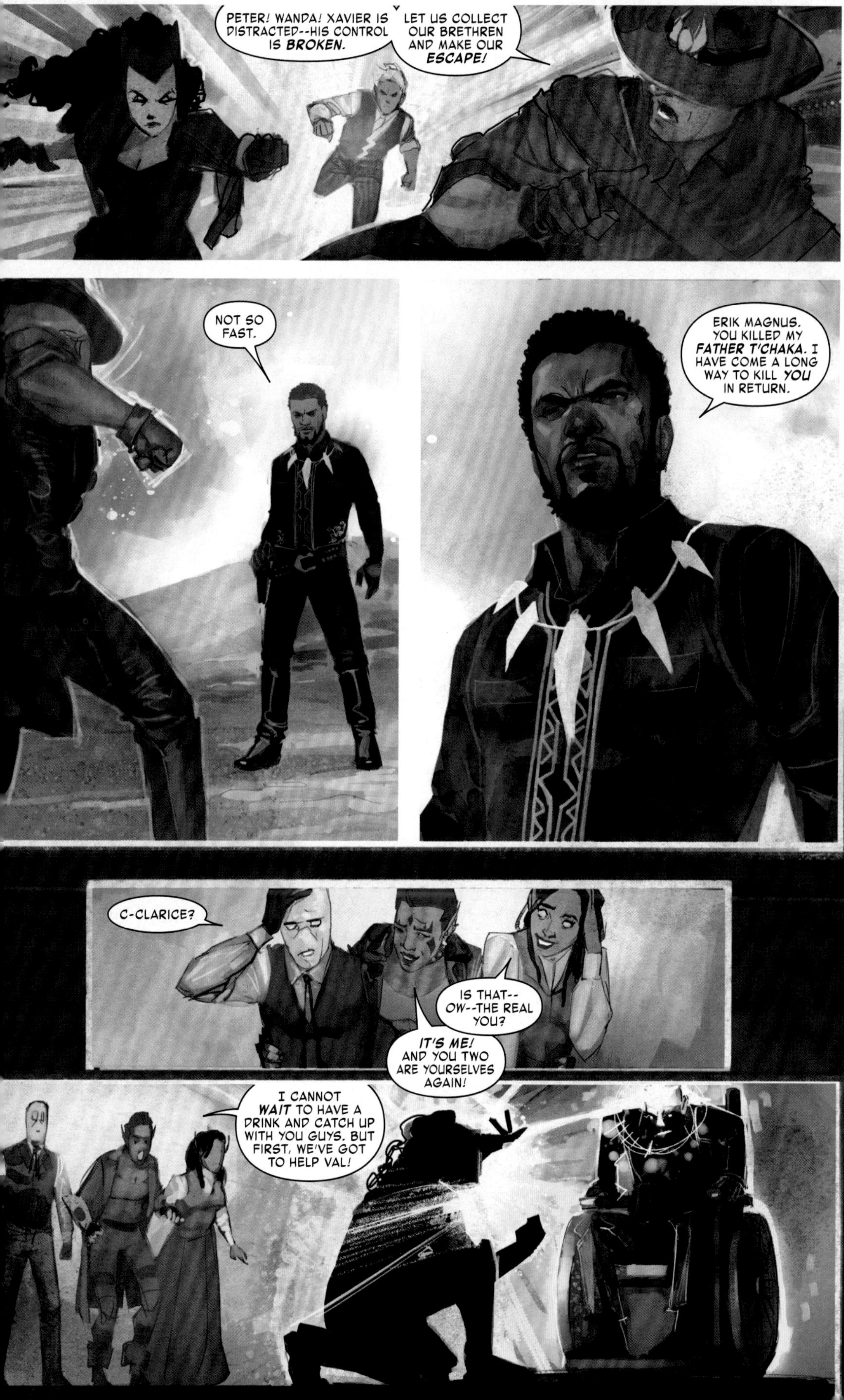
PETER! WANDA! XAVIER IS DISTRACTED--HIS CONTROL IS BROKEN.
LET US COLLECT OUR BRETHREN AND MAKE OUR ESCAPE!
NOT SO FAST.
ERIK MAGNUS. YOU KILLED MY FATHER T'CHAKA. I HAVE COME A LONG WAY TO KILL YOU IN RETURN.
C-CLARICE?
IS THAT-- OW--THE REAL YOU?
IT'S ME! AND YOU TWO ARE YOURSELVES AGAIN!
I CANNOT WAIT TO HAVE A DRINK AND CATCH UP WITH YOU GUYS. BUT FIRST, WE'VE GOT TO HELP VAL!

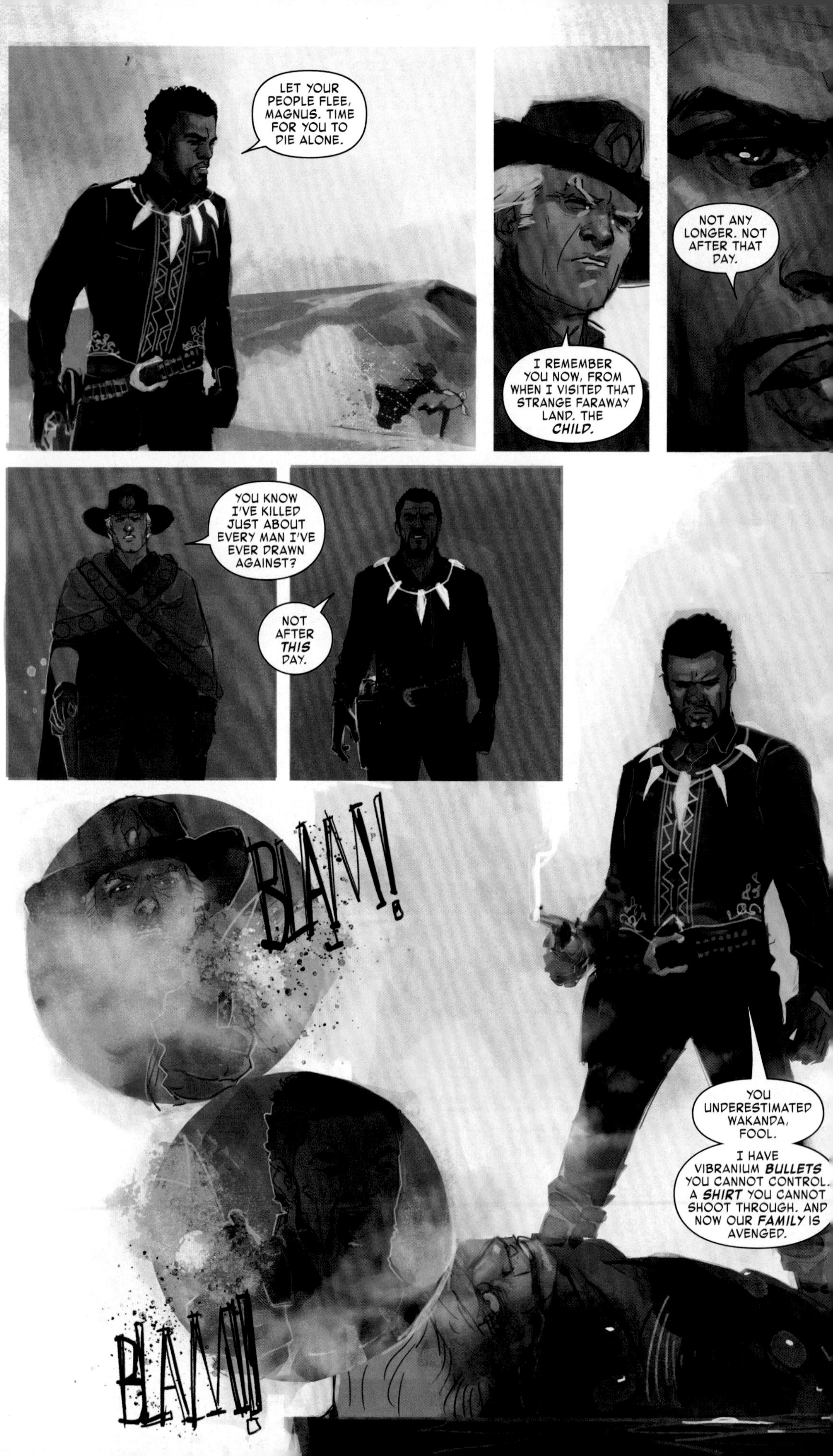
LET YOUR PEOPLE FLEE, MAGNUS. TIME FOR YOU TO DIE ALONE.
I REMEMBER YOU NOW, FROM WHEN I VISITED THAT STRANGE FARAWAY LAND. THE *CHILD.*
NOT ANY LONGER. NOT AFTER THAT DAY.
YOU KNOW I'VE KILLED JUST ABOUT EVERY MAN I'VE EVER DRAWN AGAINST?
NOT AFTER *THIS* DAY.
BLAM!
BLAM!
YOU UNDERESTIMATED WAKANDA, FOOL.
I HAVE VIBRANIUM *BULLETS* YOU CANNOT CONTROL. A *SHIRT* YOU CANNOT SHOOT THROUGH. AND NOW OUR *FAMILY* IS AVENGED.

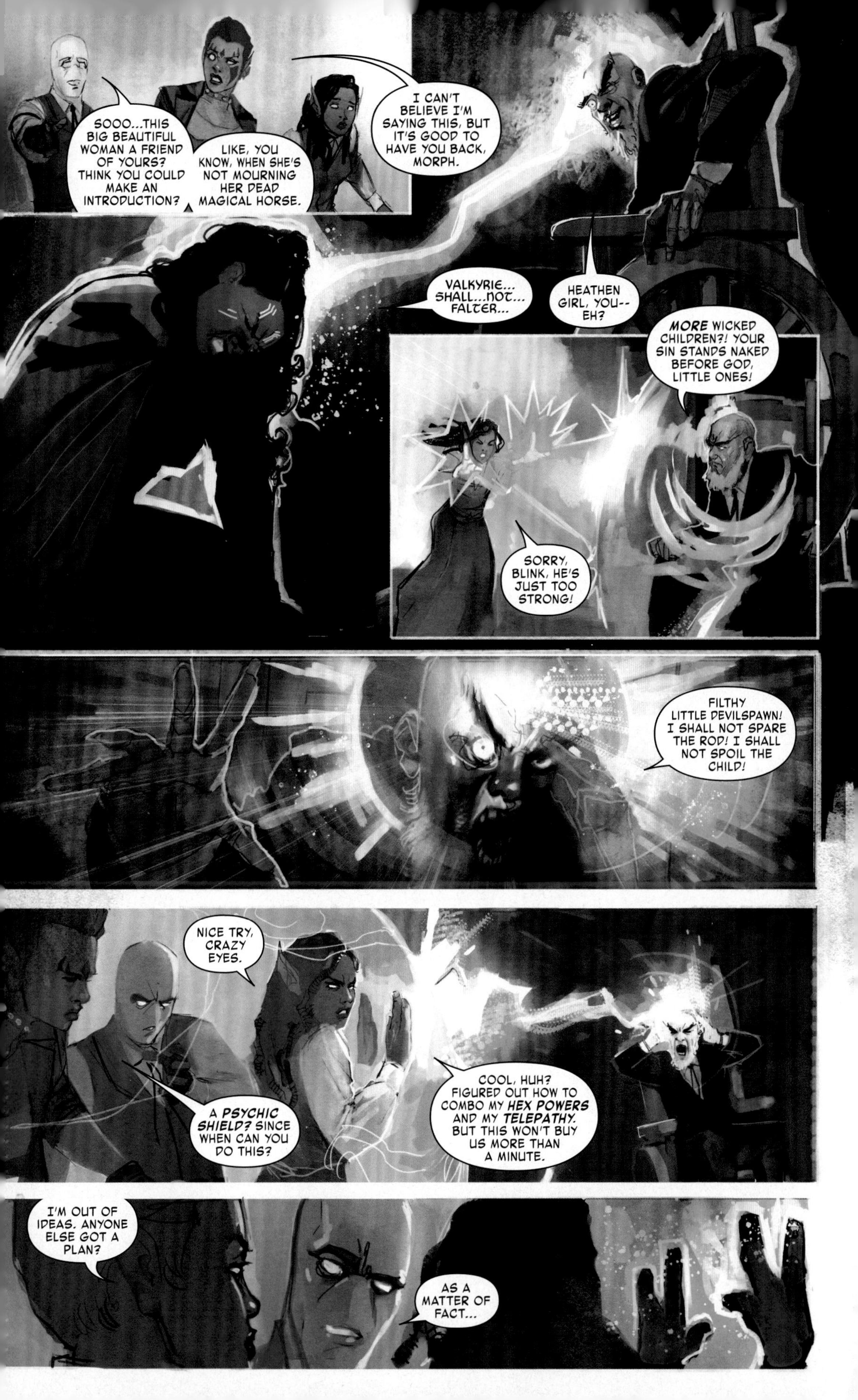
SOOO...THIS BIG BEAUTIFUL WOMAN A FRIEND OF YOURS? THINK YOU COULD MAKE AN INTRODUCTION?
LIKE, YOU KNOW, WHEN SHE'S NOT MOURNING HER DEAD MAGICAL HORSE.
I CAN'T BELIEVE I'M SAYING THIS, BUT IT'S GOOD TO HAVE YOU BACK, MORPH.
VALKYRIE... SHALL...NOT... FALTER...
HEATHEN GIRL, YOU-- EH?
MORE WICKED CHILDREN?! YOUR SIN STANDS NAKED BEFORE GOD, LITTLE ONES!
SORRY, BLINK, HE'S JUST TOO STRONG!
FILTHY LITTLE DEVILSPAWN! I SHALL NOT SPARE THE ROD! I SHALL NOT SPOIL THE CHILD!
NICE TRY, CRAZY EYES.
A PSYCHIC SHIELD? SINCE WHEN CAN YOU DO THIS?
COOL, HUH? FIGURED OUT HOW TO COMBO MY HEX POWERS AND MY TELEPATHY. BUT THIS WON'T BUY US MORE THAN A MINUTE.
I'M OUT OF IDEAS. ANYONE ELSE GOT A PLAN?
AS A MATTER OF FACT...

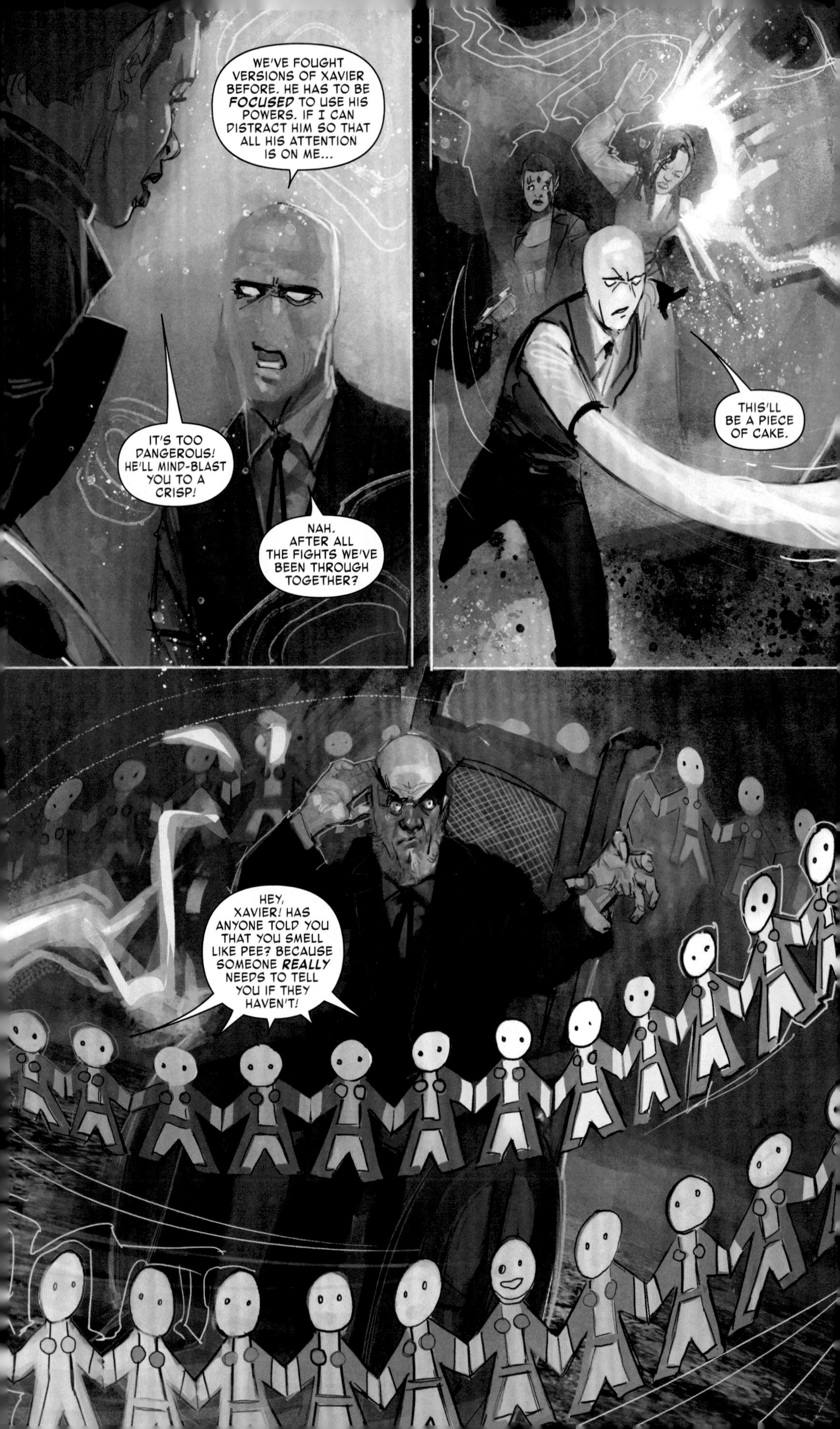
WE'VE FOUGHT VERSIONS OF XAVIER BEFORE. HE HAS TO BE FOCUSED TO USE HIS POWERS. IF I CAN DISTRACT HIM SO THAT ALL HIS ATTENTION IS ON ME...
IT'S TOO DANGEROUS! HE'LL MIND-BLAST YOU TO A CRISP!
NAH. AFTER ALL THE FIGHTS WE'VE BEEN THROUGH TOGETHER?
THIS'LL BE A PIECE OF CAKE.
HEY, XAVIER! HAS ANYONE TOLD YOU THAT YOU SMELL LIKE PEE? BECAUSE SOMEONE REALLY NEEDS TO TELL YOU IF THEY HAVEN'T!

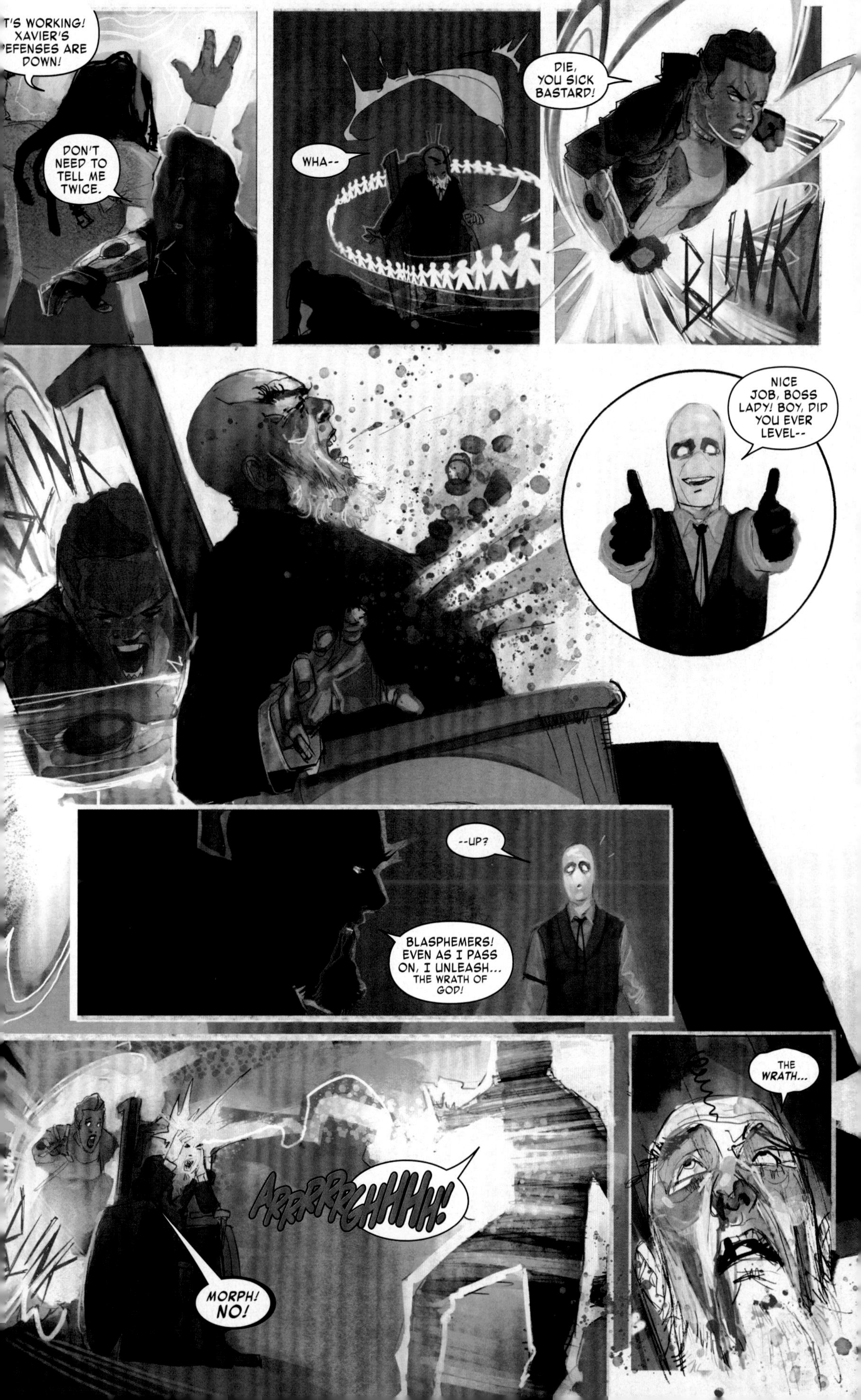

T'S WORKING! XAVIER'S 'EFENSES ARE DOWN!
DON'T NEED TO TELL ME TWICE.
WHA--
DIE, YOU SICK BASTARD!
BLINK!
NICE JOB, BOSS LADY! BOY, DID YOU EVER LEVEL--
--UP?
BLASPHEMERS! EVEN AS I PASS ON, I UNLEASH... THE WRATH OF GOD!
ARRRRRGHHHHH!
MORPH! NO!
THE WRATH...

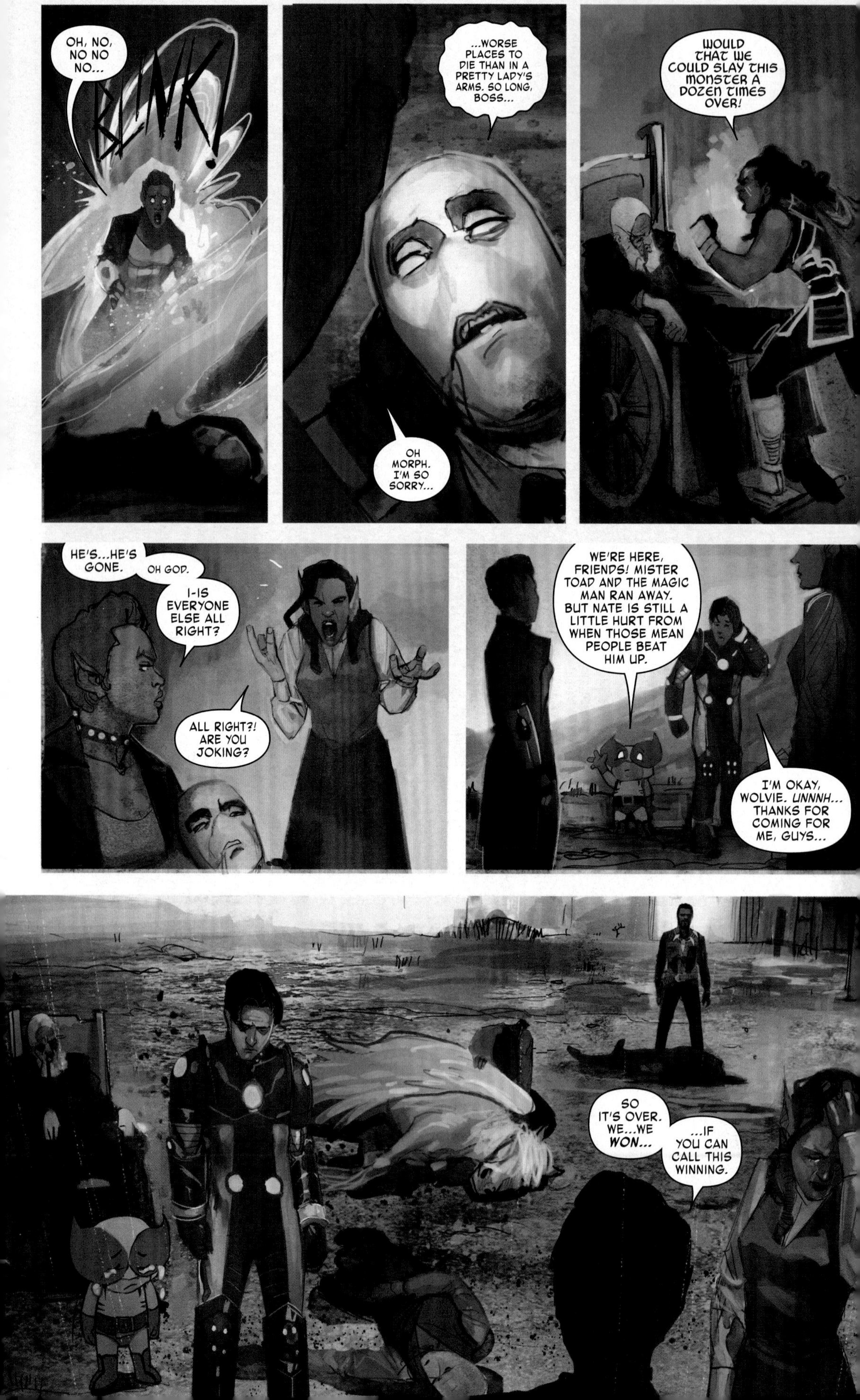

OH, NO, NO NO NO...
BLINK!
...WORSE PLACES TO DIE THAN IN A PRETTY LADY'S ARMS. SO LONG, BOSS...
OH MORPH. I'M SO SORRY...
WOULD THAT WE COULD SLAY THIS MONSTER A DOZEN TIMES OVER!
HE'S...HE'S GONE.
OH GOD.
I-IS EVERYONE ELSE ALL RIGHT?
ALL RIGHT?! ARE YOU JOKING?
WE'RE HERE, FRIENDS! MISTER TOAD AND THE MAGIC MAN RAN AWAY. BUT NATE IS STILL A LITTLE HURT FROM WHEN THOSE MEAN PEOPLE BEAT HIM UP.
I'M OKAY, WOLVIE. UNNNH... THANKS FOR COMING FOR ME, GUYS...
SO IT'S OVER. WE...WE WON...
...IF YOU CAN CALL THIS WINNING.

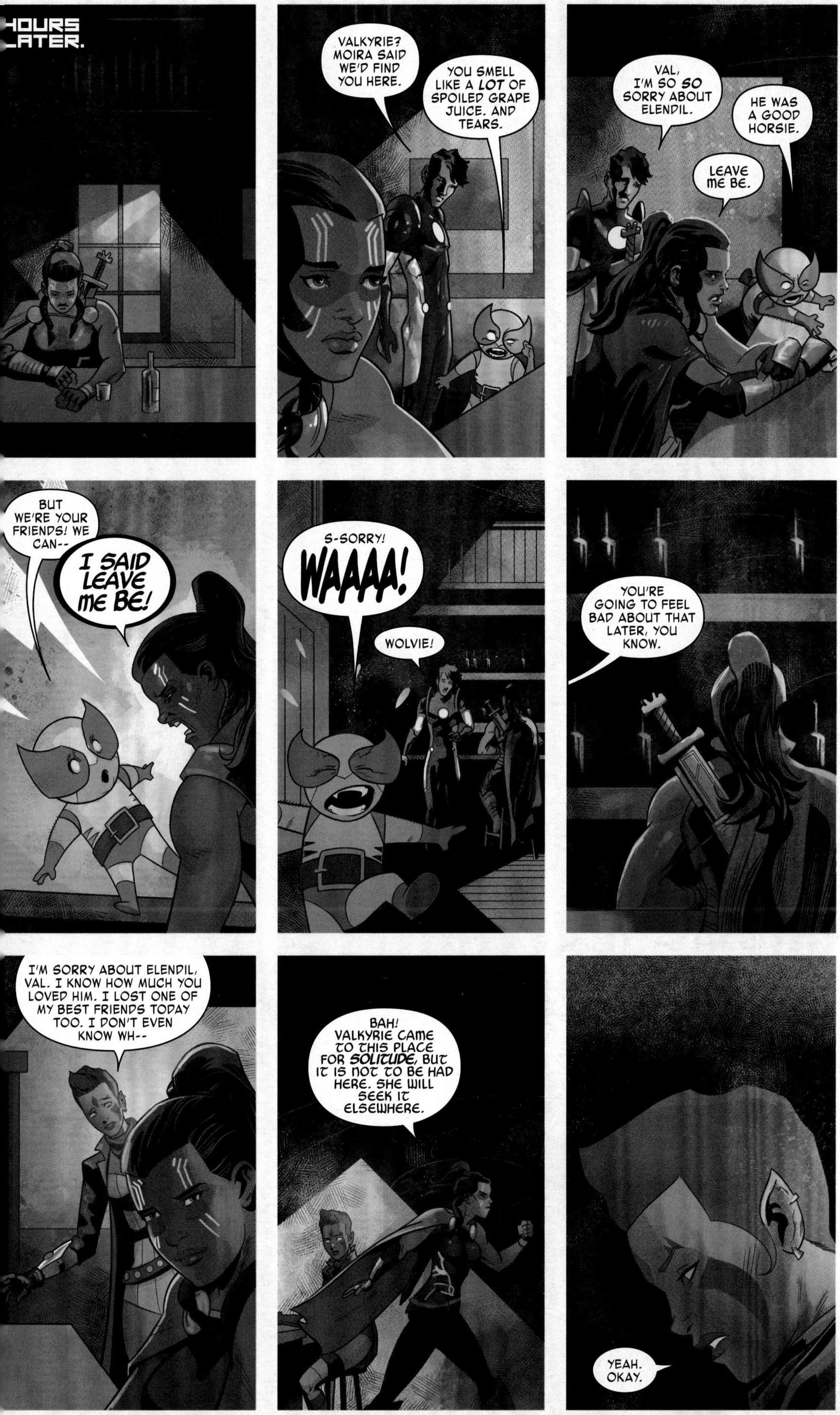
HOURS LATER.
VALKYRIE? MOIRA SAID WE'D FIND YOU HERE.
YOU SMELL LIKE A LOT OF SPOILED GRAPE JUICE. AND TEARS.
VAL, I'M SO SO SORRY ABOUT ELENDIL.
HE WAS A GOOD HORSIE.
LEAVE ME BE.
BUT WE'RE YOUR FRIENDS! WE CAN--
I SAID LEAVE ME BE!
S-SORRY!
WAAAA!
WOLVIE!
YOU'RE GOING TO FEEL BAD ABOUT THAT LATER, YOU KNOW.
I'M SORRY ABOUT ELENDIL, VAL. I KNOW HOW MUCH YOU LOVED HIM. I LOST ONE OF MY BEST FRIENDS TODAY TOO. I DON'T EVEN KNOW WH--
BAH! VALKYRIE CAME TO THIS PLACE FOR SOLITUDE, BUT IT IS NOT TO BE HAD HERE. SHE WILL SEEK IT ELSEWHERE.
YEAH. OKAY.

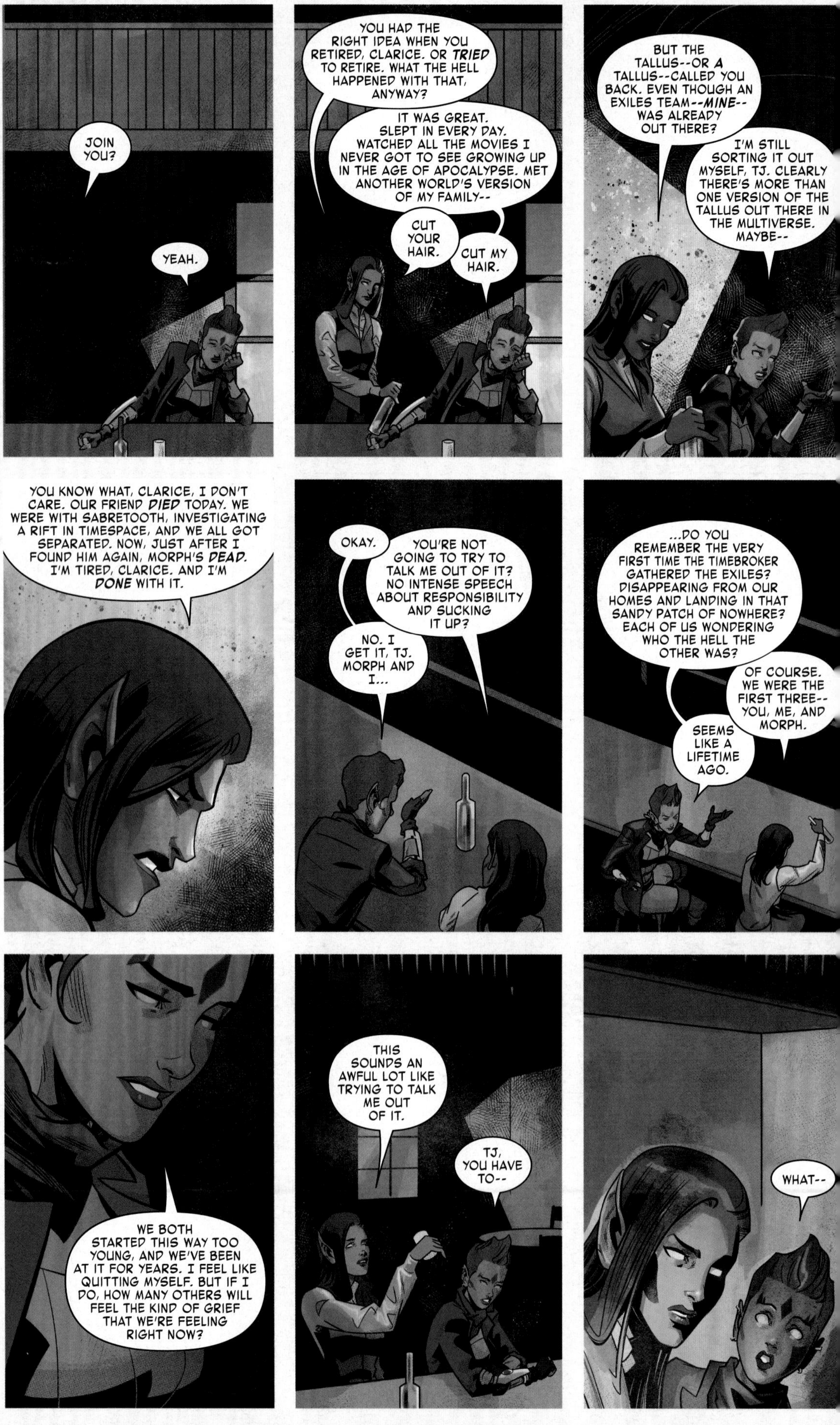
JOIN YOU?
YEAH.
YOU HAD THE RIGHT IDEA WHEN YOU RETIRED, CLARICE. OR *TRIED* TO RETIRE. WHAT THE HELL HAPPENED WITH THAT, ANYWAY?
IT WAS GREAT. SLEPT IN EVERY DAY. WATCHED ALL THE MOVIES I NEVER GOT TO SEE GROWING UP IN THE AGE OF APOCALYPSE. MET ANOTHER WORLD'S VERSION OF MY FAMILY--
CUT YOUR HAIR.
CUT MY HAIR.
BUT THE TALLUS--OR *A* TALLUS--CALLED YOU BACK. EVEN THOUGH AN EXILES TEAM--*MINE*--WAS ALREADY OUT THERE?
I'M STILL SORTING IT OUT MYSELF, TJ. CLEARLY THERE'S MORE THAN ONE VERSION OF THE TALLUS OUT THERE IN THE MULTIVERSE. MAYBE--
YOU KNOW WHAT, CLARICE, I DON'T CARE. OUR FRIEND *DIED* TODAY. WE WERE WITH SABRETOOTH, INVESTIGATING A RIFT IN TIMESPACE, AND WE ALL GOT SEPARATED. NOW, JUST AFTER I FOUND HIM AGAIN, MORPH'S *DEAD.* I'M TIRED, CLARICE. AND I'M *DONE* WITH IT.
OKAY.
YOU'RE NOT GOING TO TRY TO TALK ME OUT OF IT? NO INTENSE SPEECH ABOUT RESPONSIBILITY AND SUCKING IT UP?
NO. I GET IT, TJ. MORPH AND I...
...DO YOU REMEMBER THE VERY FIRST TIME THE TIMEBROKER GATHERED THE EXILES? DISAPPEARING FROM OUR HOMES AND LANDING IN THAT SANDY PATCH OF NOWHERE? EACH OF US WONDERING WHO THE HELL THE OTHER WAS?
OF COURSE. WE WERE THE FIRST THREE--YOU, ME, AND MORPH.
SEEMS LIKE A LIFETIME AGO.
WE BOTH STARTED THIS WAY TOO YOUNG, AND WE'VE BEEN AT IT FOR YEARS. I FEEL LIKE QUITTING MYSELF. BUT IF I DO, HOW MANY OTHERS WILL FEEL THE KIND OF GRIEF THAT WE'RE FEELING RIGHT NOW?
THIS SOUNDS AN AWFUL LOT LIKE TRYING TO TALK ME OUT OF IT.
TJ, YOU HAVE TO--
WHAT--

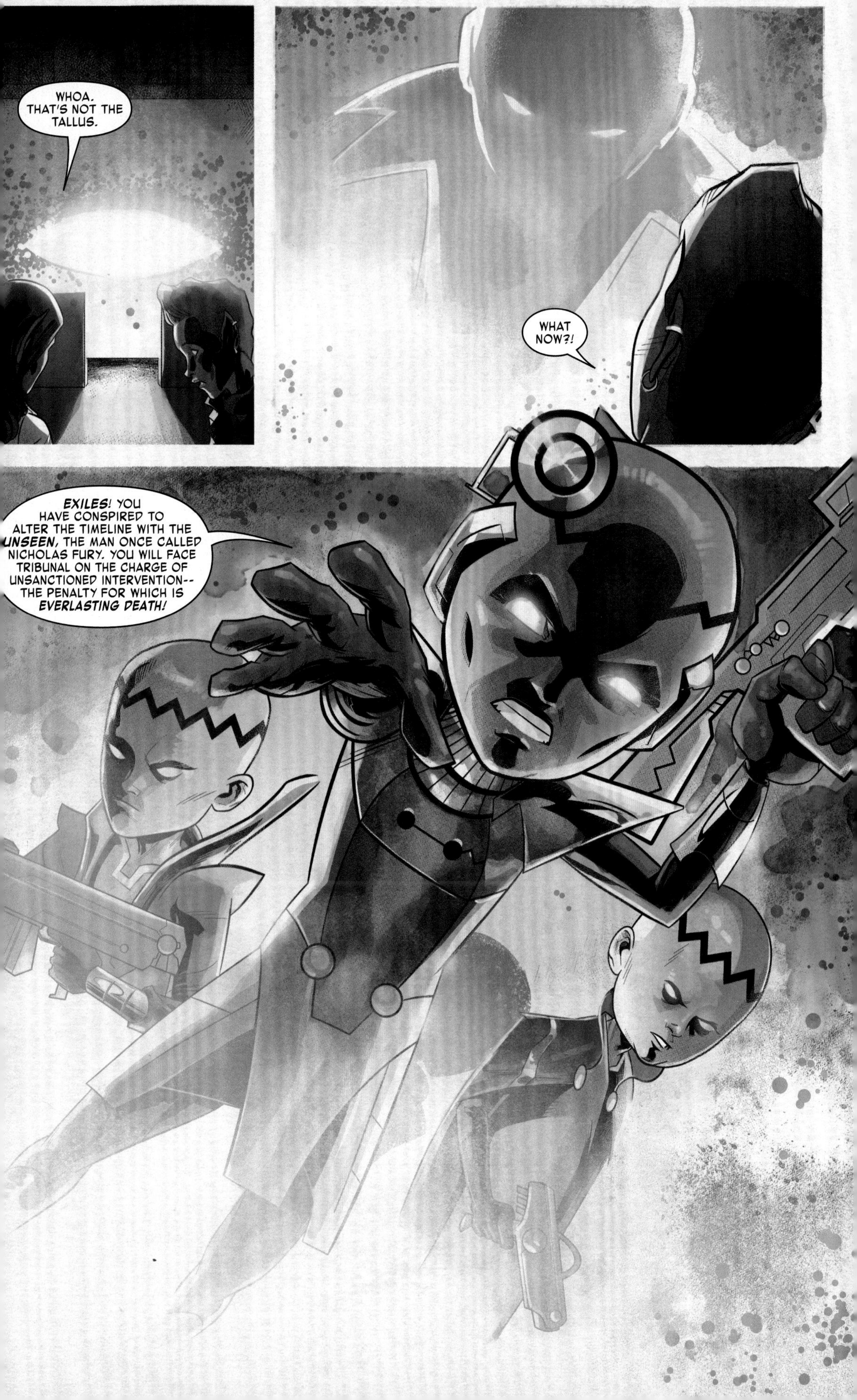
WHOA. THAT'S NOT THE TALLUS.
WHAT NOW?!
EXILES! YOU HAVE CONSPIRED TO ALTER THE TIMELINE WITH THE UNSEEN, THE MAN ONCE CALLED NICHOLAS FURY. YOU WILL FACE TRIBUNAL ON THE CHARGE OF UNSANCTIONED INTERVENTION-- THE PENALTY FOR WHICH IS EVERLASTING DEATH!

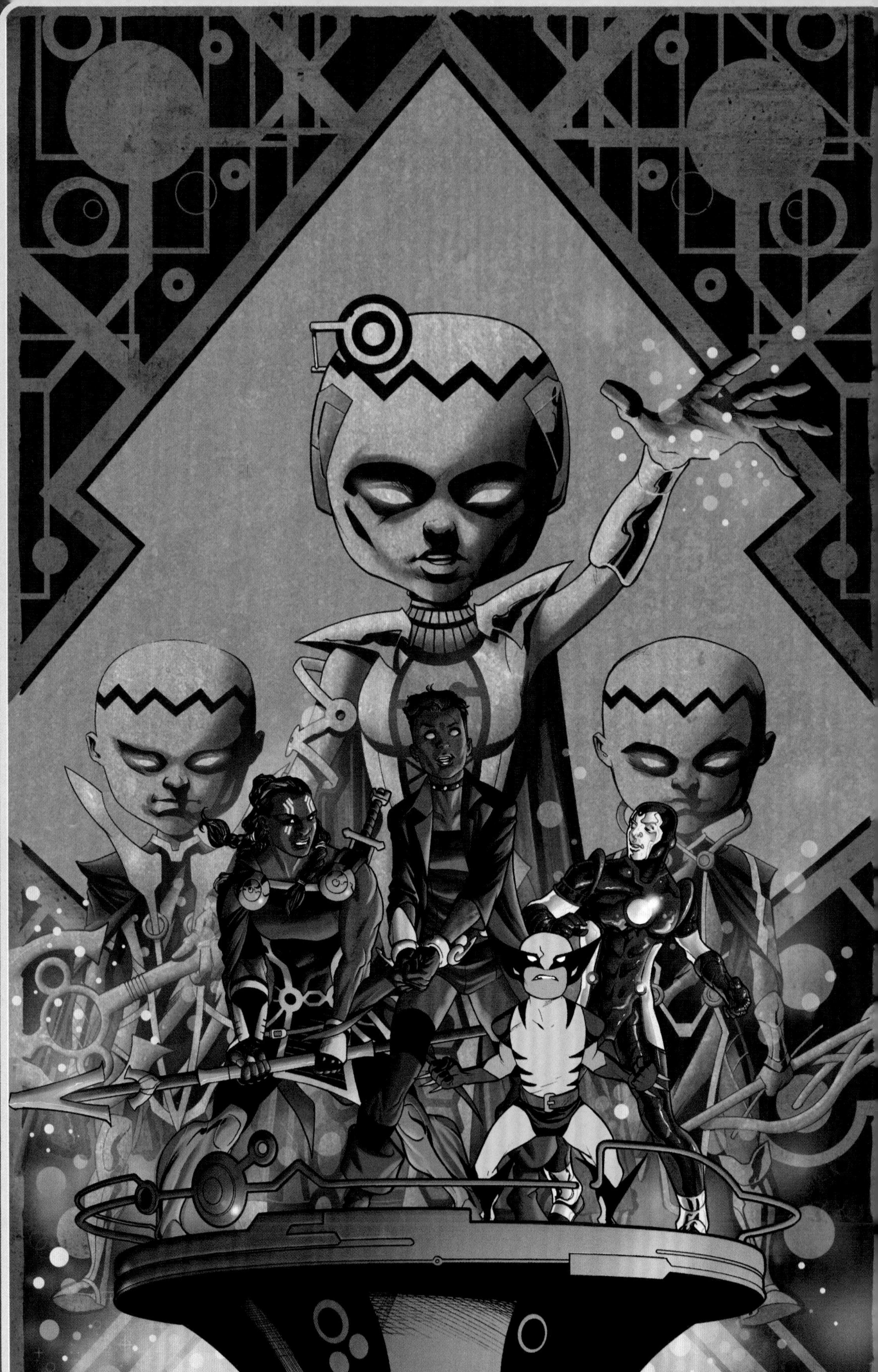

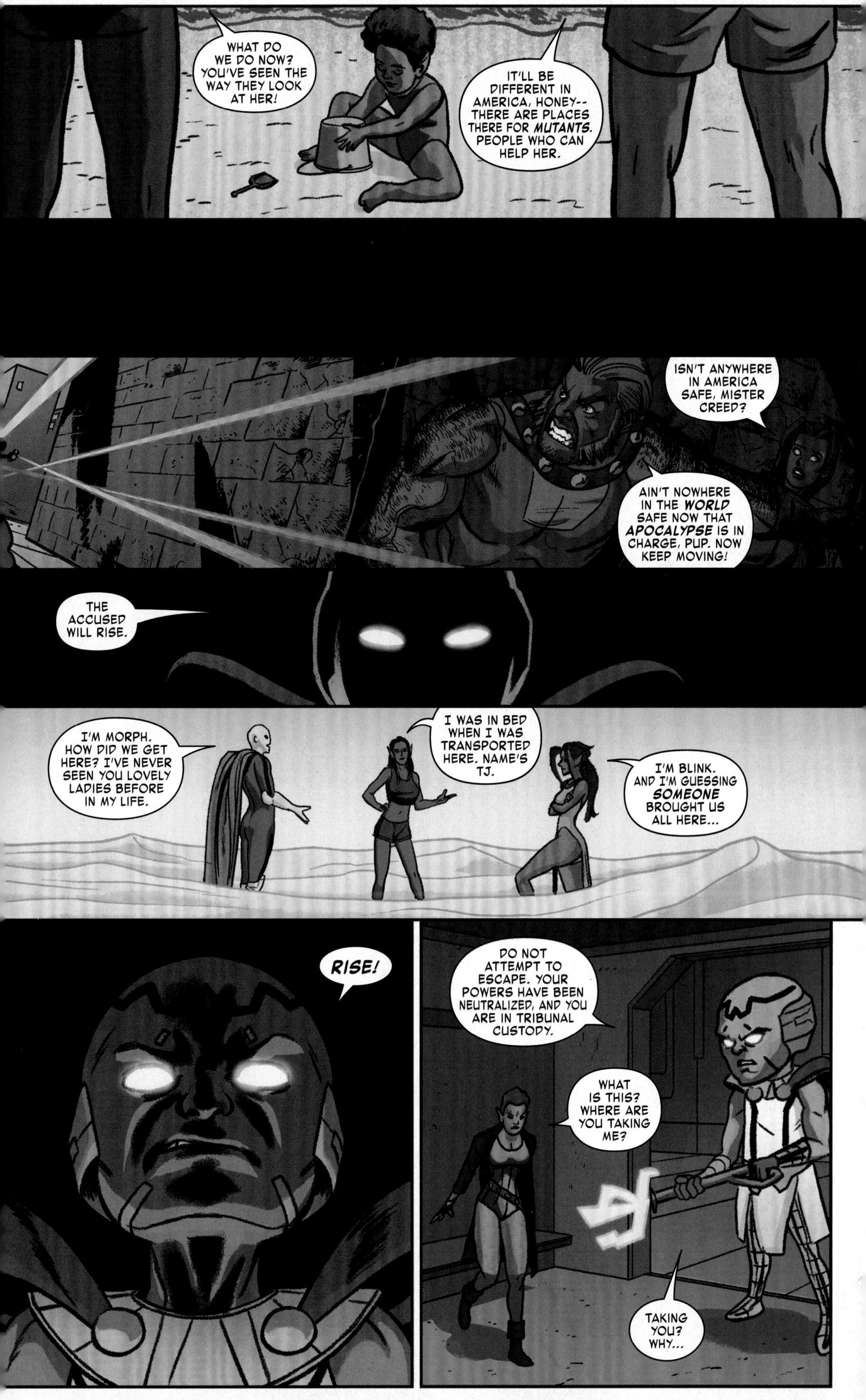

WHAT DO WE DO NOW? YOU'VE SEEN THE WAY THEY LOOK AT HER!
IT'LL BE DIFFERENT IN AMERICA, HONEY-- THERE ARE PLACES THERE FOR MUTANTS. PEOPLE WHO CAN HELP HER.
ISN'T ANYWHERE IN AMERICA SAFE, MISTER CREED?
AIN'T NOWHERE IN THE WORLD SAFE NOW THAT APOCALYPSE IS IN CHARGE, PUP. NOW KEEP MOVING!
THE ACCUSED WILL RISE.
I'M MORPH. HOW DID WE GET HERE? I'VE NEVER SEEN YOU LOVELY LADIES BEFORE IN MY LIFE.
I WAS IN BED WHEN I WAS TRANSPORTED HERE. NAME'S TJ.
I'M BLINK. AND I'M GUESSING SOMEONE BROUGHT US ALL HERE...
RISE!
DO NOT ATTEMPT TO ESCAPE. YOUR POWERS HAVE BEEN NEUTRALIZED, AND YOU ARE IN TRIBUNAL CUSTODY.
WHAT IS THIS? WHERE ARE YOU TAKING ME?
TAKING YOU? WHY...

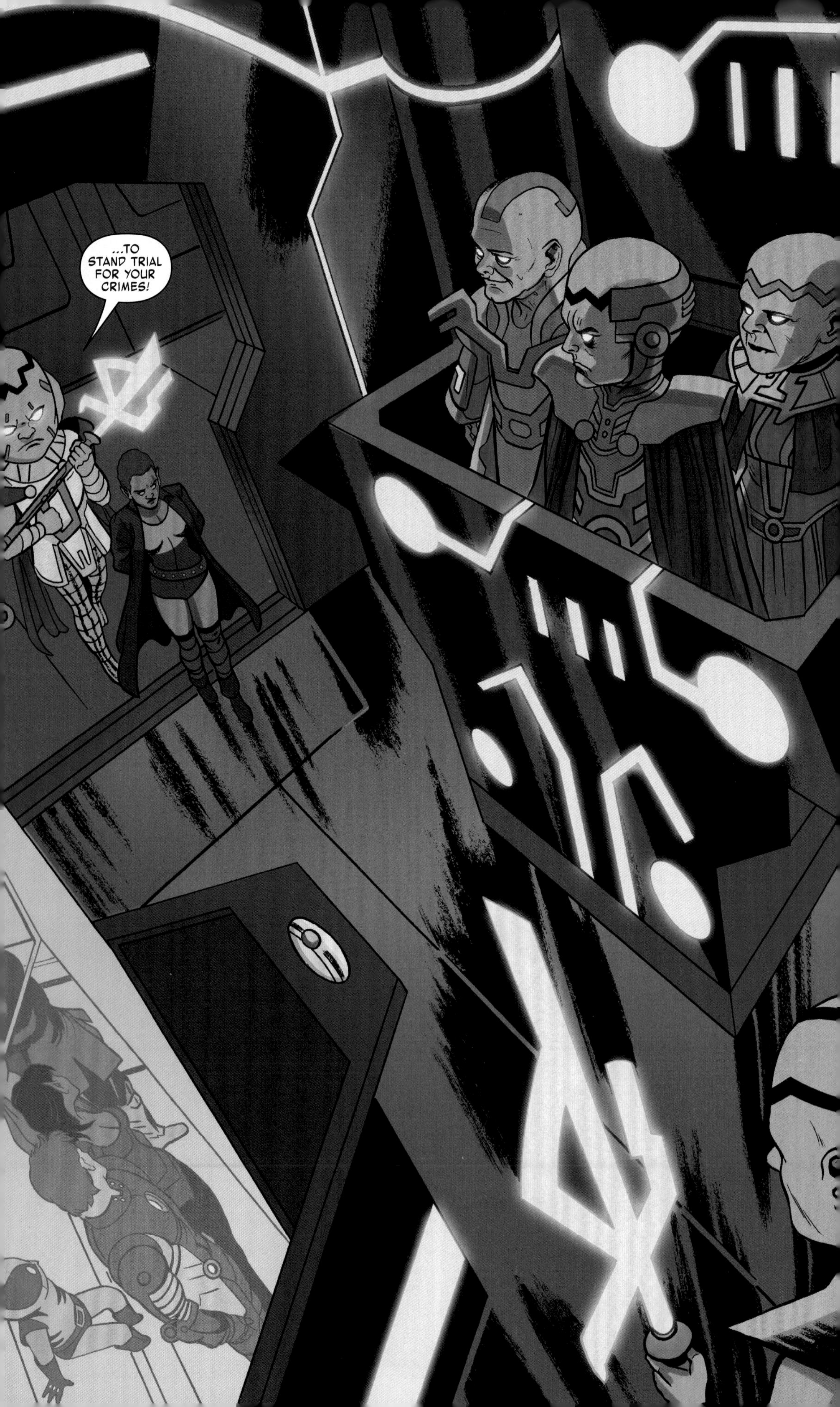
...TO STAND TRIAL FOR YOUR CRIMES!

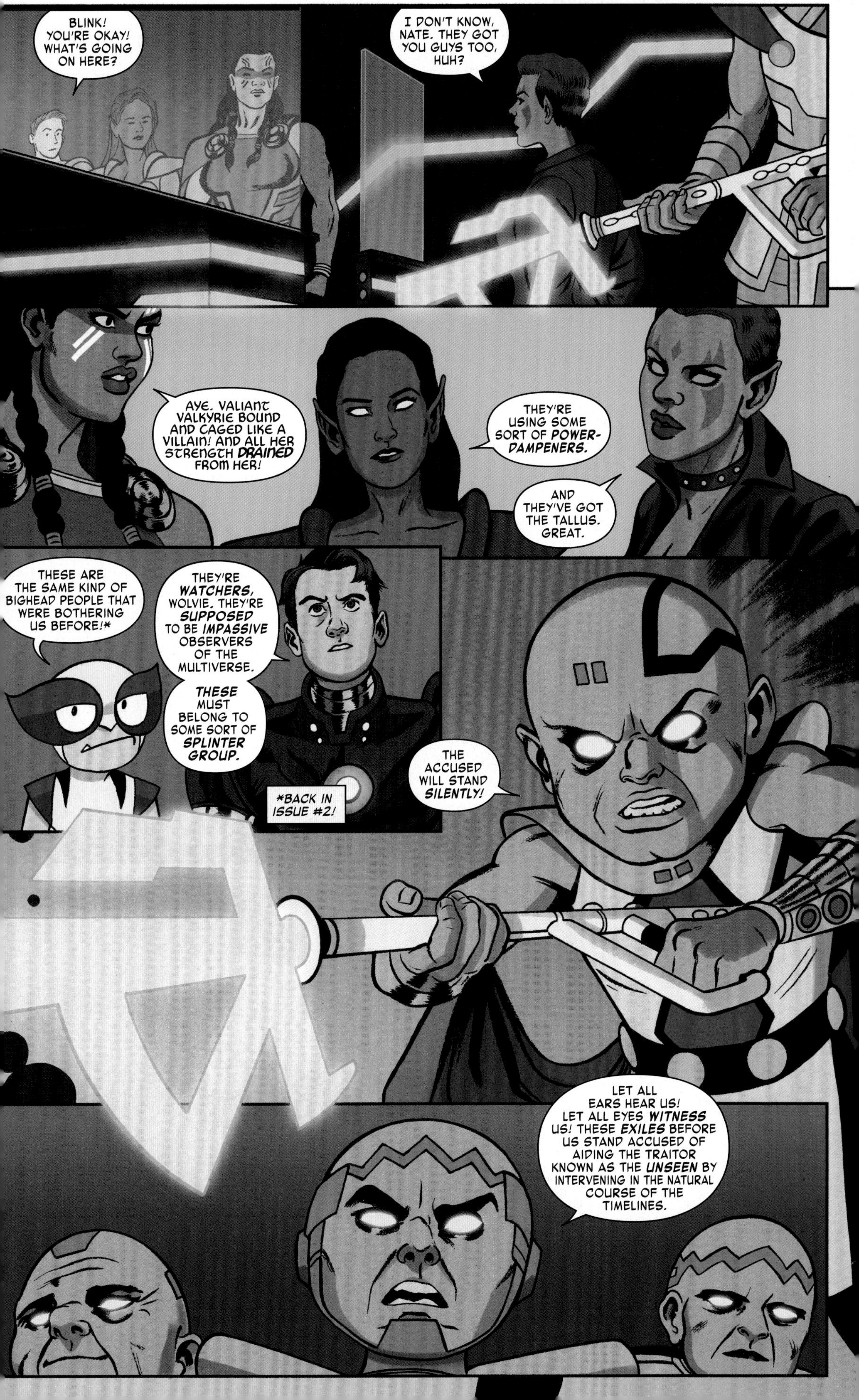

BLINK! YOU'RE OKAY! WHAT'S GOING ON HERE?
I DON'T KNOW, NATE. THEY GOT YOU GUYS TOO, HUH?
AYE. VALIANT VALKYRIE BOUND AND CAGED LIKE A VILLAIN! AND ALL HER STRENGTH DRAINED FROM HER!
THEY'RE USING SOME SORT OF POWER-DAMPENERS.
AND THEY'VE GOT THE TALLUS. GREAT.
THESE ARE THE SAME KIND OF BIGHEAD PEOPLE THAT WERE BOTHERING US BEFORE!*
THEY'RE WATCHERS, WOLVIE. THEY'RE SUPPOSED TO BE IMPASSIVE OBSERVERS OF THE MULTIVERSE.
THESE MUST BELONG TO SOME SORT OF SPLINTER GROUP.
*BACK IN ISSUE #2!
THE ACCUSED WILL STAND SILENTLY!
LET ALL EARS HEAR US! LET ALL EYES WITNESS US! THESE EXILES BEFORE US STAND ACCUSED OF AIDING THE TRAITOR KNOWN AS THE UNSEEN BY INTERVENING IN THE NATURAL COURSE OF THE TIMELINES.

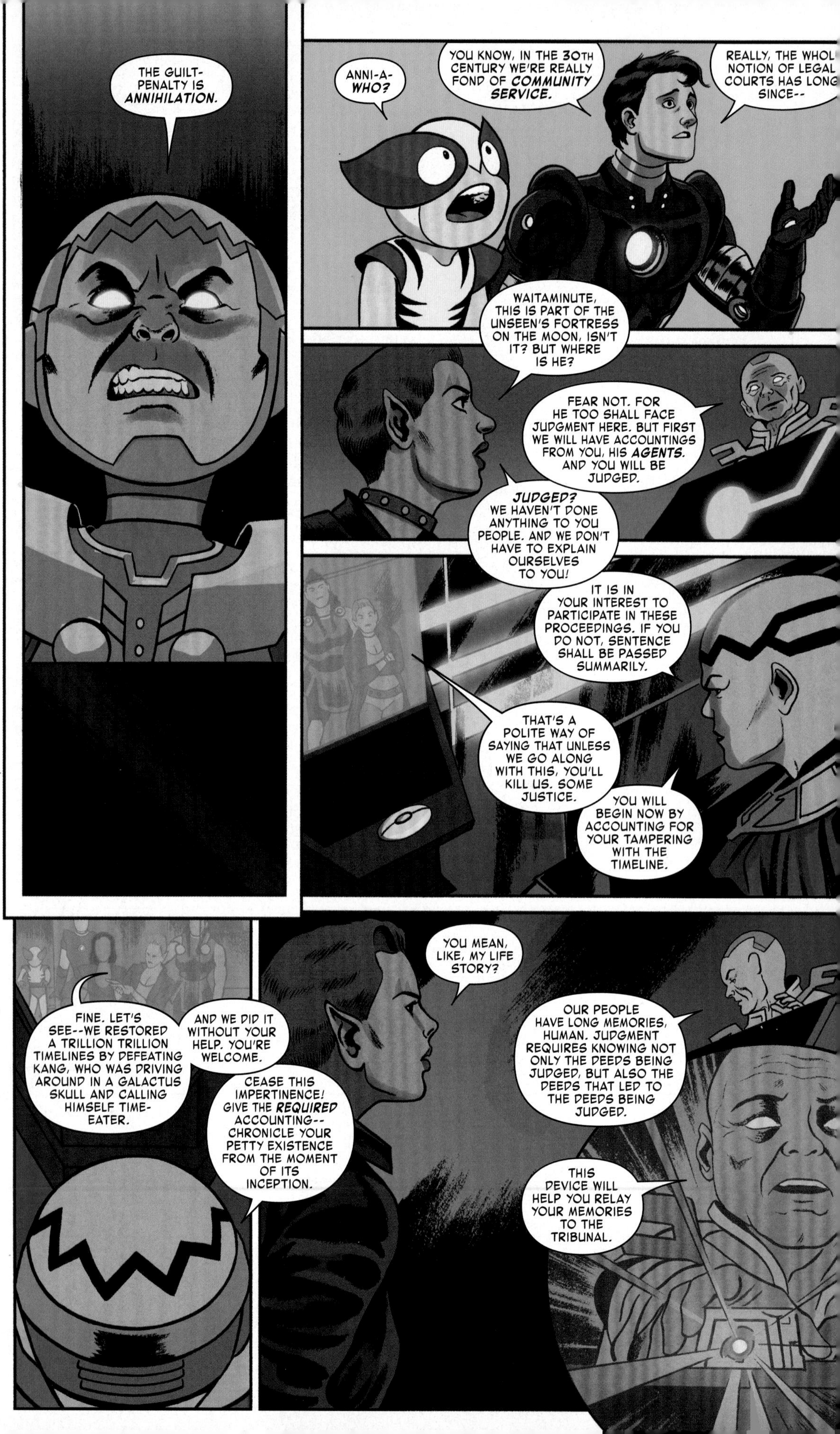

THE GUILT-PENALTY IS ANNIHILATION.
ANNI-A-WHO?
YOU KNOW, IN THE 30TH CENTURY WE'RE REALLY FOND OF COMMUNITY SERVICE.
REALLY, THE WHOL NOTION OF LEGAL COURTS HAS LONG SINCE--
WAITAMINUTE, THIS IS PART OF THE UNSEEN'S FORTRESS ON THE MOON, ISN'T IT? BUT WHERE IS HE?
FEAR NOT. FOR HE TOO SHALL FACE JUDGMENT HERE. BUT FIRST WE WILL HAVE ACCOUNTINGS FROM YOU, HIS AGENTS. AND YOU WILL BE JUDGED.
JUDGED? WE HAVEN'T DONE ANYTHING TO YOU PEOPLE. AND WE DON'T HAVE TO EXPLAIN OURSELVES TO YOU!
IT IS IN YOUR INTEREST TO PARTICIPATE IN THESE PROCEEDINGS. IF YOU DO NOT, SENTENCE SHALL BE PASSED SUMMARILY.
THAT'S A POLITE WAY OF SAYING THAT UNLESS WE GO ALONG WITH THIS, YOU'LL KILL US. SOME JUSTICE.
YOU WILL BEGIN NOW BY ACCOUNTING FOR YOUR TAMPERING WITH THE TIMELINE.
FINE. LET'S SEE--WE RESTORED A TRILLION TRILLION TIMELINES BY DEFEATING KANG, WHO WAS DRIVING AROUND IN A GALACTUS SKULL AND CALLING HIMSELF TIME-EATER.
AND WE DID IT WITHOUT YOUR HELP. YOU'RE WELCOME.
CEASE THIS IMPERTINENCE! GIVE THE REQUIRED ACCOUNTING--CHRONICLE YOUR PETTY EXISTENCE FROM THE MOMENT OF ITS INCEPTION.
YOU MEAN, LIKE, MY LIFE STORY?
OUR PEOPLE HAVE LONG MEMORIES, HUMAN. JUDGMENT REQUIRES KNOWING NOT ONLY THE DEEDS BEING JUDGED, BUT ALSO THE DEEDS THAT LED TO THE DEEDS BEING JUDGED.
THIS DEVICE WILL HELP YOU RELAY YOUR MEMORIES TO THE TRIBUNAL.

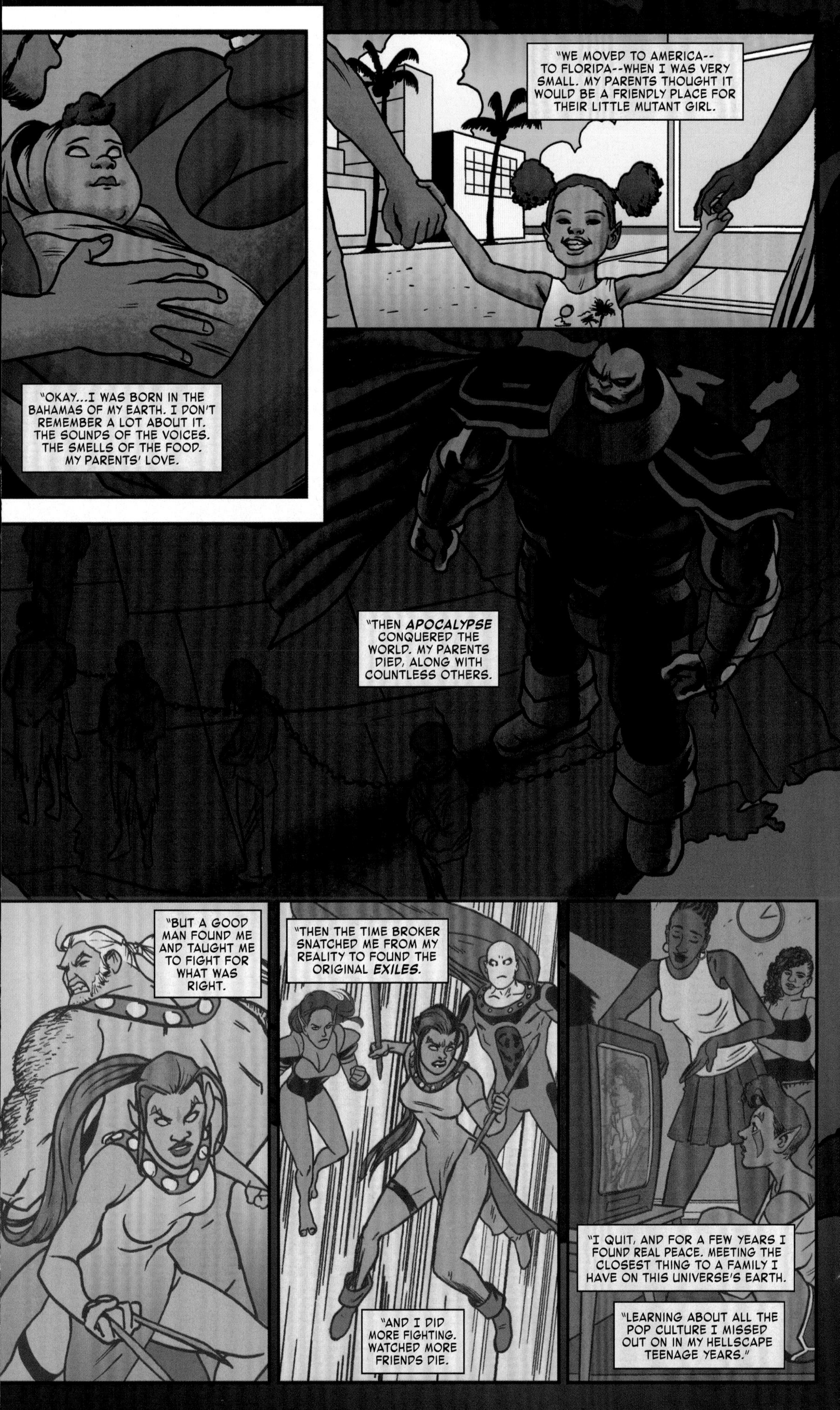
"OKAY...I WAS BORN IN THE BAHAMAS OF MY EARTH. I DON'T REMEMBER A LOT ABOUT IT. THE SOUNDS OF THE VOICES. THE SMELLS OF THE FOOD. MY PARENTS' LOVE.
"WE MOVED TO AMERICA-- TO FLORIDA--WHEN I WAS VERY SMALL. MY PARENTS THOUGHT IT WOULD BE A FRIENDLY PLACE FOR THEIR LITTLE MUTANT GIRL.
"THEN APOCALYPSE CONQUERED THE WORLD. MY PARENTS DIED, ALONG WITH COUNTLESS OTHERS.
"BUT A GOOD MAN FOUND ME AND TAUGHT ME TO FIGHT FOR WHAT WAS RIGHT.
"THEN THE TIME BROKER SNATCHED ME FROM MY REALITY TO FOUND THE ORIGINAL EXILES.
"AND I DID MORE FIGHTING. WATCHED MORE FRIENDS DIE.
"I QUIT, AND FOR A FEW YEARS I FOUND REAL PEACE. MEETING THE CLOSEST THING TO A FAMILY I HAVE ON THIS UNIVERSE'S EARTH.
"LEARNING ABOUT ALL THE POP CULTURE I MISSED OUT ON IN MY HELLSCAPE TEENAGE YEARS."

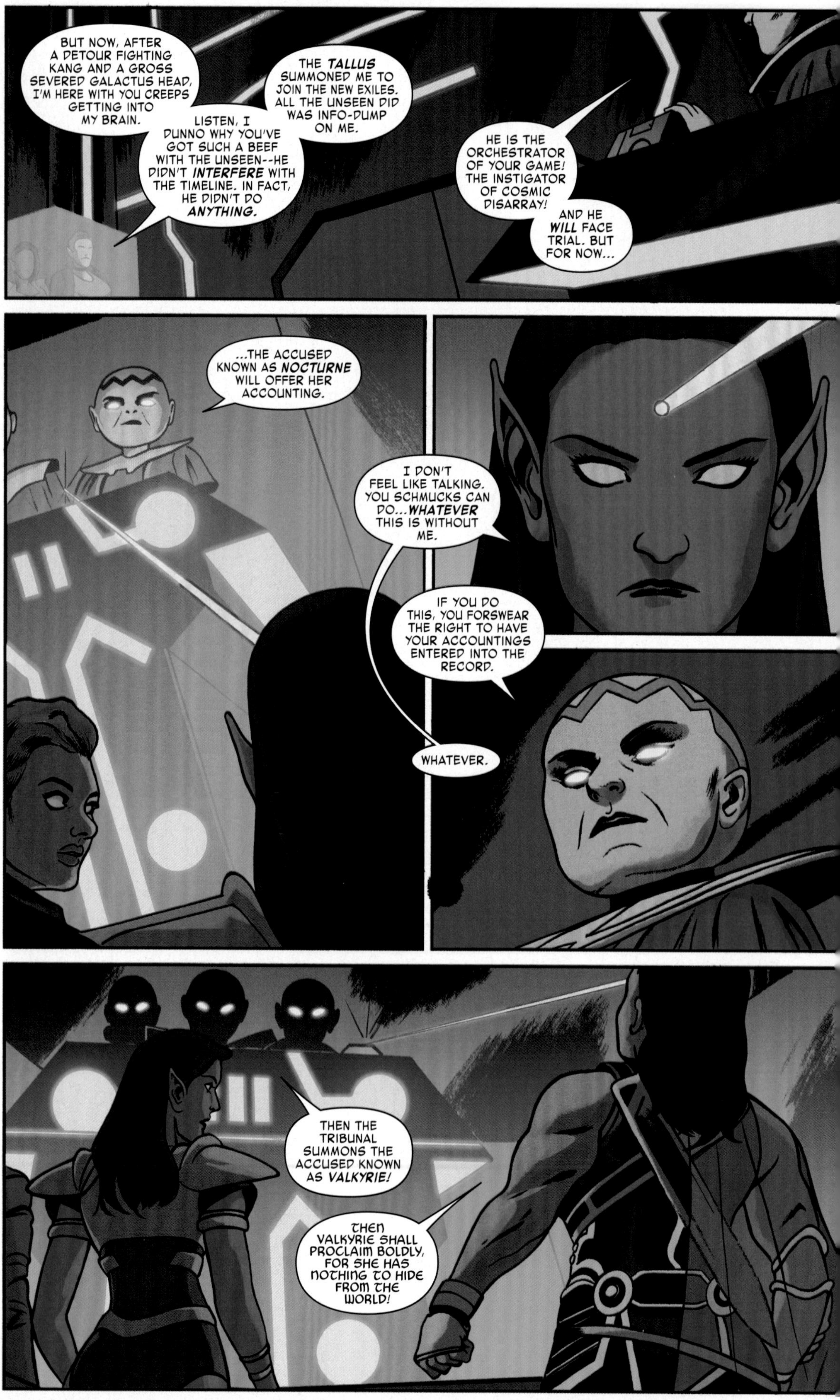
BUT NOW, AFTER A DETOUR FIGHTING KANG AND A GROSS SEVERED GALACTUS HEAD, I'M HERE WITH YOU CREEPS GETTING INTO MY BRAIN.
THE TALLUS SUMMONED ME TO JOIN THE NEW EXILES. ALL THE UNSEEN DID WAS INFO-DUMP ON ME.
LISTEN, I DUNNO WHY YOU'VE GOT SUCH A BEEF WITH THE UNSEEN--HE DIDN'T INTERFERE WITH THE TIMELINE. IN FACT, HE DIDN'T DO ANYTHING.
HE IS THE ORCHESTRATOR OF YOUR GAME! THE INSTIGATOR OF COSMIC DISARRAY!
AND HE WILL FACE TRIAL. BUT FOR NOW...
...THE ACCUSED KNOWN AS NOCTURNE WILL OFFER HER ACCOUNTING.
I DON'T FEEL LIKE TALKING. YOU SCHMUCKS CAN DO...WHATEVER THIS IS WITHOUT ME.
IF YOU DO THIS, YOU FORSWEAR THE RIGHT TO HAVE YOUR ACCOUNTINGS ENTERED INTO THE RECORD.
WHATEVER.
THEN THE TRIBUNAL SUMMONS THE ACCUSED KNOWN AS VALKYRIE!
THEN VALKYRIE SHALL PROCLAIM BOLDLY, FOR SHE HAS NOTHING TO HIDE FROM THE WORLD!

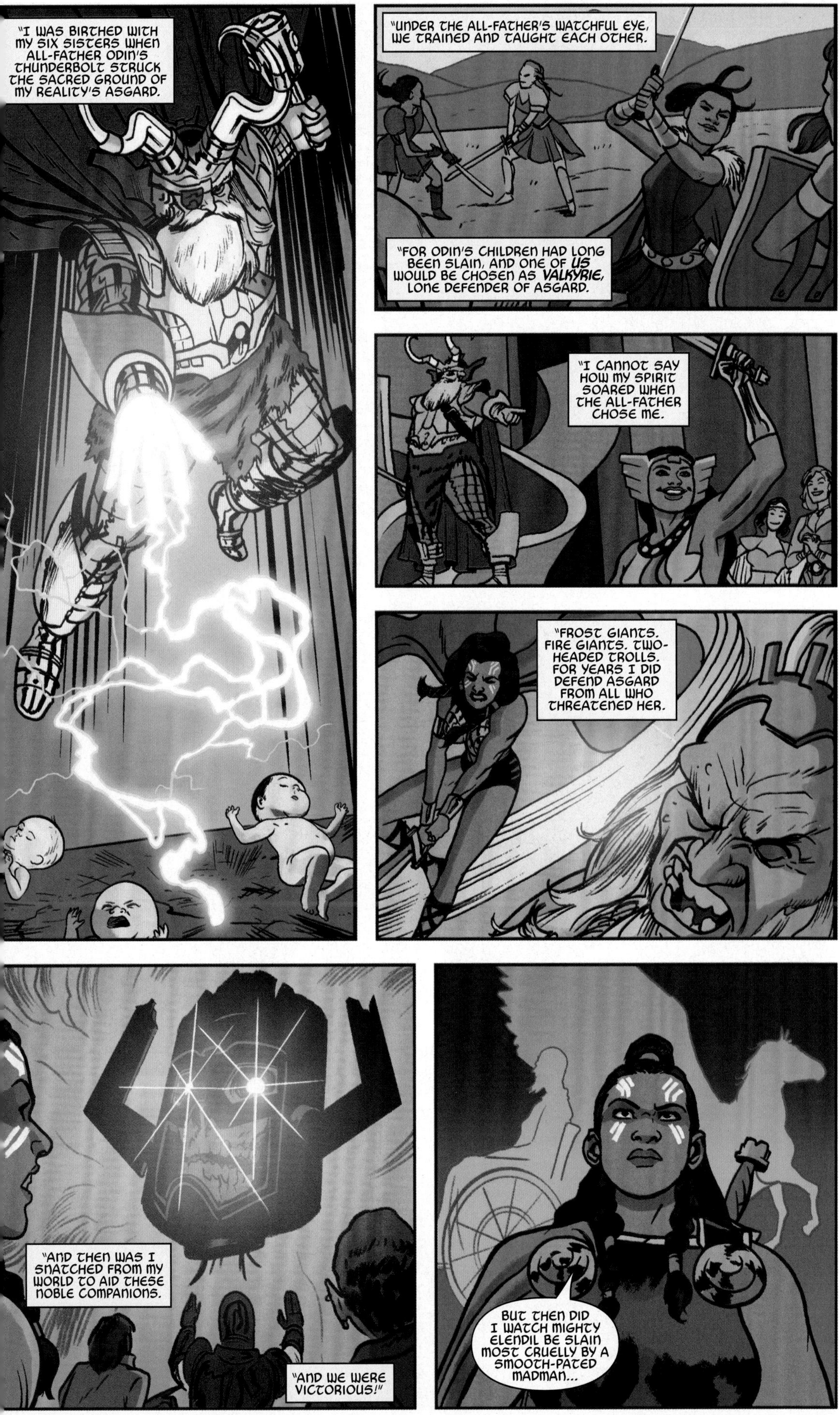
"I WAS BIRTHED WITH MY SIX SISTERS WHEN ALL-FATHER ODIN'S THUNDERBOLT STRUCK THE SACRED GROUND OF MY REALITY'S ASGARD.
"UNDER THE ALL-FATHER'S WATCHFUL EYE, WE TRAINED AND TAUGHT EACH OTHER.
"FOR ODIN'S CHILDREN HAD LONG BEEN SLAIN, AND ONE OF US WOULD BE CHOSEN AS VALKYRIE, LONE DEFENDER OF ASGARD.
"I CANNOT SAY HOW MY SPIRIT SOARED WHEN THE ALL-FATHER CHOSE ME.
"FROST GIANTS. FIRE GIANTS. TWO-HEADED TROLLS. FOR YEARS I DID DEFEND ASGARD FROM ALL WHO THREATENED HER.
"AND THEN WAS I SNATCHED FROM MY WORLD TO AID THESE NOBLE COMPANIONS.
"AND WE WERE VICTORIOUS!"
BUT THEN DID I WATCH MIGHTY ELENDIL BE SLAIN MOST CRUELLY BY A SMOOTH-PATED MADMAN...

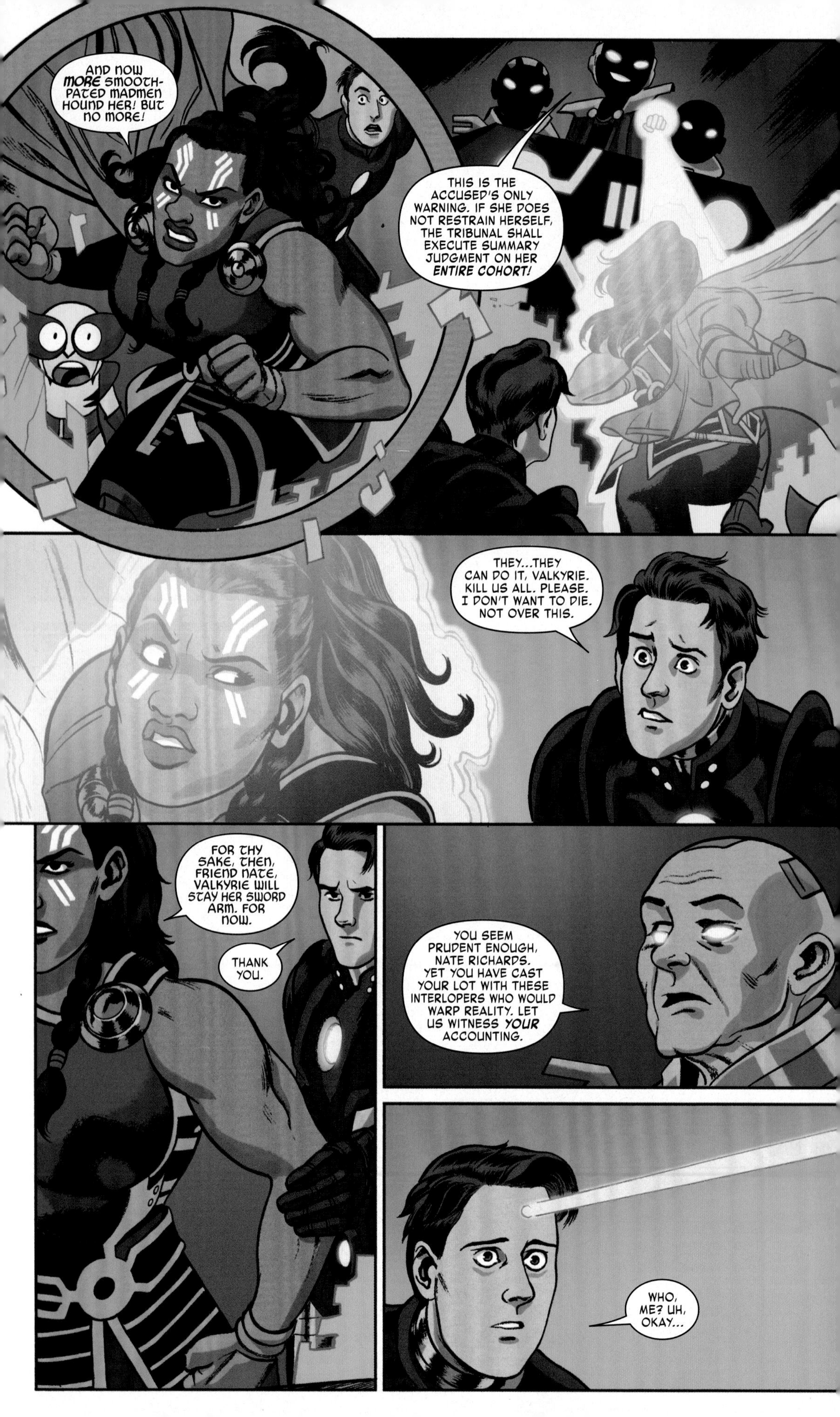
AND NOW MORE SMOOTH-PATED MADMEN HOUND HER! BUT NO MORE!
THIS IS THE ACCUSED'S ONLY WARNING. IF SHE DOES NOT RESTRAIN HERSELF, THE TRIBUNAL SHALL EXECUTE SUMMARY JUDGMENT ON HER ENTIRE COHORT!
THEY...THEY CAN DO IT, VALKYRIE. KILL US ALL. PLEASE. I DON'T WANT TO DIE. NOT OVER THIS.
FOR THY SAKE, THEN, FRIEND NATE, VALKYRIE WILL STAY HER SWORD ARM. FOR NOW.
THANK YOU.
YOU SEEM PRUDENT ENOUGH, NATE RICHARDS. YET YOU HAVE CAST YOUR LOT WITH THESE INTERLOPERS WHO WOULD WARP REALITY. LET US WITNESS YOUR ACCOUNTING.
WHO, ME? UH, OKAY...

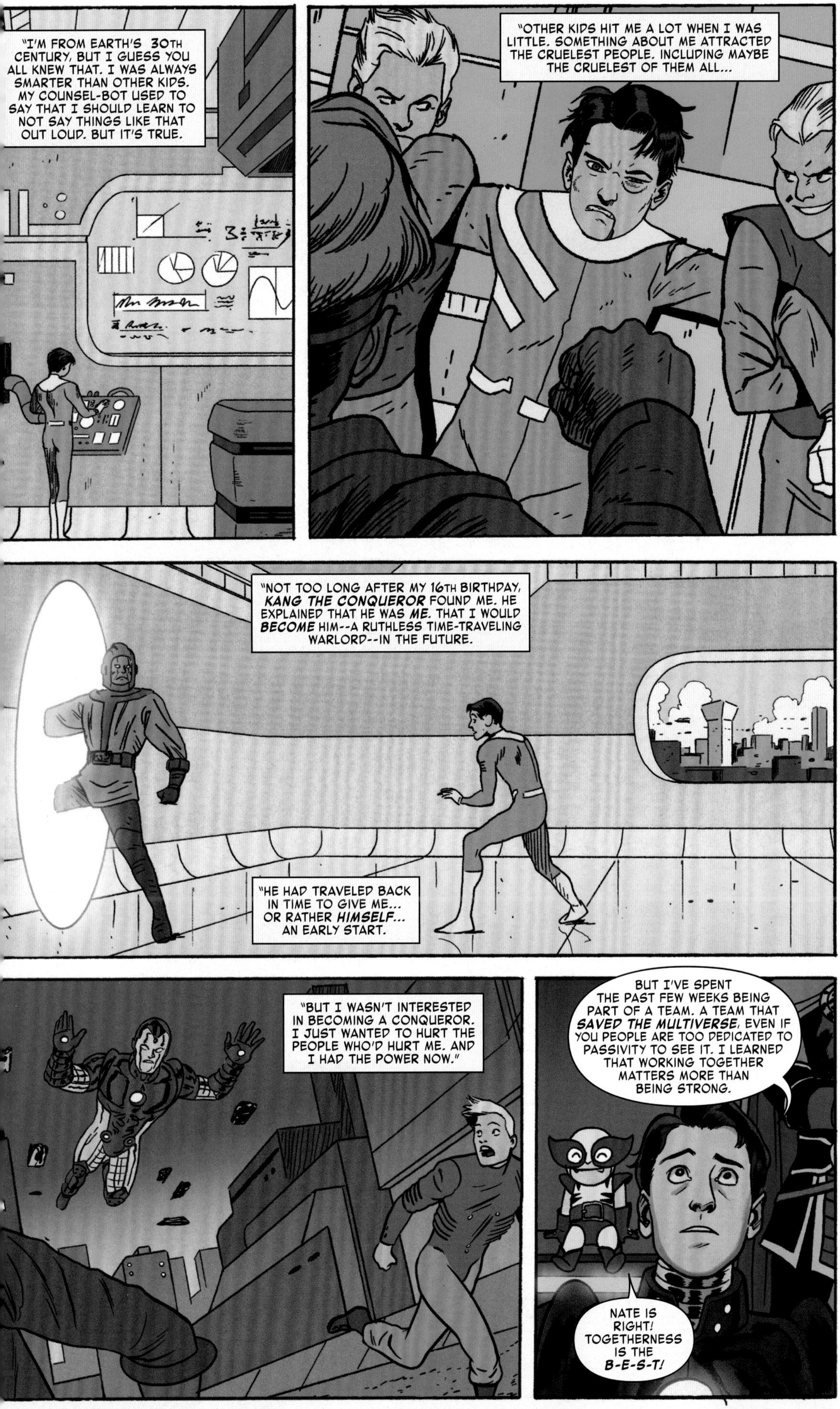
"I'M FROM EARTH'S 30TH CENTURY, BUT I GUESS YOU ALL KNEW THAT. I WAS ALWAYS SMARTER THAN OTHER KIDS. MY COUNSEL-BOT USED TO SAY THAT I SHOULD LEARN TO NOT SAY THINGS LIKE THAT OUT LOUD. BUT IT'S TRUE.
"OTHER KIDS HIT ME A LOT WHEN I WAS LITTLE. SOMETHING ABOUT ME ATTRACTED THE CRUELEST PEOPLE. INCLUDING MAYBE THE CRUELEST OF THEM ALL...
"NOT TOO LONG AFTER MY 16TH BIRTHDAY, ***KANG THE CONQUEROR*** FOUND ME. HE EXPLAINED THAT HE WAS ***ME.*** THAT I WOULD ***BECOME*** HIM--A RUTHLESS TIME-TRAVELING WARLORD--IN THE FUTURE.
"HE HAD TRAVELED BACK IN TIME TO GIVE ME... OR RATHER ***HIMSELF***... AN EARLY START.
"BUT I WASN'T INTERESTED IN BECOMING A CONQUEROR. I JUST WANTED TO HURT THE PEOPLE WHO'D HURT ME. AND I HAD THE POWER NOW."
BUT I'VE SPENT THE PAST FEW WEEKS BEING PART OF A TEAM. A TEAM THAT ***SAVED THE MULTIVERSE***, EVEN IF YOU PEOPLE ARE TOO DEDICATED TO PASSIVITY TO SEE IT. I LEARNED THAT WORKING TOGETHER MATTERS MORE THAN BEING STRONG.
NATE IS RIGHT! TOGETHERNESS IS THE ***B-E-S-T!***

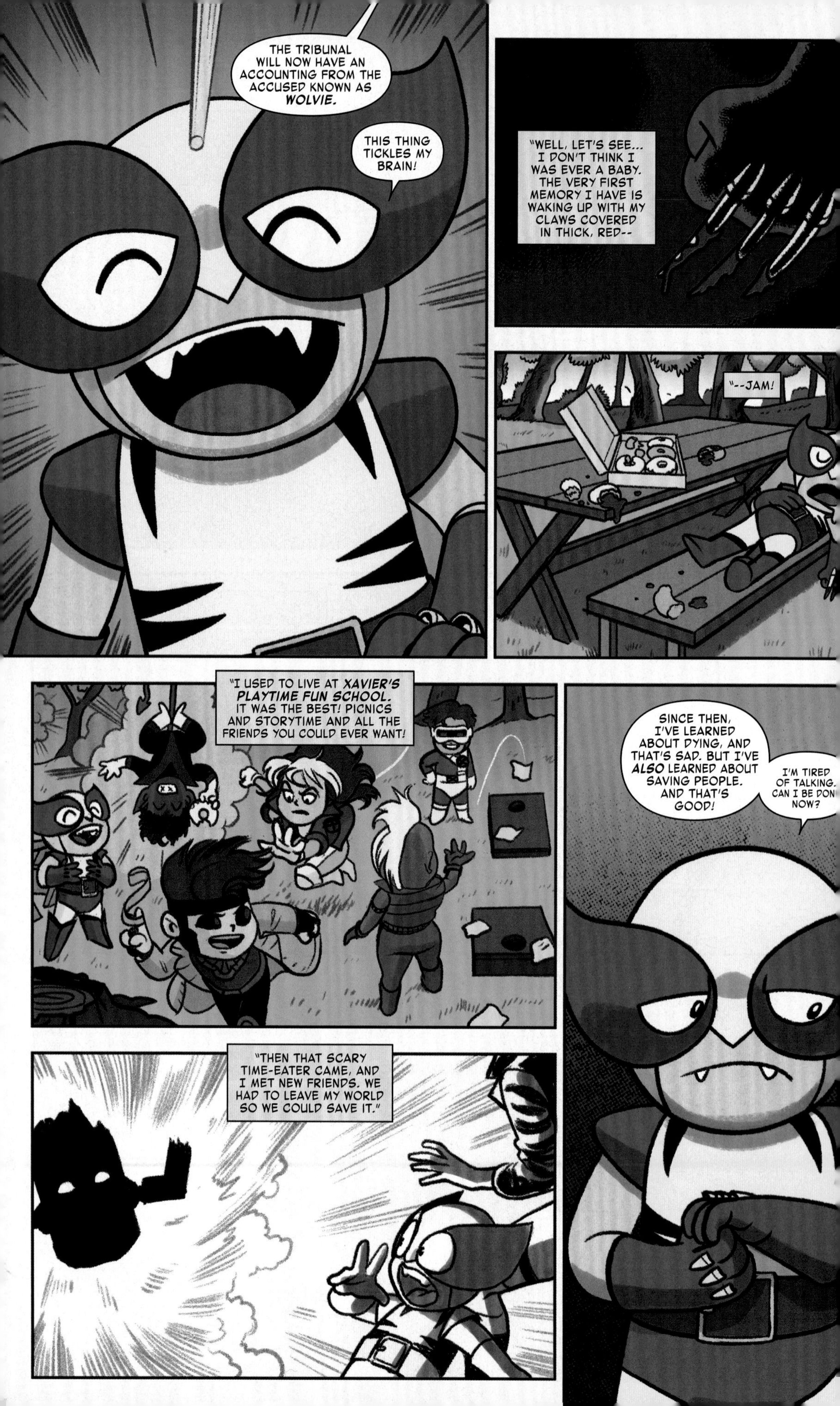

THE TRIBUNAL WILL NOW HAVE AN ACCOUNTING FROM THE ACCUSED KNOWN AS WOLVIE.
THIS THING TICKLES MY BRAIN!
"WELL, LET'S SEE... I DON'T THINK I WAS EVER A BABY. THE VERY FIRST MEMORY I HAVE IS WAKING UP WITH MY CLAWS COVERED IN THICK, RED--
"--JAM!
"I USED TO LIVE AT XAVIER'S PLAYTIME FUN SCHOOL. IT WAS THE BEST! PICNICS AND STORYTIME AND ALL THE FRIENDS YOU COULD EVER WANT!
"THEN THAT SCARY TIME-EATER CAME, AND I MET NEW FRIENDS. WE HAD TO LEAVE MY WORLD SO WE COULD SAVE IT."
SINCE THEN, I'VE LEARNED ABOUT DYING, AND THAT'S SAD. BUT I'VE ALSO LEARNED ABOUT SAVING PEOPLE. AND THAT'S GOOD!
I'M TIRED OF TALKING. CAN I BE DON NOW?

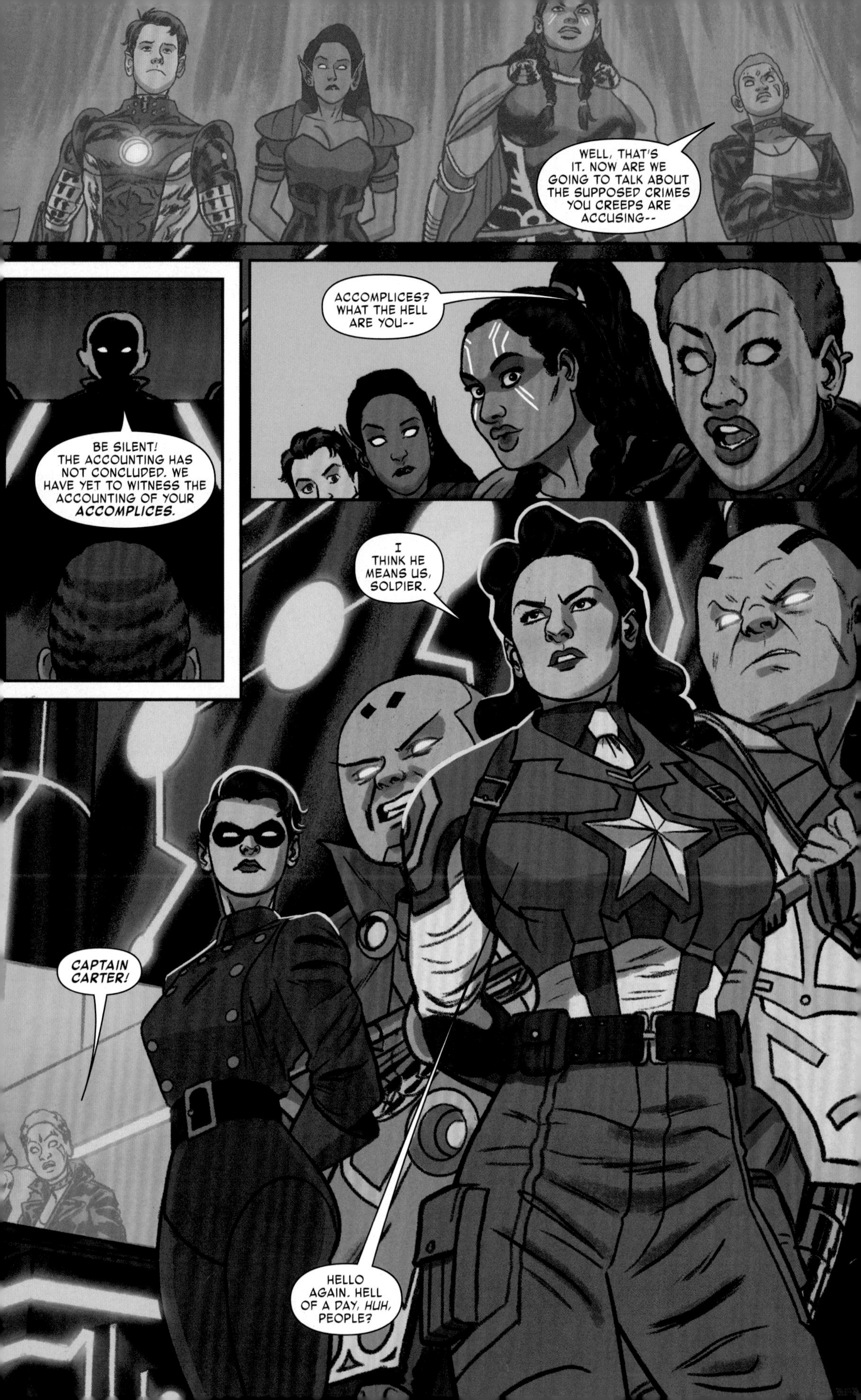
WELL, THAT'S IT. NOW ARE WE GOING TO TALK ABOUT THE SUPPOSED CRIMES YOU CREEPS ARE ACCUSING--
BE SILENT! THE ACCOUNTING HAS NOT CONCLUDED. WE HAVE YET TO WITNESS THE ACCOUNTING OF YOUR *ACCOMPLICES.*
ACCOMPLICES? WHAT THE HELL ARE YOU--
I THINK HE MEANS US, SOLDIER.
CAPTAIN CARTER!
HELLO AGAIN. HELL OF A DAY, *HUH,* PEOPLE?

YOU'RE ALIVE! AFTER THE EXPLOSION* WE DIDN'T KNOW IF--

WHAT THE BLOODY HELL IS GOING ON? I SAW THE BOMB GO OFF, AND THEN BECKY AND I WERE *HERE*--WITH THESE UGLY FELLOWS. AT FIRST WE THOUGHT THIS WAS SOME HYDRA PLOT, BUT...

I ONLY KNOW HALF OF IT, CAPTAIN, AND THAT HALF WOULD TAKE FOREVER TO EXPLAIN.

*BACK IN ISSUE #3!

MUSCLES! BOY ARE YOU A SIGHT FOR SORE EYES.

SWEET BECKY! THE SIGHT OF THEE IS A BALM FOR VALKYRIE'S WOUNDED HEART AS WELL! WOULD THAT MINE HANDS WERE FREE, I WOULD LIFT THEE IN MINE ARMS.

WE'LL GET TIME FOR THAT.

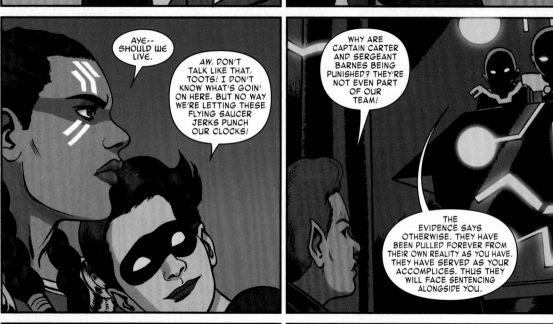

AYE-- SHOULD WE LIVE.

AW, DON'T TALK LIKE THAT, TOOTS! I DON'T KNOW WHAT'S GOIN' ON HERE, BUT NO WAY WE'RE LETTING THESE FLYING SAUCER JERKS PUNCH OUR CLOCKS!

WHY ARE CAPTAIN CARTER AND SERGEANT BARNES BEING PUNISHED? THEY'RE NOT EVEN PART OF OUR TEAM!

THE EVIDENCE SAYS OTHERWISE. THEY HAVE BEEN PULLED FOREVER FROM THEIR OWN REALITY AS YOU HAVE. THEY HAVE SERVED AS YOUR ACCOMPLICES. THUS THEY WILL FACE SENTENCING ALONGSIDE YOU.

AND NOW THEY WILL GIVE THEIR ACCOUNTS.

I DON'T KNOW WHO THE HELL YOU PEOPLE ARE, BUT NAME, RANK AND SERIAL NUMBER ARE ALL YOU ARE GOING TO GET OUT OF ME.

≥SNIFF≤

CAPTAIN, PLEASE--THEY'RE RUNNING OUT OF PATIENCE. REALLY THINK THEY'RE GOING TO KILL US IF WE DON'T GO ALONG WITH THIS. *ALL* OF US.

ALL RIGHT. THIS MOON-MEN STUFF ISN'T MY TERRITORY, SO I'LL FOLLOW YOUR LEAD. FOR NOW.

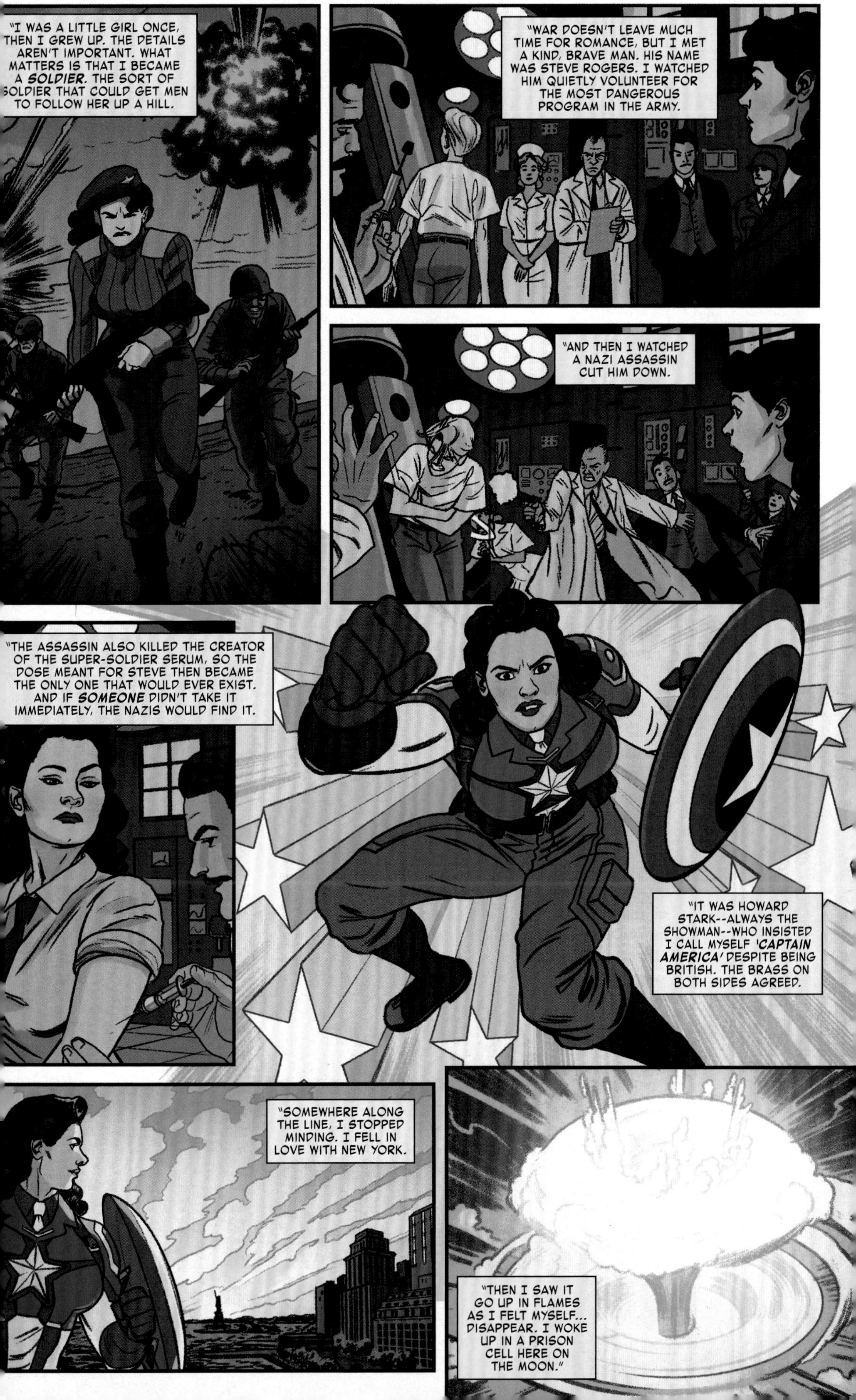
"I WAS A LITTLE GIRL ONCE, THEN I GREW UP. THE DETAILS AREN'T IMPORTANT. WHAT MATTERS IS THAT I BECAME A *SOLDIER*. THE SORT OF SOLDIER THAT COULD GET MEN TO FOLLOW HER UP A HILL.
"WAR DOESN'T LEAVE MUCH TIME FOR ROMANCE, BUT I MET A KIND, BRAVE MAN. HIS NAME WAS STEVE ROGERS. I WATCHED HIM QUIETLY VOLUNTEER FOR THE MOST DANGEROUS PROGRAM IN THE ARMY.
"AND THEN I WATCHED A NAZI ASSASSIN CUT HIM DOWN.
"THE ASSASSIN ALSO KILLED THE CREATOR OF THE SUPER-SOLDIER SERUM, SO THE DOSE MEANT FOR STEVE THEN BECAME THE ONLY ONE THAT WOULD EVER EXIST. AND IF *SOMEONE* DIDN'T TAKE IT IMMEDIATELY, THE NAZIS WOULD FIND IT.
"IT WAS HOWARD STARK--ALWAYS THE SHOWMAN--WHO INSISTED I CALL MYSELF *'CAPTAIN AMERICA'* DESPITE BEING BRITISH. THE BRASS ON BOTH SIDES AGREED.
"SOMEWHERE ALONG THE LINE, I STOPPED MINDING. I FELL IN LOVE WITH NEW YORK.
"THEN I SAW IT GO UP IN FLAMES AS I FELT MYSELF... DISAPPEAR. I WOKE UP IN A PRISON CELL HERE ON THE MOON."

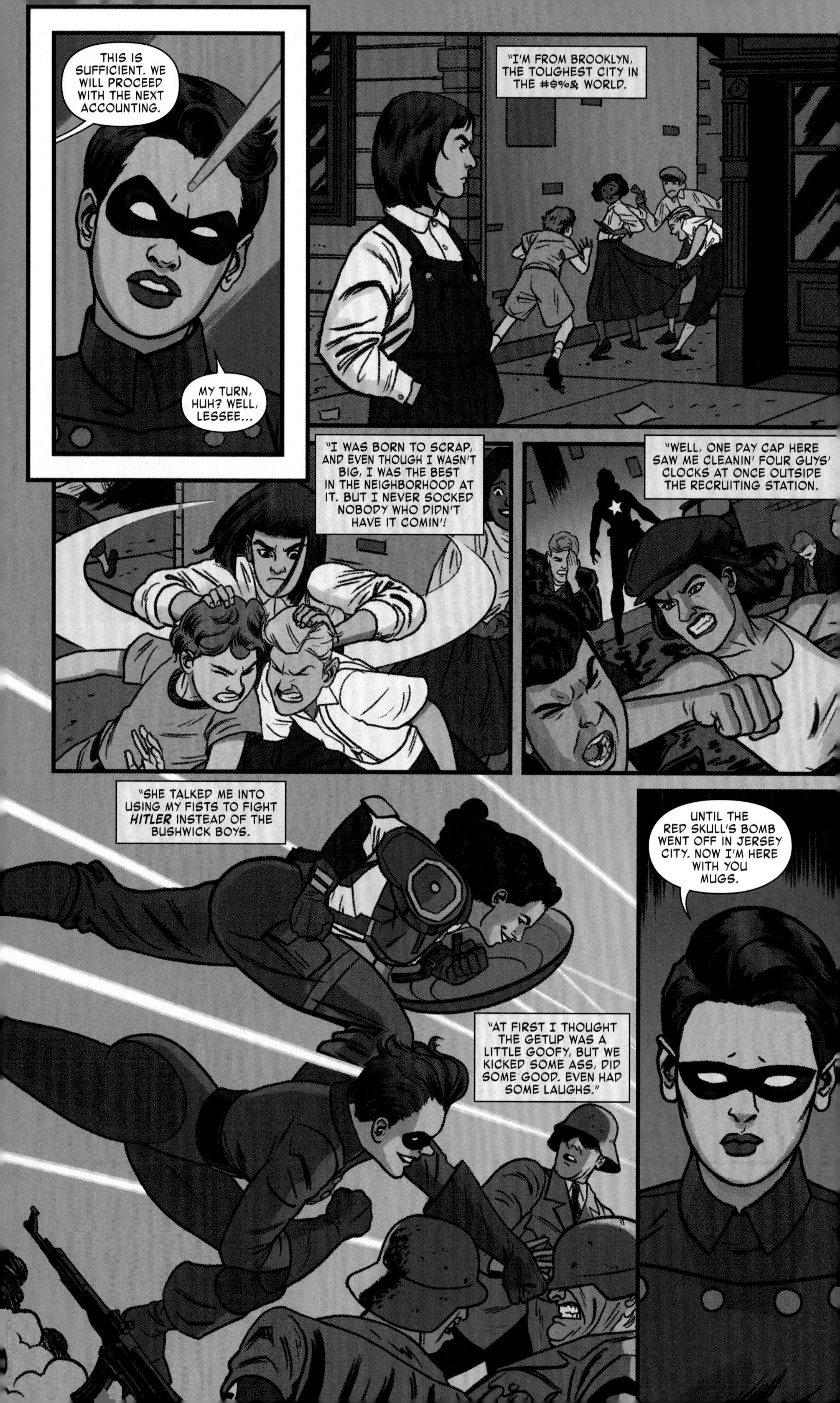
THIS IS SUFFICIENT. WE WILL PROCEED WITH THE NEXT ACCOUNTING.
MY TURN, HUH? WELL, LESSEE...
"I'M FROM BROOKLYN, THE TOUGHEST CITY IN THE #$%& WORLD.
"I WAS BORN TO SCRAP, AND EVEN THOUGH I WASN'T BIG, I WAS THE BEST IN THE NEIGHBORHOOD AT IT. BUT I NEVER SOCKED NOBODY WHO DIDN'T HAVE IT COMIN'!
"WELL, ONE DAY CAP HERE SAW ME CLEANIN' FOUR GUYS' CLOCKS AT ONCE OUTSIDE THE RECRUITING STATION.
"SHE TALKED ME INTO USING MY FISTS TO FIGHT *HITLER* INSTEAD OF THE BUSHWICK BOYS.
"AT FIRST I THOUGHT THE GETUP WAS A LITTLE GOOFY, BUT WE KICKED SOME ASS, DID SOME GOOD. EVEN HAD SOME LAUGHS."
UNTIL THE RED SKULL'S BOMB WENT OFF IN JERSEY CITY. NOW I'M HERE WITH YOU MUGS.

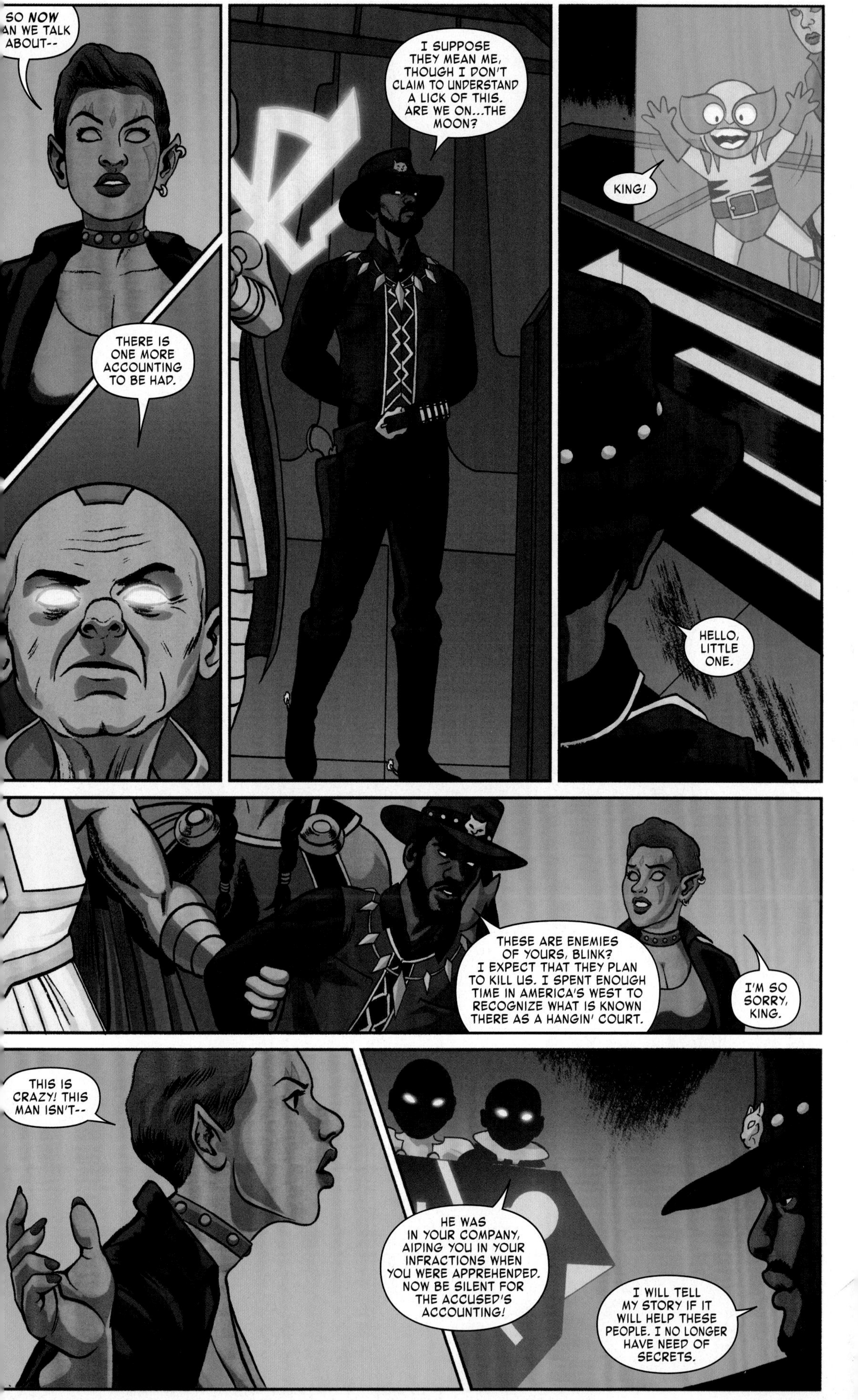

SO NOW
AN WE TALK
ABOUT--
THERE IS
ONE MORE
ACCOUNTING
TO BE HAD.
I SUPPOSE
THEY MEAN ME,
THOUGH I DON'T
CLAIM TO UNDERSTAND
A LICK OF THIS.
ARE WE ON...THE
MOON?
KING!
HELLO,
LITTLE
ONE.
THESE ARE ENEMIES
OF YOURS, BLINK?
I EXPECT THAT THEY PLAN
TO KILL US. I SPENT ENOUGH
TIME IN AMERICA'S WEST TO
RECOGNIZE WHAT IS KNOWN
THERE AS A HANGIN' COURT.
I'M SO
SORRY,
KING.
THIS IS
CRAZY! THIS
MAN ISN'T--
HE WAS
IN YOUR COMPANY,
AIDING YOU IN YOUR
INFRACTIONS WHEN
YOU WERE APPREHENDED.
NOW BE SILENT FOR
THE ACCUSED'S
ACCOUNTING!
I WILL TELL
MY STORY IF IT
WILL HELP THESE
PEOPLE. I NO LONGER
HAVE NEED OF
SECRETS.

THIS TECHNOLOGY... IT'S *REMARKABLE*. I WISH THAT MY *SISTER* COULD SEE THIS.

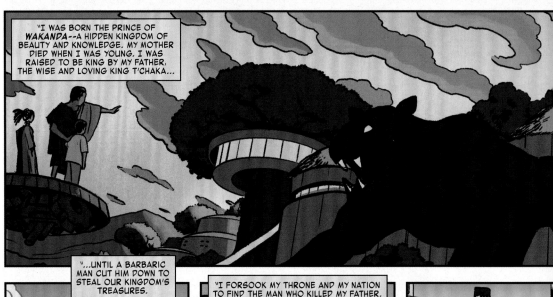

"I WAS BORN THE PRINCE OF *WAKANDA*--A HIDDEN KINGDOM OF BEAUTY AND KNOWLEDGE. MY MOTHER DIED WHEN I WAS YOUNG. I WAS RAISED TO BE KING BY MY FATHER, THE WISE AND LOVING KING T'CHAKA...

"...UNTIL A BARBARIC MAN CUT HIM DOWN TO STEAL OUR KINGDOM'S TREASURES.

"I FORSOOK MY THRONE AND MY NATION TO FIND THE MAN WHO KILLED MY FATHER. ACCORDING TO OUR WAYS, I CAN NEVER RETURN TO HIDDEN WAKANDA AGAIN.

"FOR YEARS I HUNTED MAGNUS. BUT AT LAST I FOUND HIM, AND MY FATHER HAS BEEN AVENGED."

I CROSSED OCEANS AND DESERTS IN PURSUIT OF THAT MAN. I HAVE SEEN HORRORS OF THE SPIRIT AND WONDERS OF THE MIND. BUT EVEN HERE ON THE MOON, I KNOW WRONG WHEN I SEE IT. AND THIS FARCE IS *WRONG*.

RENDER YOUR VERDICT. I HAVE SAID ENOUGH, I THINK.

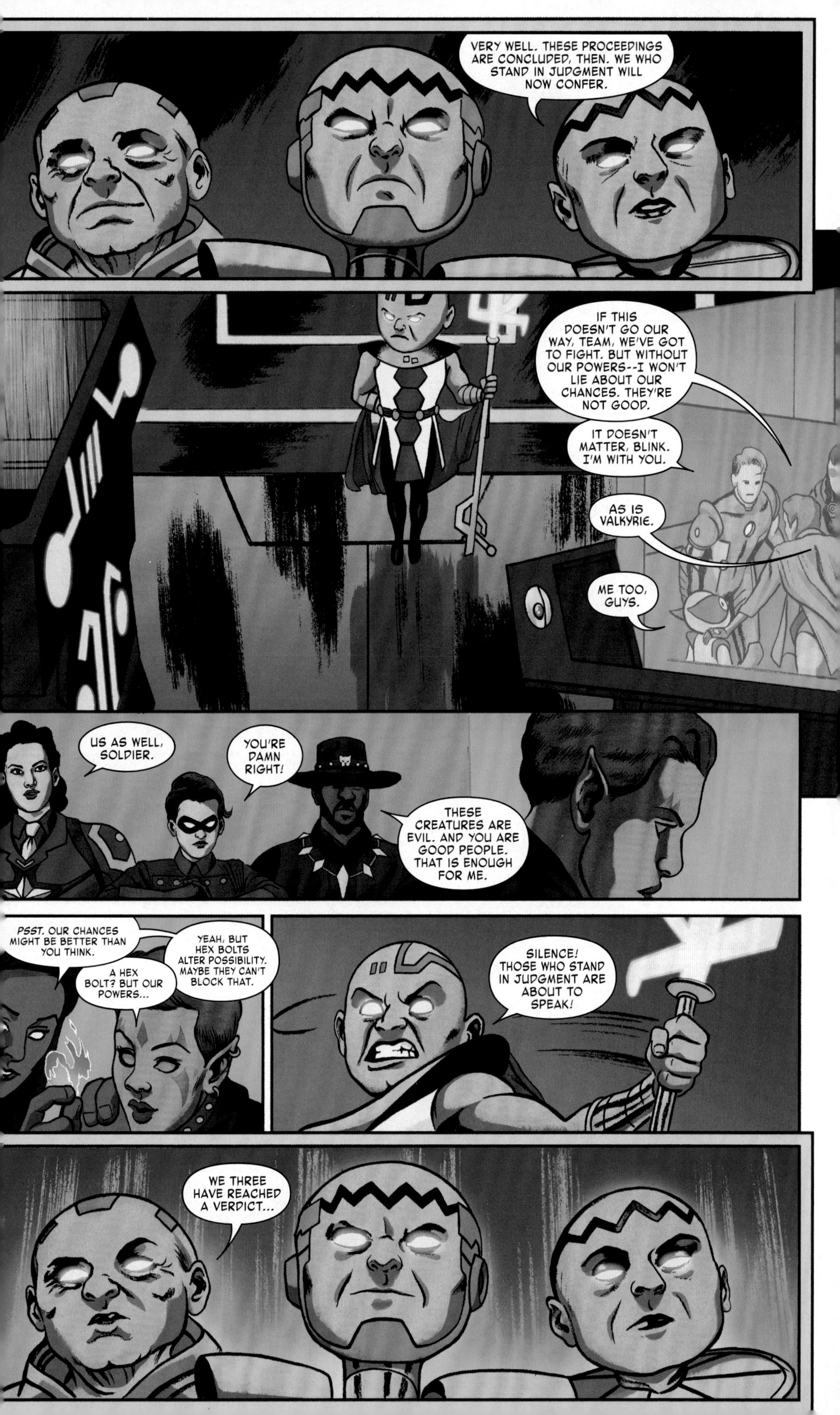
VERY WELL. THESE PROCEEDINGS ARE CONCLUDED, THEN. WE WHO STAND IN JUDGMENT WILL NOW CONFER.
IF THIS DOESN'T GO OUR WAY, TEAM, WE'VE GOT TO FIGHT. BUT WITHOUT OUR POWERS--I WON'T LIE ABOUT OUR CHANCES. THEY'RE NOT GOOD.
IT DOESN'T MATTER, BLINK. I'M WITH YOU.
AS IS VALKYRIE.
ME TOO, GUYS.
US AS WELL, SOLDIER.
YOU'RE DAMN RIGHT!
THESE CREATURES ARE EVIL. AND YOU ARE GOOD PEOPLE. THAT IS ENOUGH FOR ME.
PSST. OUR CHANCES MIGHT BE BETTER THAN YOU THINK.
A HEX BOLT? BUT OUR POWERS...
YEAH, BUT HEX BOLTS ALTER POSSIBILITY. MAYBE THEY CAN'T BLOCK THAT.
SILENCE! THOSE WHO STAND IN JUDGMENT ARE ABOUT TO SPEAK!
WE THREE HAVE REACHED A VERDICT...

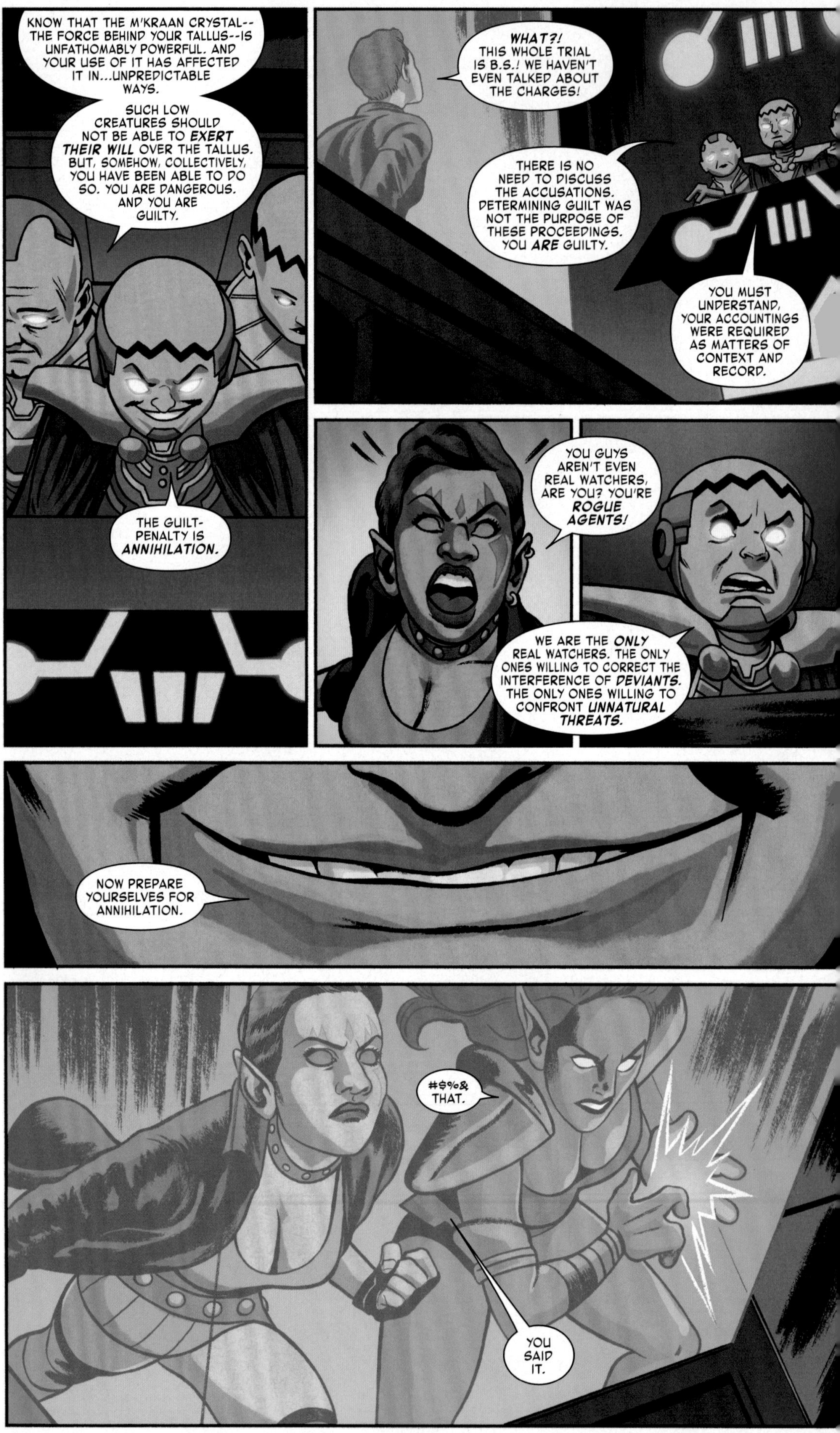
KNOW THAT THE M'KRAAN CRYSTAL--THE FORCE BEHIND YOUR TALLUS--IS UNFATHOMABLY POWERFUL. AND YOUR USE OF IT HAS AFFECTED IT IN...UNPREDICTABLE WAYS.
SUCH LOW CREATURES SHOULD NOT BE ABLE TO EXERT THEIR WILL OVER THE TALLUS. BUT, SOMEHOW, COLLECTIVELY, YOU HAVE BEEN ABLE TO DO SO. YOU ARE DANGEROUS. AND YOU ARE GUILTY.
THE GUILT-PENALTY IS ANNIHILATION.
WHAT?! THIS WHOLE TRIAL IS B.S.! WE HAVEN'T EVEN TALKED ABOUT THE CHARGES!
THERE IS NO NEED TO DISCUSS THE ACCUSATIONS. DETERMINING GUILT WAS NOT THE PURPOSE OF THESE PROCEEDINGS. YOU ARE GUILTY.
YOU MUST UNDERSTAND, YOUR ACCOUNTINGS WERE REQUIRED AS MATTERS OF CONTEXT AND RECORD.
YOU GUYS AREN'T EVEN REAL WATCHERS, ARE YOU? YOU'RE ROGUE AGENTS!
WE ARE THE ONLY REAL WATCHERS. THE ONLY ONES WILLING TO CORRECT THE INTERFERENCE OF DEVIANTS. THE ONLY ONES WILLING TO CONFRONT UNNATURAL THREATS.
NOW PREPARE YOURSELVES FOR ANNIHILATION.
#$%& THAT.
YOU SAID IT.

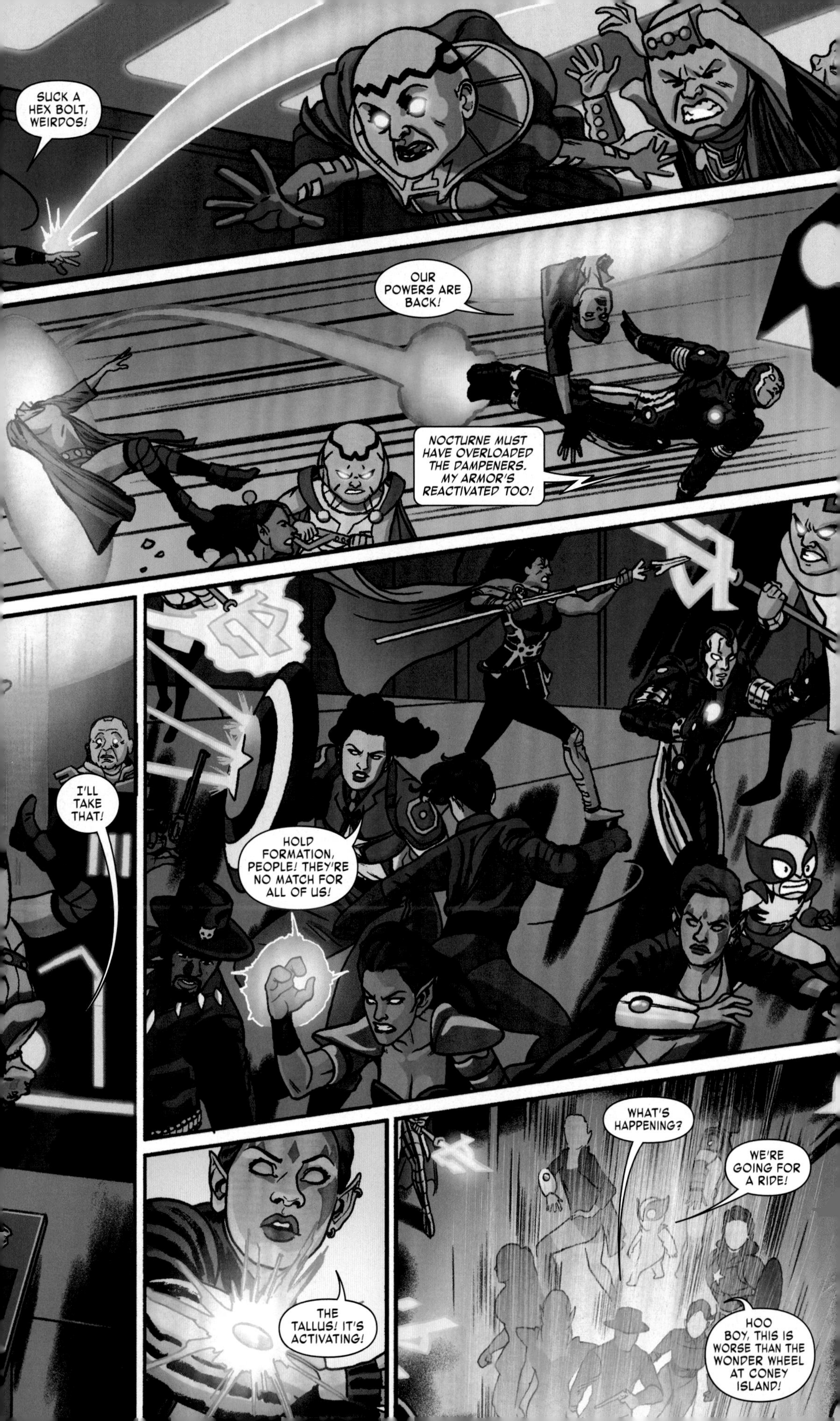
SUCK A HEX BOLT, WEIRDOS!
OUR POWERS ARE BACK!
NOCTURNE MUST HAVE OVERLOADED THE DAMPENERS. MY ARMOR'S REACTIVATED TOO!
I'LL TAKE THAT!
HOLD FORMATION, PEOPLE! THEY'RE NO MATCH FOR ALL OF US!
THE TALLUS! IT'S ACTIVATING!
WHAT'S HAPPENING?
WE'RE GOING FOR A RIDE!
HOO BOY, THIS IS WORSE THAN THE WONDER WHEEL AT CONEY ISLAND!

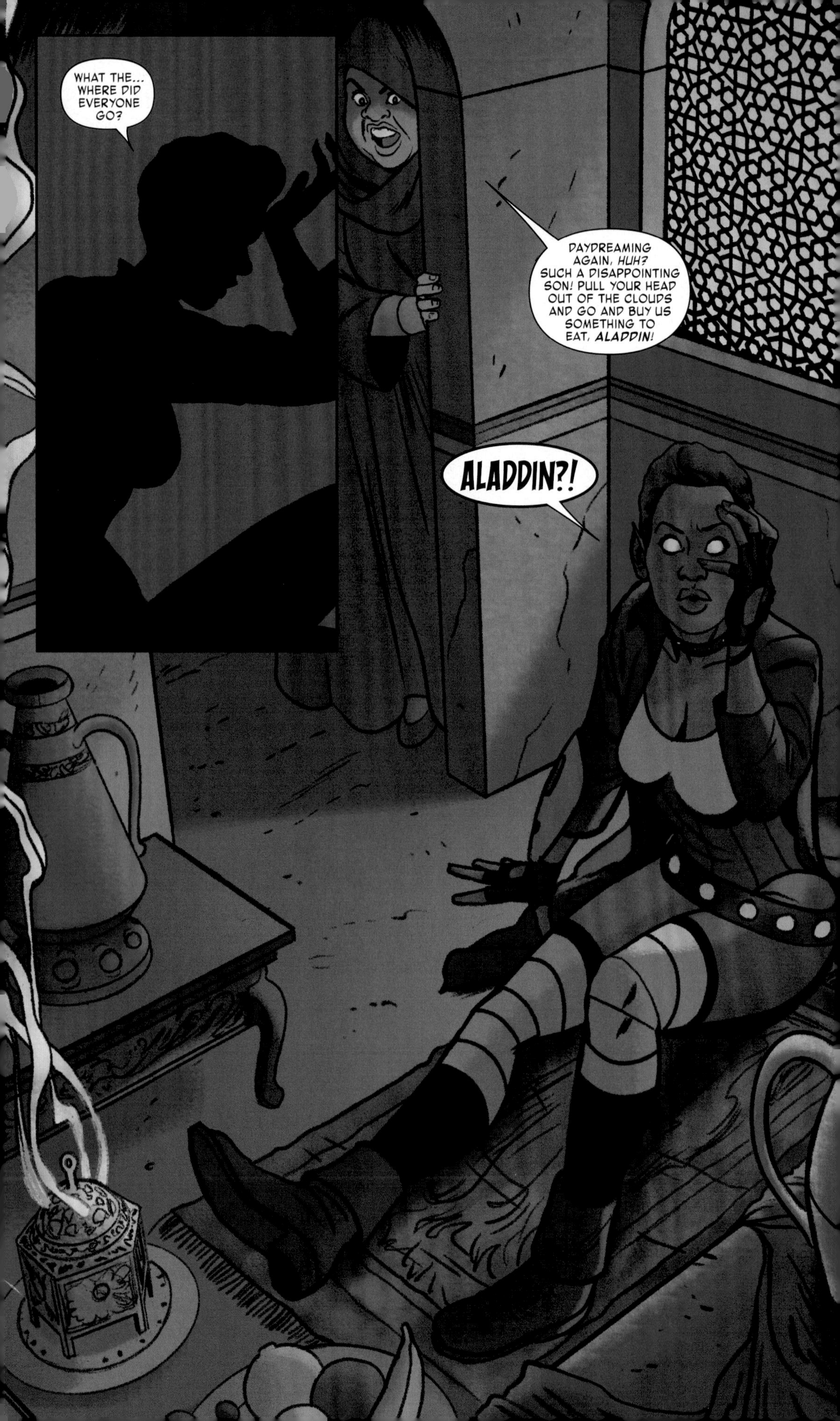
WHAT THE... WHERE DID EVERYONE GO?
DAYDREAMING AGAIN, HUH? SUCH A DISAPPOINTING SON! PULL YOUR HEAD OUT OF THE CLOUDS AND GO AND BUY US SOMETHING TO EAT, ALADDIN!
ALADDIN?!

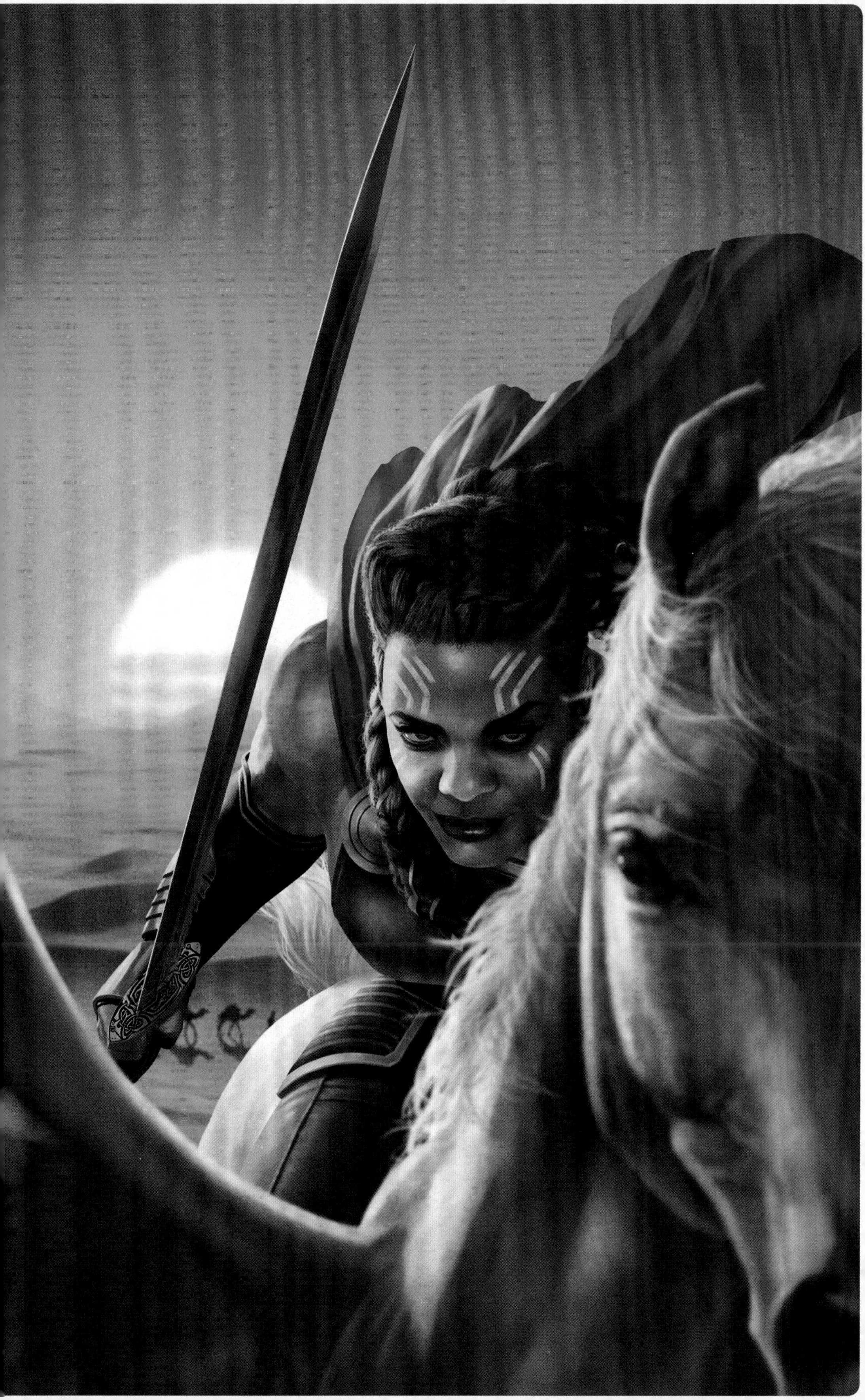

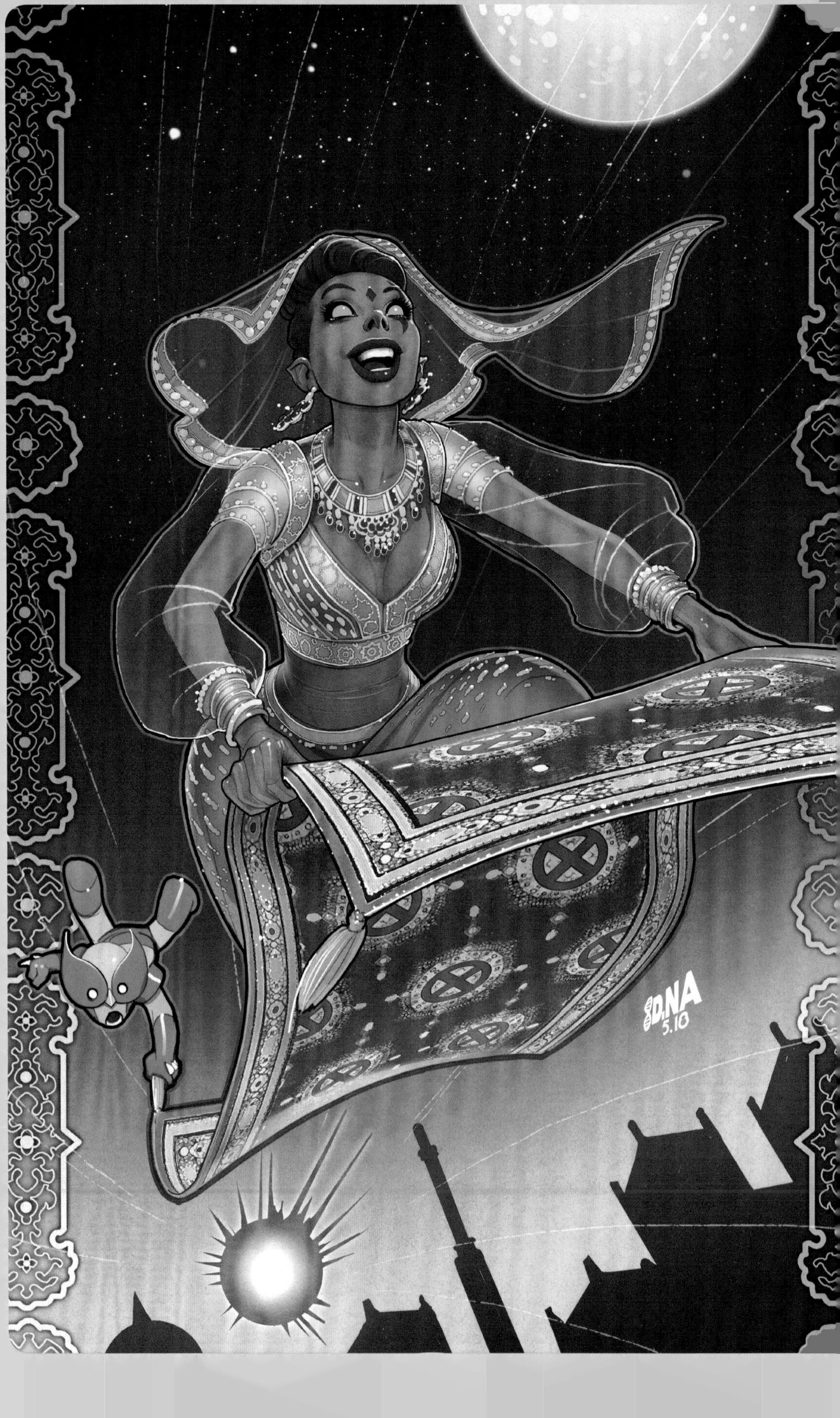
D.NA
5.18

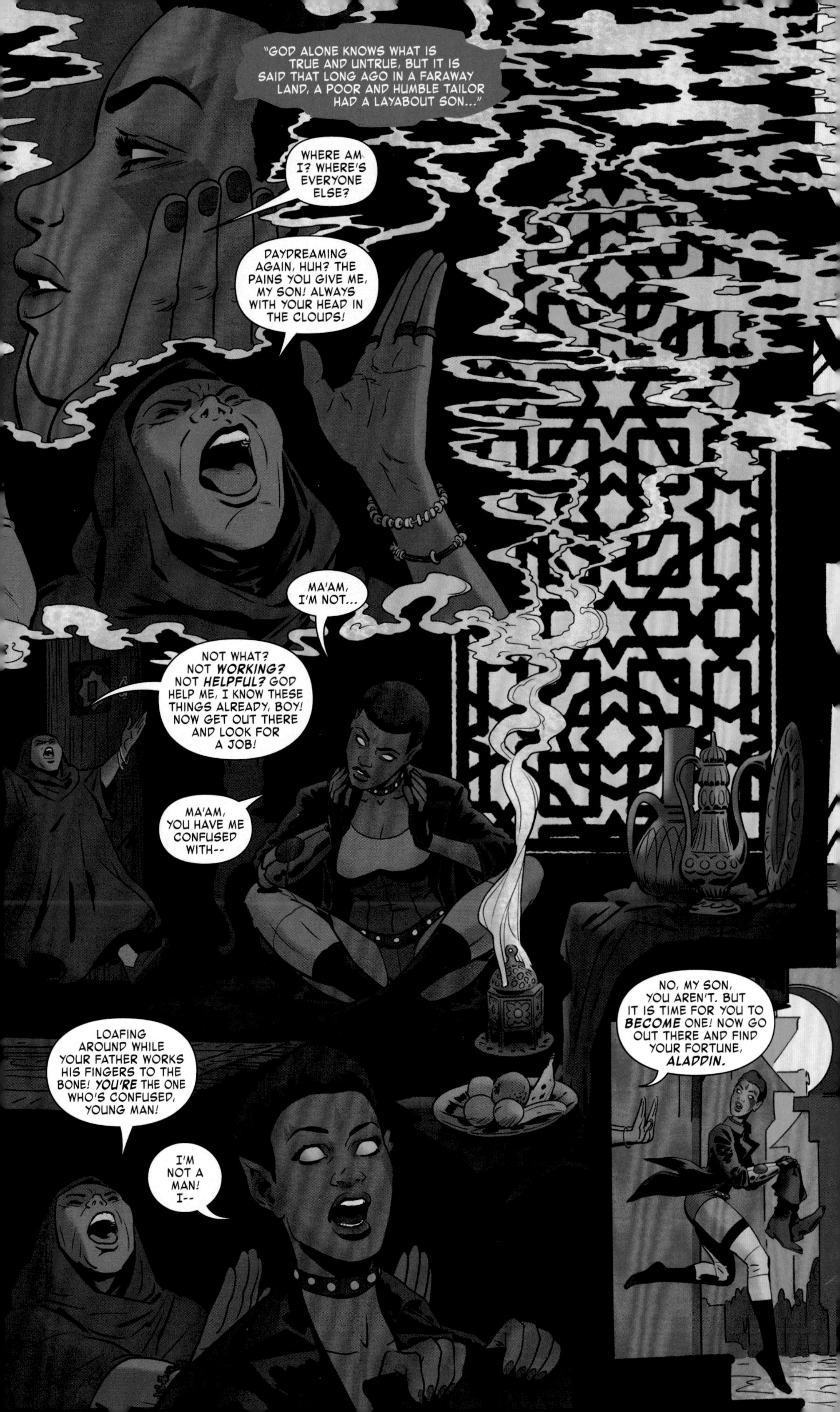

"GOD ALONE KNOWS WHAT IS TRUE AND UNTRUE, BUT IT IS SAID THAT LONG AGO IN A FARAWAY LAND, A POOR AND HUMBLE TAILOR HAD A LAYABOUT SON..."
WHERE AM I? WHERE'S EVERYONE ELSE?
DAYDREAMING AGAIN, HUH? THE PAINS YOU GIVE ME, MY SON! ALWAYS WITH YOUR HEAD IN THE CLOUDS!
MA'AM, I'M NOT...
NOT WHAT? NOT **WORKING?** NOT **HELPFUL?** GOD HELP ME, I KNOW THESE THINGS ALREADY, BOY! NOW GET OUT THERE AND LOOK FOR A JOB!
MA'AM, YOU HAVE ME CONFUSED WITH--
LOAFING AROUND WHILE YOUR FATHER WORKS HIS FINGERS TO THE BONE! **YOU'RE** THE ONE WHO'S CONFUSED, YOUNG MAN!
I'M NOT A MAN! I--
NO, MY SON, YOU AREN'T. BUT IT IS TIME FOR YOU TO **BECOME** ONE! NOW GO OUT THERE AND FIND YOUR FORTUNE, **ALADDIN.**

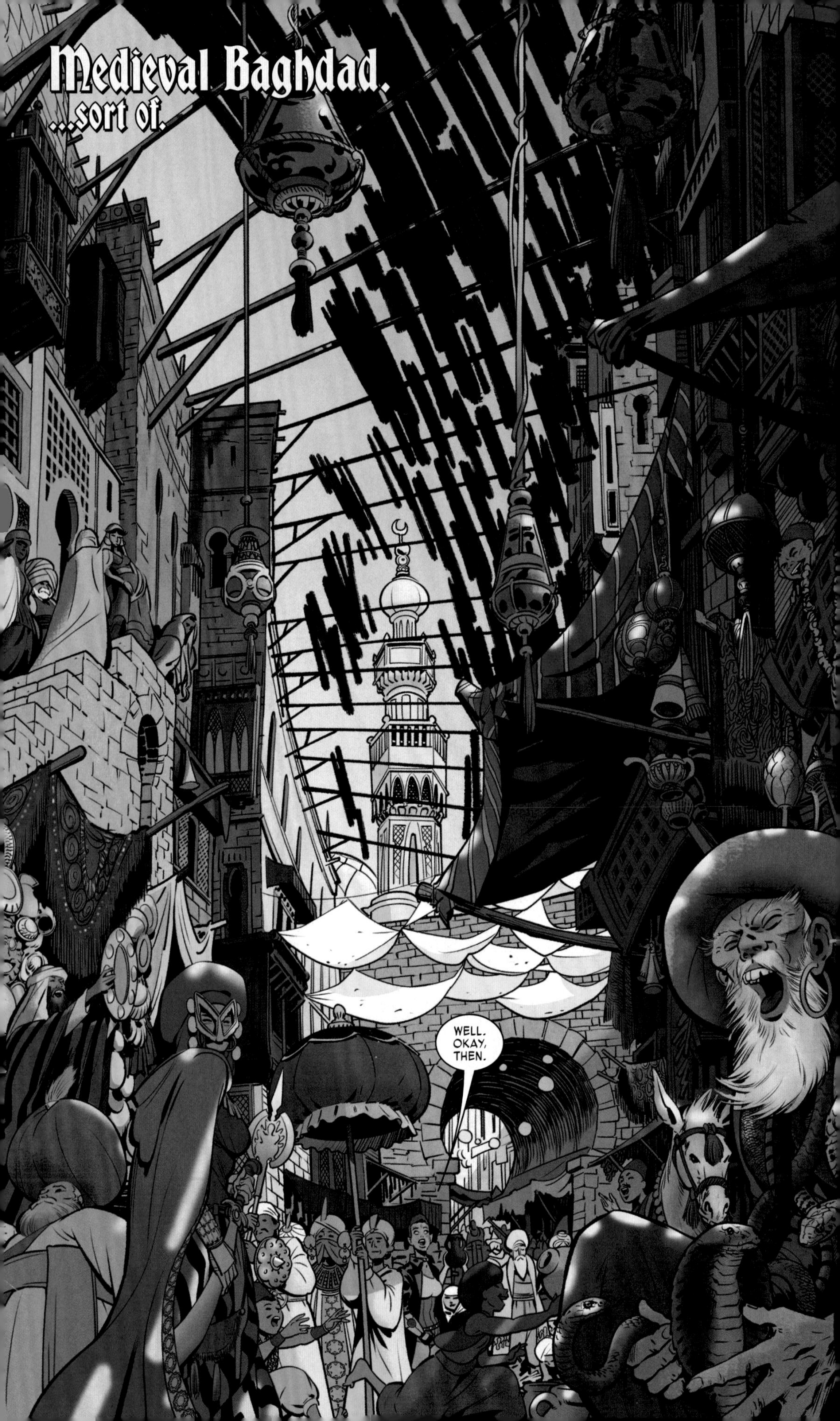
Medieval Baghdad.
...sort of.
WELL. OKAY, THEN.

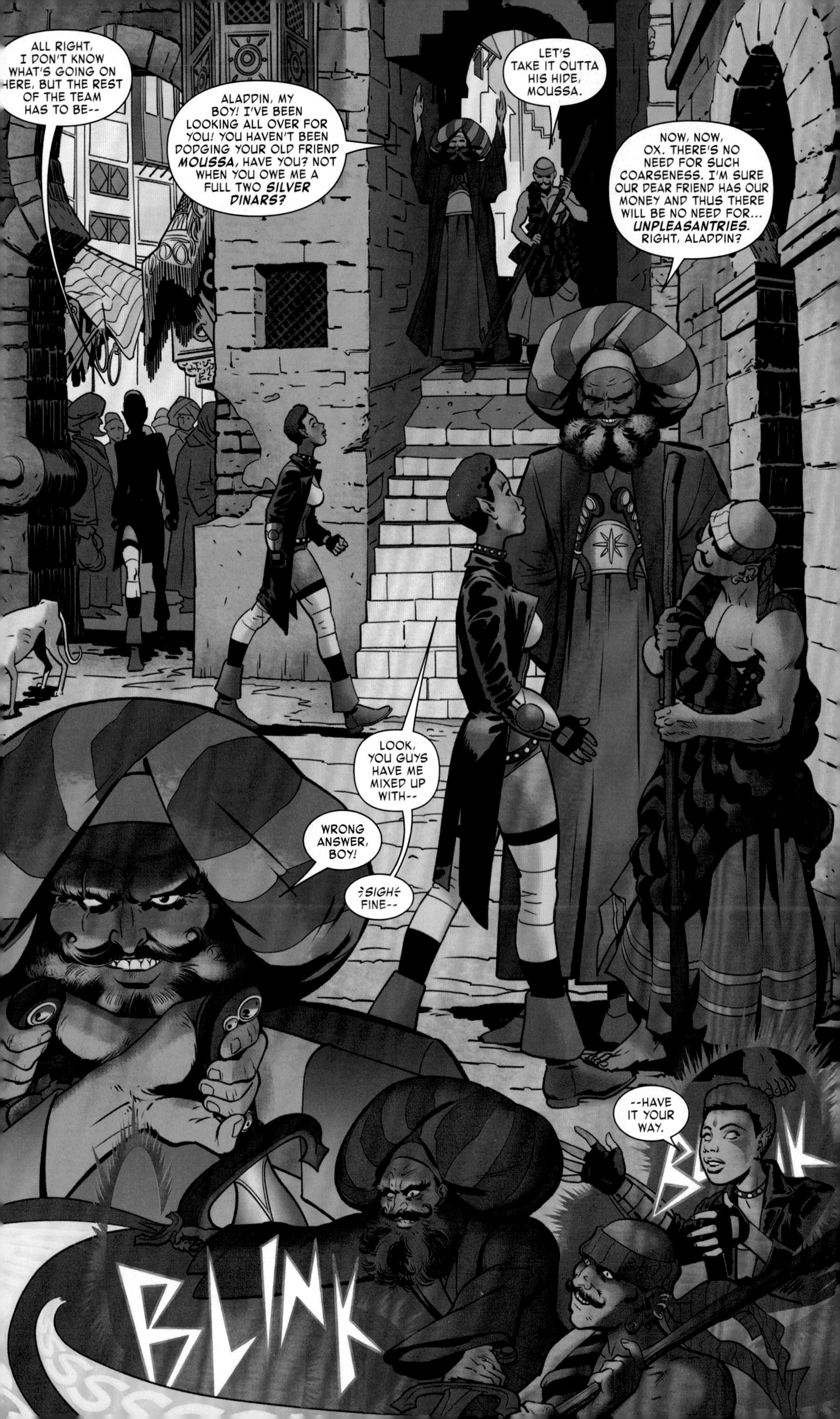
ALL RIGHT, I DON'T KNOW WHAT'S GOING ON HERE, BUT THE REST OF THE TEAM HAS TO BE--
ALADDIN, MY BOY! I'VE BEEN LOOKING ALL OVER FOR YOU! YOU HAVEN'T BEEN DODGING YOUR OLD FRIEND MOUSSA, HAVE YOU? NOT WHEN YOU OWE ME A FULL TWO SILVER DINARS?
LET'S TAKE IT OUTTA HIS HIDE, MOUSSA.
NOW, NOW, OX. THERE'S NO NEED FOR SUCH COARSENESS. I'M SURE OUR DEAR FRIEND HAS OUR MONEY AND THUS THERE WILL BE NO NEED FOR... UNPLEASANTRIES. RIGHT, ALADDIN?
LOOK, YOU GUYS HAVE ME MIXED UP WITH--
WRONG ANSWER, BOY!
SIGH FINE--
--HAVE IT YOUR WAY.
BLINK
BLINK

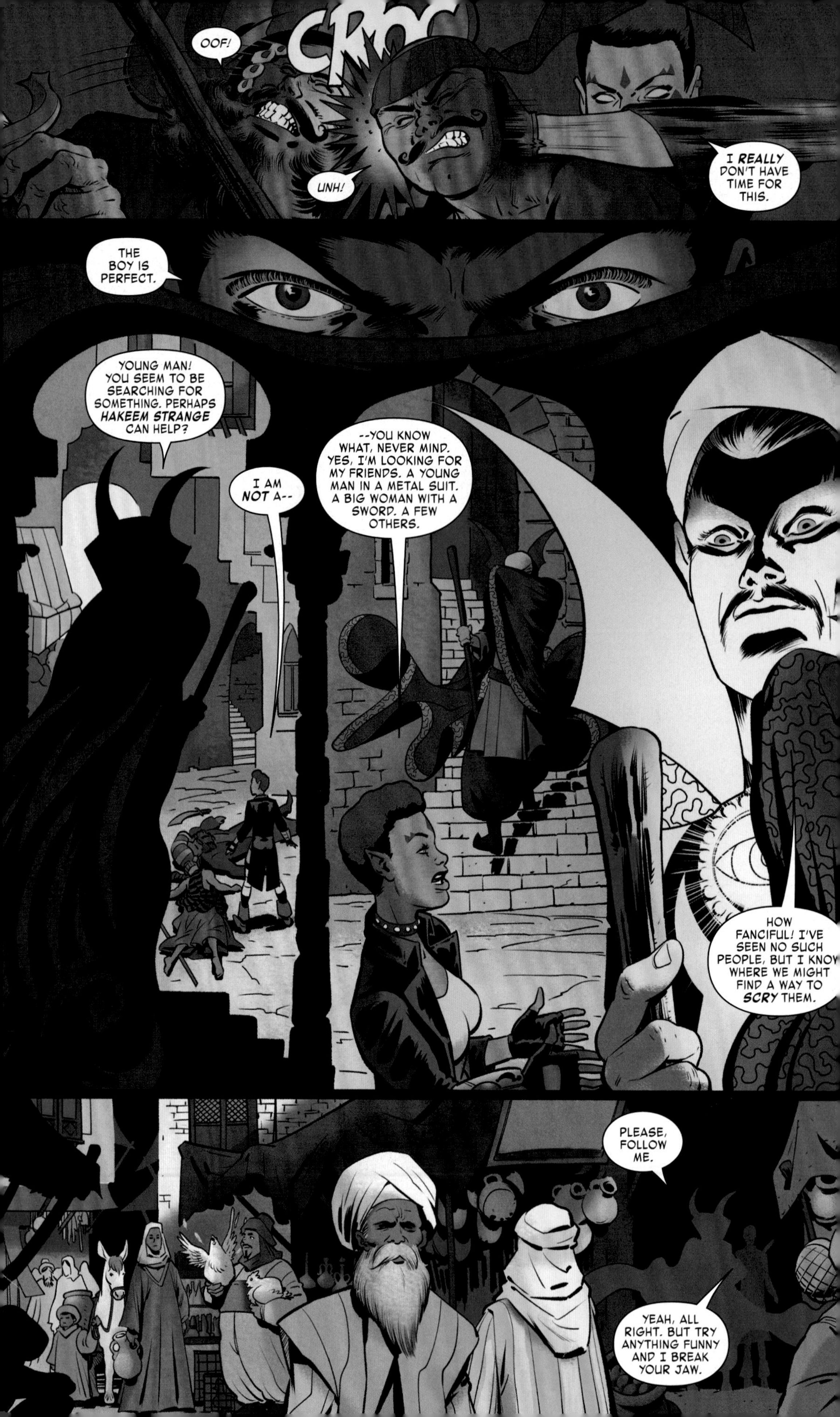
OOF!
CROC
UNH!
I REALLY DON'T HAVE TIME FOR THIS.
THE BOY IS PERFECT.
YOUNG MAN! YOU SEEM TO BE SEARCHING FOR SOMETHING. PERHAPS HAKEEM STRANGE CAN HELP?
I AM NOT A--
--YOU KNOW WHAT, NEVER MIND. YES, I'M LOOKING FOR MY FRIENDS. A YOUNG MAN IN A METAL SUIT. A BIG WOMAN WITH A SWORD. A FEW OTHERS.
HOW FANCIFUL! I'VE SEEN NO SUCH PEOPLE, BUT I KNOW WHERE WE MIGHT FIND A WAY TO SCRY THEM.
PLEASE, FOLLOW ME.
YEAH, ALL RIGHT. BUT TRY ANYTHING FUNNY AND I BREAK YOUR JAW.

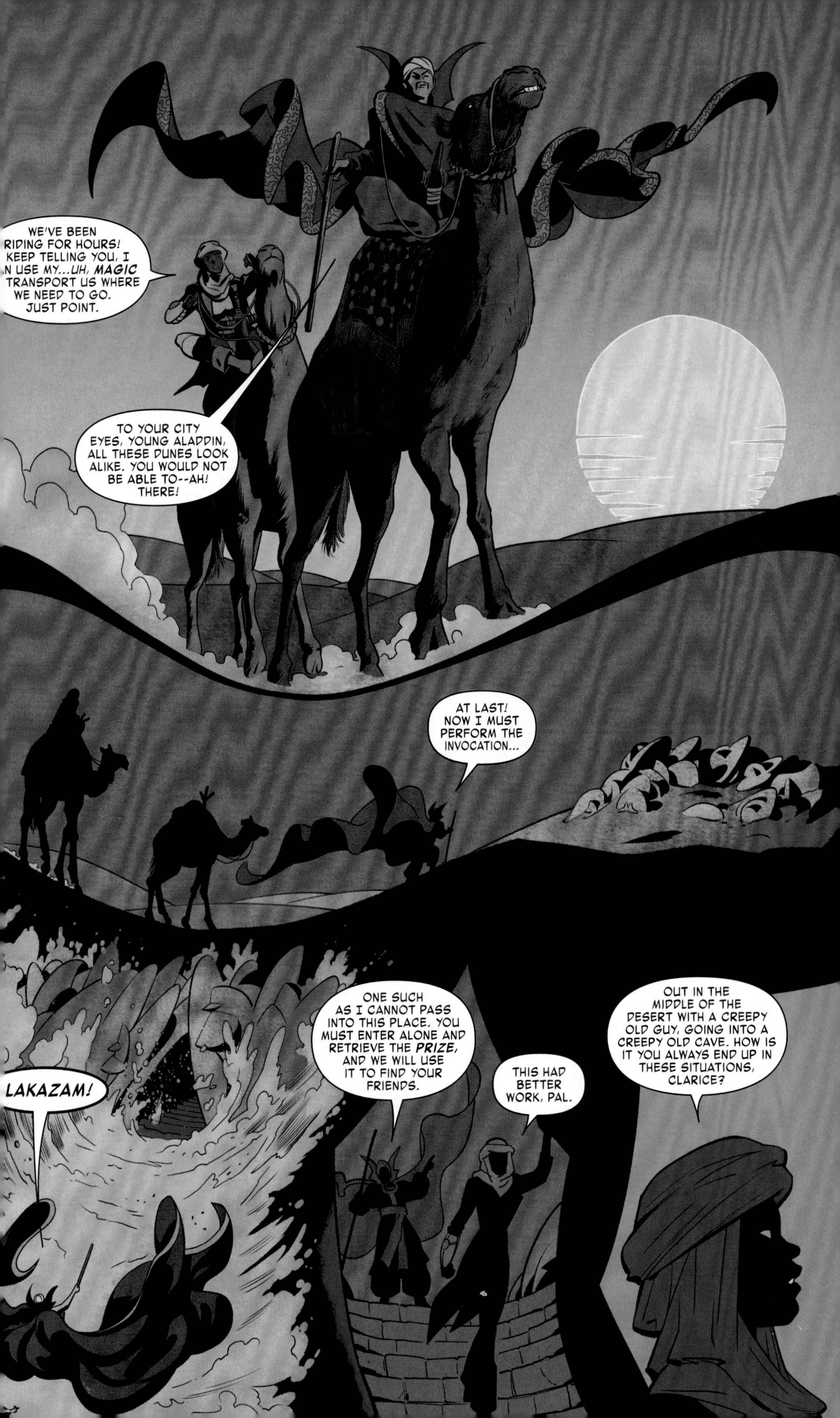
WE'VE BEEN RIDING FOR HOURS! KEEP TELLING YOU, I N USE MY...UH, MAGIC TRANSPORT US WHERE WE NEED TO GO. JUST POINT.
TO YOUR CITY EYES, YOUNG ALADDIN, ALL THESE DUNES LOOK ALIKE. YOU WOULD NOT BE ABLE TO--AH! THERE!
AT LAST! NOW I MUST PERFORM THE INVOCATION...
LAKAZAM!
ONE SUCH AS I CANNOT PASS INTO THIS PLACE. YOU MUST ENTER ALONE AND RETRIEVE THE PRIZE, AND WE WILL USE IT TO FIND YOUR FRIENDS.
THIS HAD BETTER WORK, PAL.
OUT IN THE MIDDLE OF THE DESERT WITH A CREEPY OLD GUY, GOING INTO A CREEPY OLD CAVE. HOW IS IT YOU ALWAYS END UP IN THESE SITUATIONS, CLARICE?

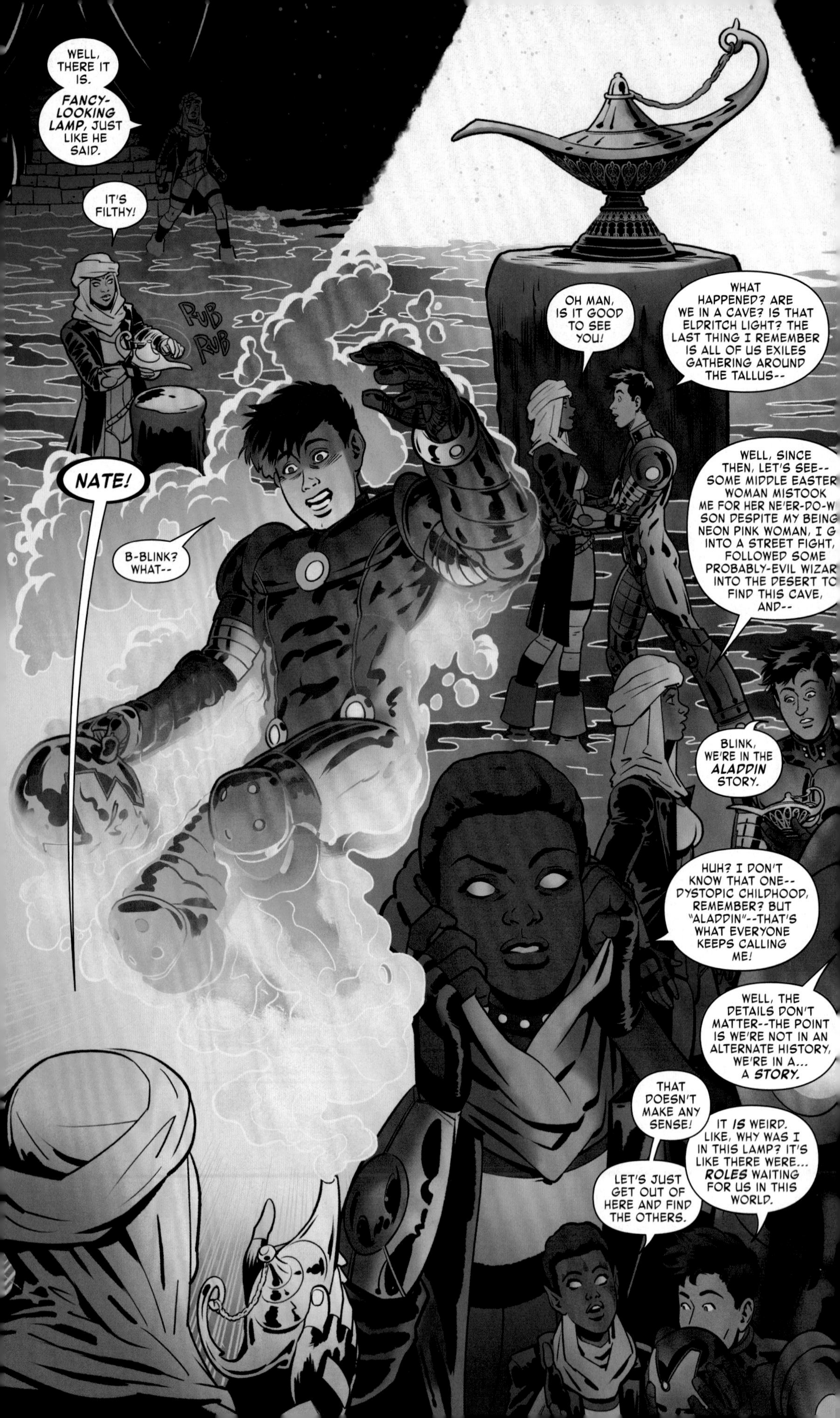
WELL, THERE IT IS. FANCY-LOOKING LAMP, JUST LIKE HE SAID.
IT'S FILTHY!
RUB RUB
NATE!
B-BLINK? WHAT--
OH MAN, IS IT GOOD TO SEE YOU!
WHAT HAPPENED? ARE WE IN A CAVE? IS THAT ELDRITCH LIGHT? THE LAST THING I REMEMBER IS ALL OF US EXILES GATHERING AROUND THE TALLUS--
WELL, SINCE THEN, LET'S SEE-- SOME MIDDLE EASTER WOMAN MISTOOK ME FOR HER NE'ER-DO-W SON DESPITE MY BEING NEON PINK WOMAN, I G INTO A STREET FIGHT, FOLLOWED SOME PROBABLY-EVIL WIZAR INTO THE DESERT TO FIND THIS CAVE, AND--
BLINK, WE'RE IN THE ALADDIN STORY.
HUH? I DON'T KNOW THAT ONE-- DYSTOPIC CHILDHOOD, REMEMBER? BUT "ALADDIN"--THAT'S WHAT EVERYONE KEEPS CALLING ME!
WELL, THE DETAILS DON'T MATTER--THE POINT IS WE'RE NOT IN AN ALTERNATE HISTORY, WE'RE IN A... A STORY.
THAT DOESN'T MAKE ANY SENSE!
LET'S JUST GET OUT OF HERE AND FIND THE OTHERS.
IT IS WEIRD. LIKE, WHY WAS I IN THIS LAMP? IT'S LIKE THERE WERE... ROLES WAITING FOR US IN THIS WORLD.

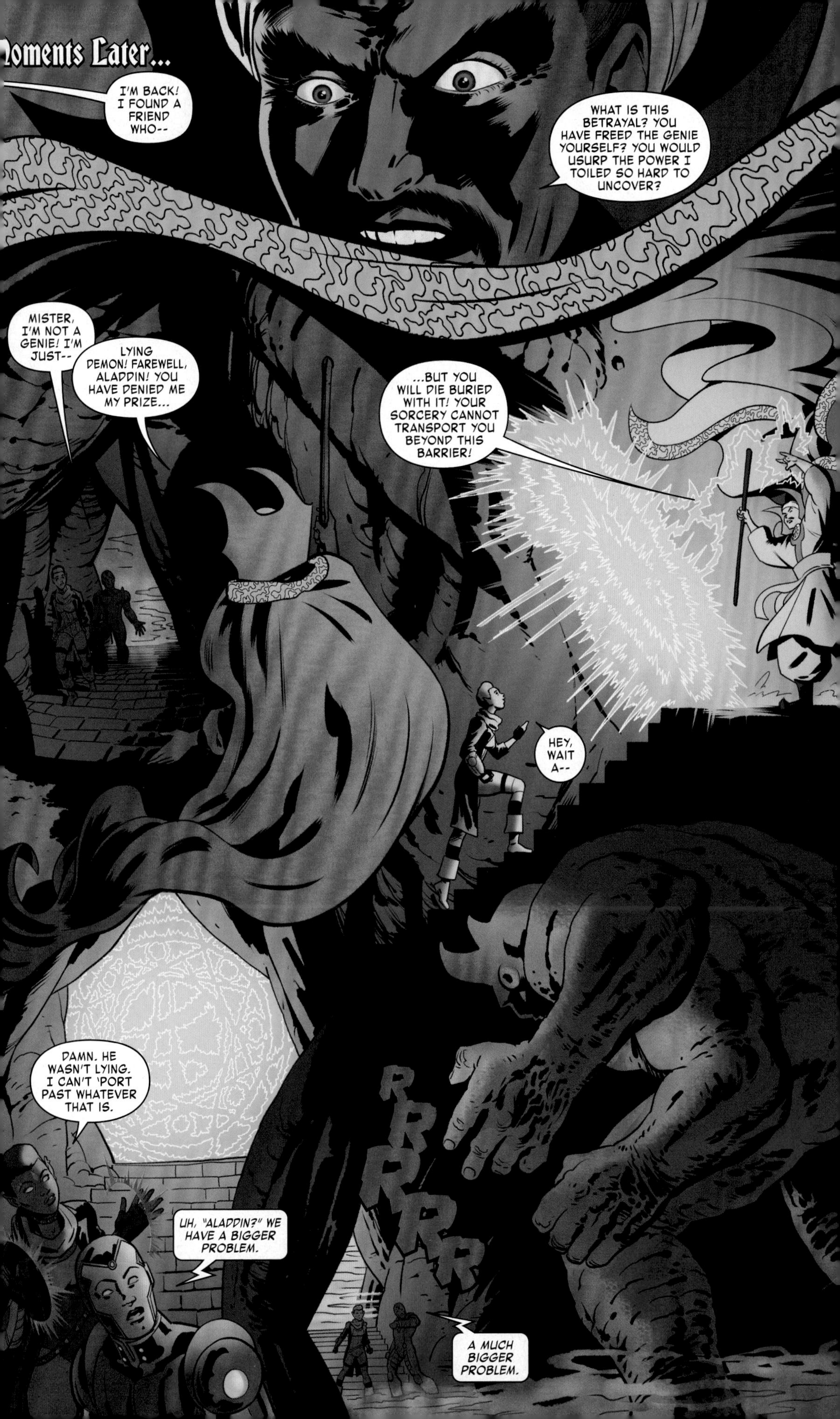

Moments Later...
I'M BACK! I FOUND A FRIEND WHO--
WHAT IS THIS BETRAYAL? YOU HAVE FREED THE GENIE YOURSELF? YOU WOULD USURP THE POWER I TOILED SO HARD TO UNCOVER?
MISTER, I'M NOT A GENIE! I'M JUST--
LYING DEMON! FAREWELL, ALADDIN! YOU HAVE DENIED ME MY PRIZE...
...BUT YOU WILL DIE BURIED WITH IT! YOUR SORCERY CANNOT TRANSPORT YOU BEYOND THIS BARRIER!
HEY, WAIT A--
DAMN. HE WASN'T LYING. I CAN'T 'PORT PAST WHATEVER THAT IS.
RRRRR
UH, "ALADDIN?" WE HAVE A BIGGER PROBLEM.
A MUCH BIGGER PROBLEM.

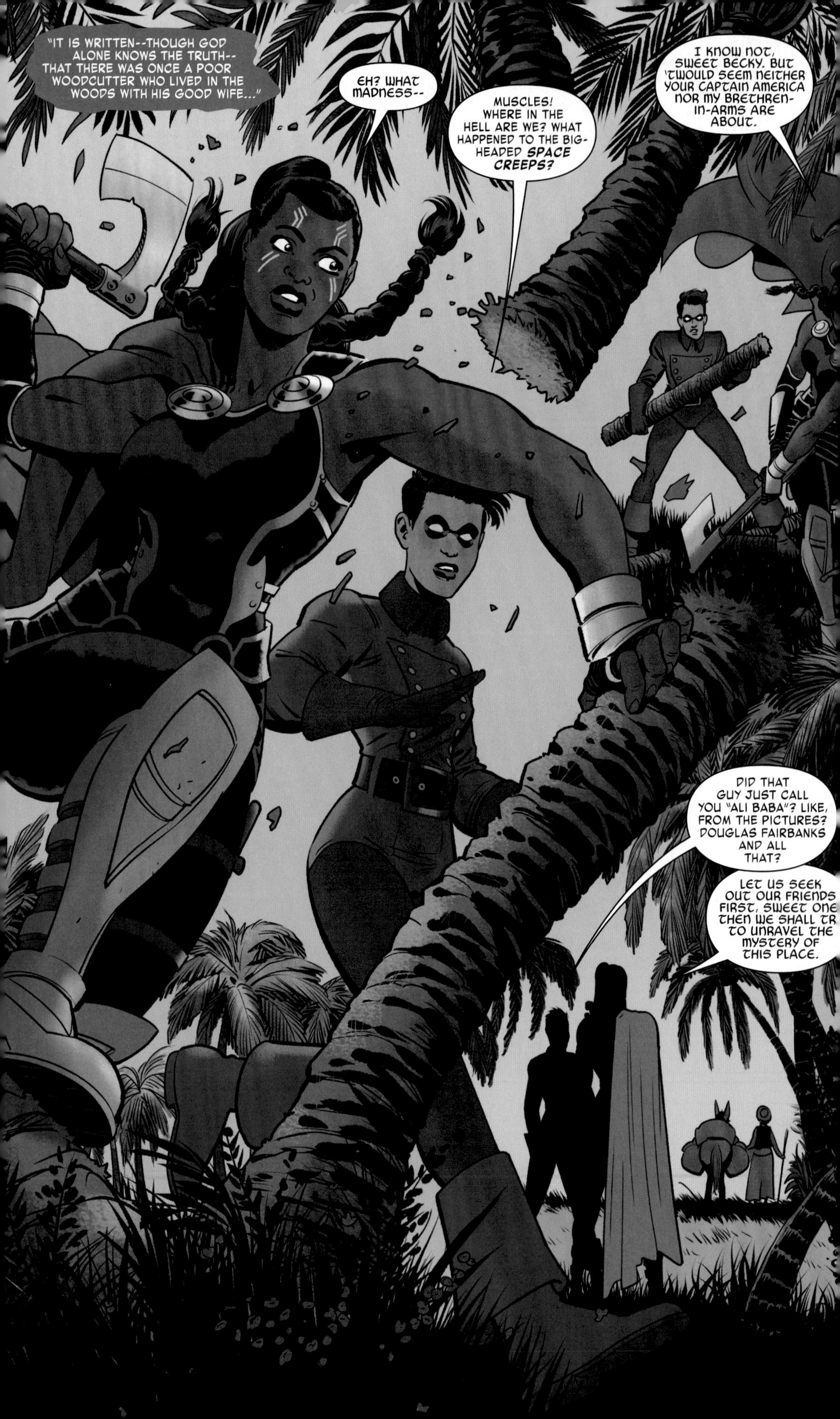
"IT IS WRITTEN--THOUGH GOD ALONE KNOWS THE TRUTH--THAT THERE WAS ONCE A POOR WOODCUTTER WHO LIVED IN THE WOODS WITH HIS GOOD WIFE..."
EH? WHAT MADNESS--
MUSCLES! WHERE IN THE HELL ARE WE? WHAT HAPPENED TO THE BIG-HEADED SPACE CREEPS?
I KNOW NOT, SWEET BECKY. BUT 'TWOULD SEEM NEITHER YOUR CAPTAIN AMERICA NOR MY BRETHREN-IN-ARMS ARE ABOUT.
DID THAT GUY JUST CALL YOU "ALI BABA"? LIKE, FROM THE PICTURES? DOUGLAS FAIRBANKS AND ALL THAT?
LET US SEEK OUT OUR FRIENDS FIRST, SWEET ONE. THEN WE SHALL TR TO UNRAVEL THE MYSTERY OF THIS PLACE.

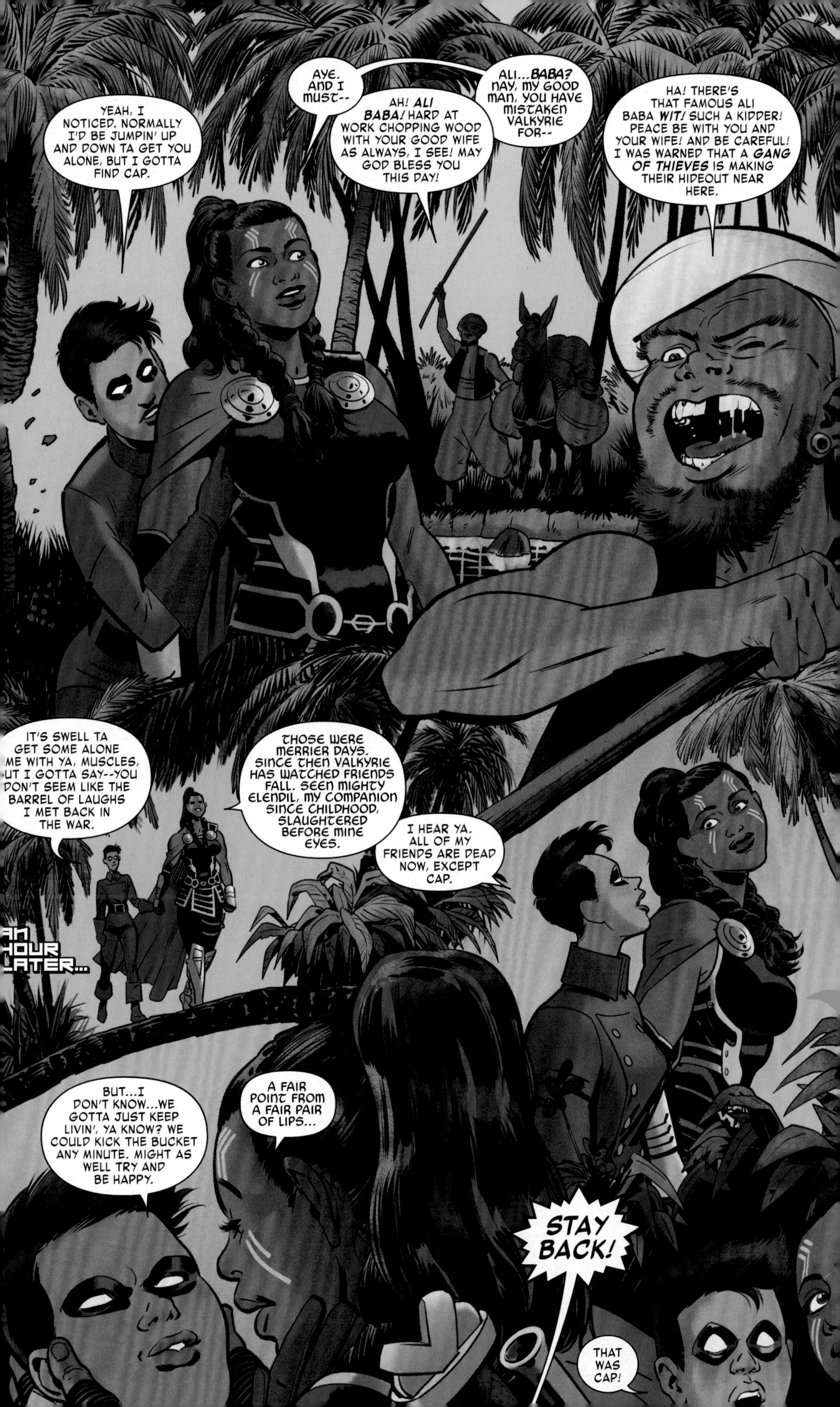
YEAH, I NOTICED. NORMALLY I'D BE JUMPIN' UP AND DOWN TA GET YOU ALONE, BUT I GOTTA FIND CAP.
AYE. AND I MUST--
AH! ALI BABA! HARD AT WORK CHOPPING WOOD WITH YOUR GOOD WIFE AS ALWAYS, I SEE! MAY GOD BLESS YOU THIS DAY!
ALI...BABA? NAY, MY GOOD MAN, YOU HAVE MISTAKEN VALKYRIE FOR--
HA! THERE'S THAT FAMOUS ALI BABA WIT! SUCH A KIDDER! PEACE BE WITH YOU AND YOUR WIFE! AND BE CAREFUL! I WAS WARNED THAT A GANG OF THIEVES IS MAKING THEIR HIDEOUT NEAR HERE.
AN HOUR LATER...
IT'S SWELL TA GET SOME ALONE ME WITH YA, MUSCLES, UT I GOTTA SAY--YOU DON'T SEEM LIKE THE BARREL OF LAUGHS I MET BACK IN THE WAR.
THOSE WERE MERRIER DAYS. SINCE THEN VALKYRIE HAS WATCHED FRIENDS FALL. SEEN MIGHTY ELENDIL, MY COMPANION SINCE CHILDHOOD, SLAUGHTERED BEFORE MINE EYES.
I HEAR YA. ALL OF MY FRIENDS ARE DEAD NOW, EXCEPT CAP.
BUT...I DON'T KNOW...WE GOTTA JUST KEEP LIVIN', YA KNOW? WE COULD KICK THE BUCKET ANY MINUTE. MIGHT AS WELL TRY AND BE HAPPY.
A FAIR POINT FROM A FAIR PAIR OF LIPS...
STAY BACK!
THAT WAS CAP!

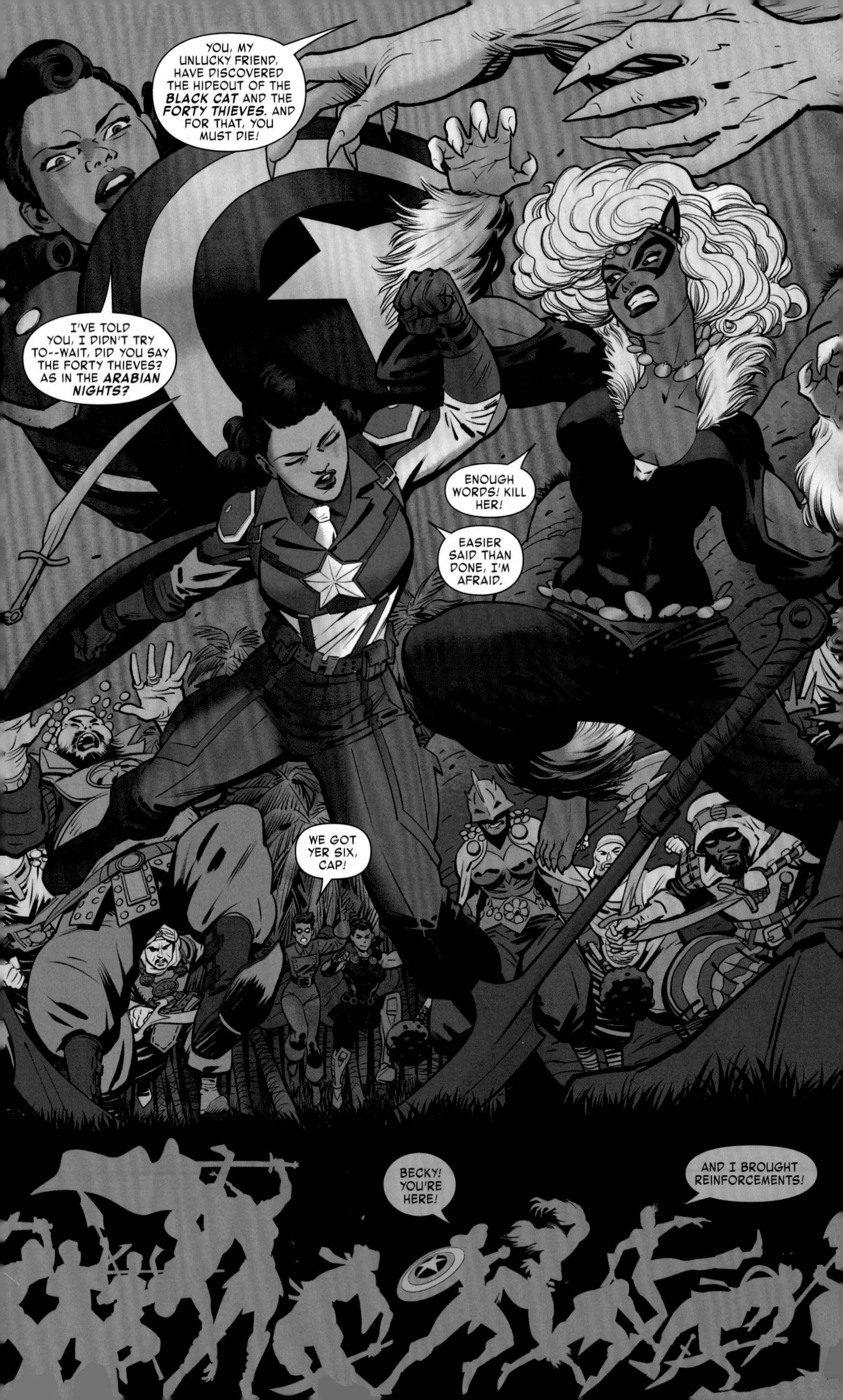
YOU, MY UNLUCKY FRIEND, HAVE DISCOVERED THE HIDEOUT OF THE BLACK CAT AND THE FORTY THIEVES. AND FOR THAT, YOU MUST DIE!
I'VE TOLD YOU, I DIDN'T TRY TO--WAIT, DID YOU SAY THE FORTY THIEVES? AS IN THE ARABIAN NIGHTS?
ENOUGH WORDS! KILL HER!
EASIER SAID THAN DONE, I'M AFRAID.
WE GOT YER SIX, CAP!
BECKY! YOU'RE HERE!
AND I BROUGHT REINFORCEMENTS!

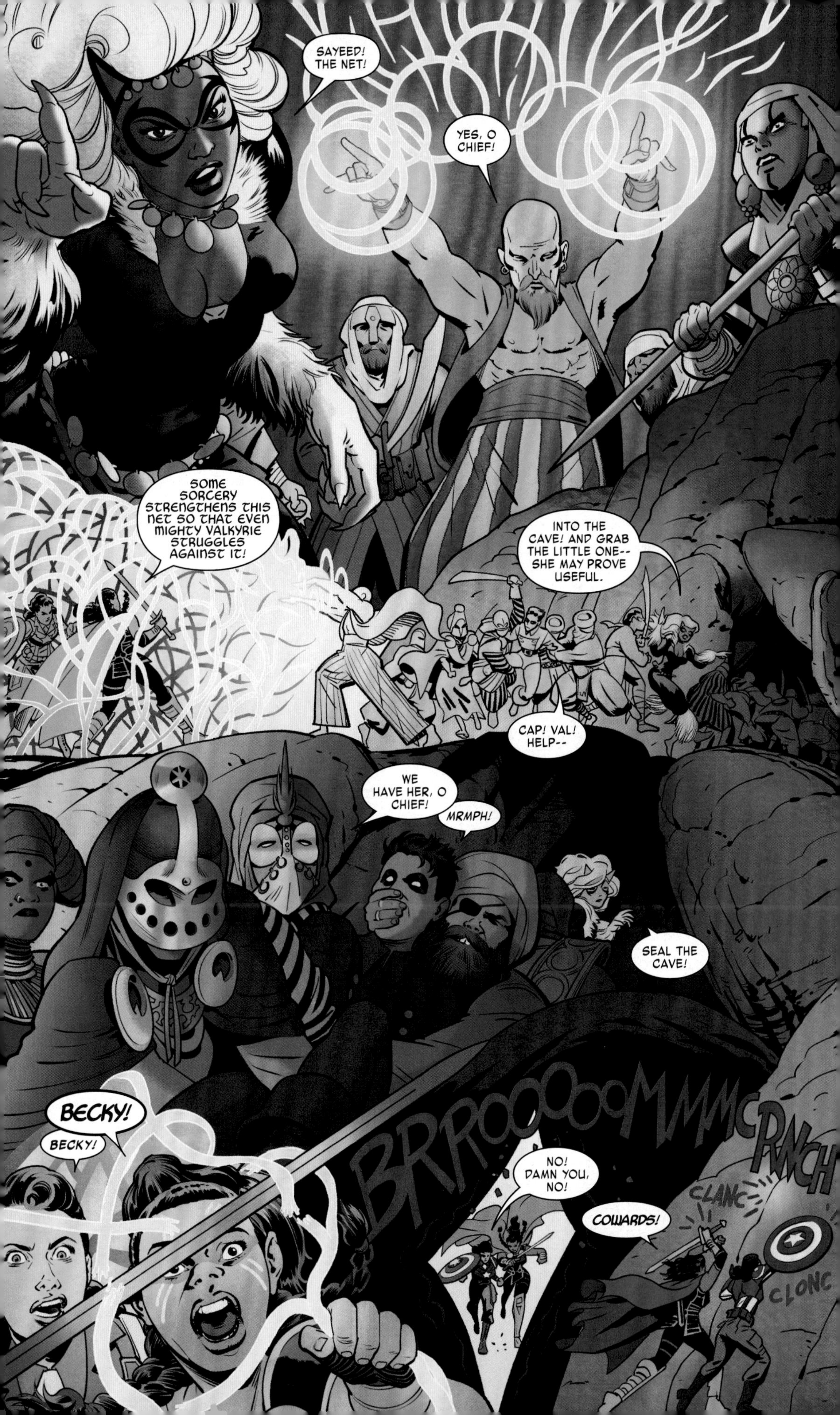
SAYEED! THE NET!
YES, O CHIEF!
SOME SORCERY STRENGTHENS THIS NET SO THAT EVEN MIGHTY VALKYRIE STRUGGLES AGAINST IT!
INTO THE CAVE! AND GRAB THE LITTLE ONE-- SHE MAY PROVE USEFUL.
CAP! VAL! HELP--
WE HAVE HER, O CHIEF!
MRMPH!
SEAL THE CAVE!
BRROOOOOOMMMMCRNCH
BECKY!
BECKY!
NO! DAMN YOU, NO!
COWARDS!
CLANC
CLONC

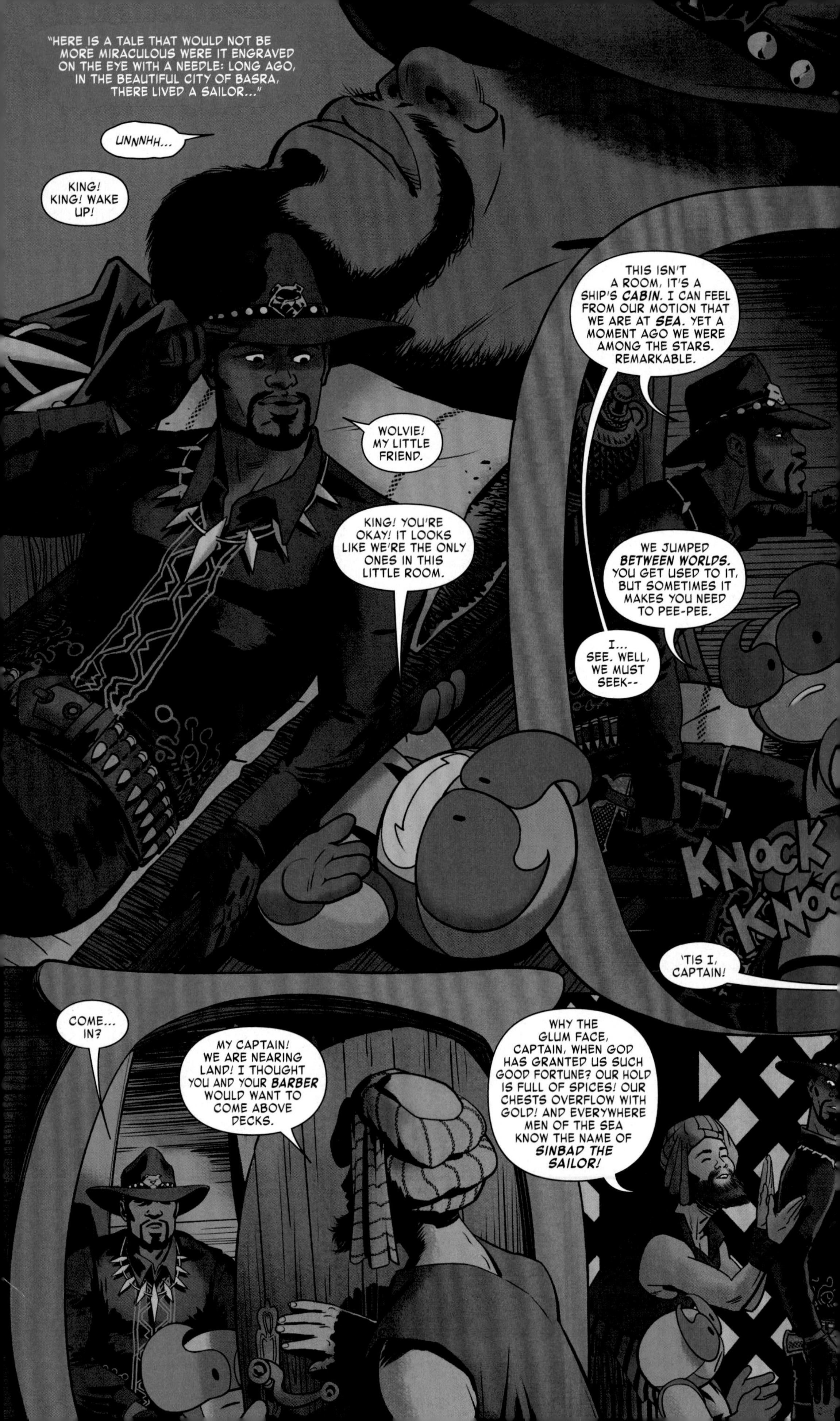
"HERE IS A TALE THAT WOULD NOT BE MORE MIRACULOUS WERE IT ENGRAVED ON THE EYE WITH A NEEDLE: LONG AGO, IN THE BEAUTIFUL CITY OF BASRA, THERE LIVED A SAILOR..."
UNNNHH...
KING! KING! WAKE UP!
WOLVIE! MY LITTLE FRIEND.
KING! YOU'RE OKAY! IT LOOKS LIKE WE'RE THE ONLY ONES IN THIS LITTLE ROOM.
THIS ISN'T A ROOM, IT'S A SHIP'S CABIN. I CAN FEEL FROM OUR MOTION THAT WE ARE AT SEA. YET A MOMENT AGO WE WERE AMONG THE STARS. REMARKABLE.
WE JUMPED BETWEEN WORLDS. YOU GET USED TO IT, BUT SOMETIMES IT MAKES YOU NEED TO PEE-PEE.
I... SEE. WELL, WE MUST SEEK--
KNOCK
'TIS I, CAPTAIN!
COME... IN?
MY CAPTAIN! WE ARE NEARING LAND! I THOUGHT YOU AND YOUR BARBER WOULD WANT TO COME ABOVE DECKS.
WHY THE GLUM FACE, CAPTAIN, WHEN GOD HAS GRANTED US SUCH GOOD FORTUNE? OUR HOLD IS FULL OF SPICES! OUR CHESTS OVERFLOW WITH GOLD! AND EVERYWHERE MEN OF THE SEA KNOW THE NAME OF SINBAD THE SAILOR!

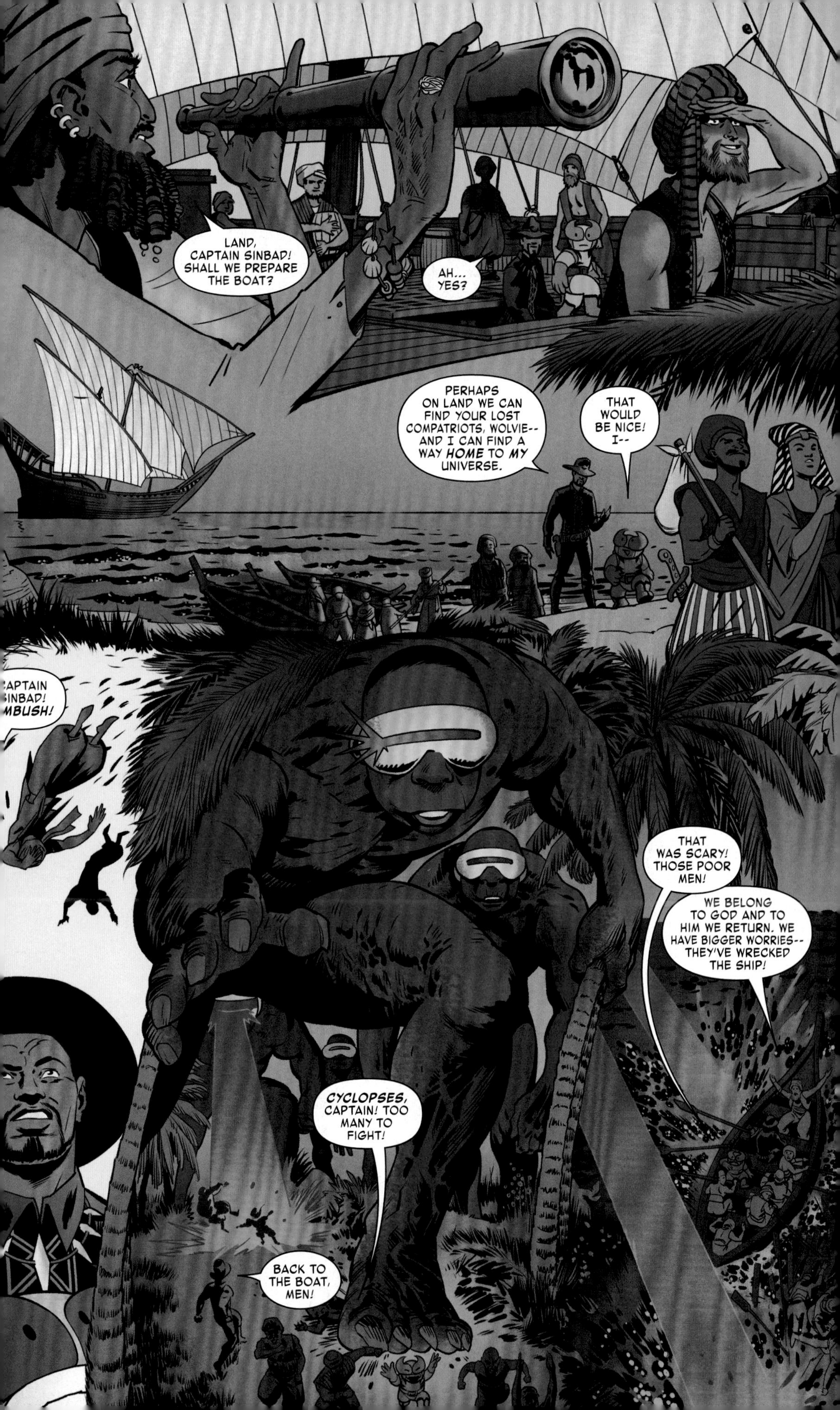
LAND, CAPTAIN SINBAD! SHALL WE PREPARE THE BOAT?
AH... YES?
PERHAPS ON LAND WE CAN FIND YOUR LOST COMPATRIOTS, WOLVIE-- AND I CAN FIND A WAY HOME TO MY UNIVERSE.
THAT WOULD BE NICE! I--
APTAIN SINBAD! MBUSH!
THAT WAS SCARY! THOSE POOR MEN!
WE BELONG TO GOD AND TO HIM WE RETURN. WE HAVE BIGGER WORRIES-- THEY'VE WRECKED THE SHIP!
CYCLOPSES, CAPTAIN! TOO MANY TO FIGHT!
BACK TO THE BOAT, MEN!

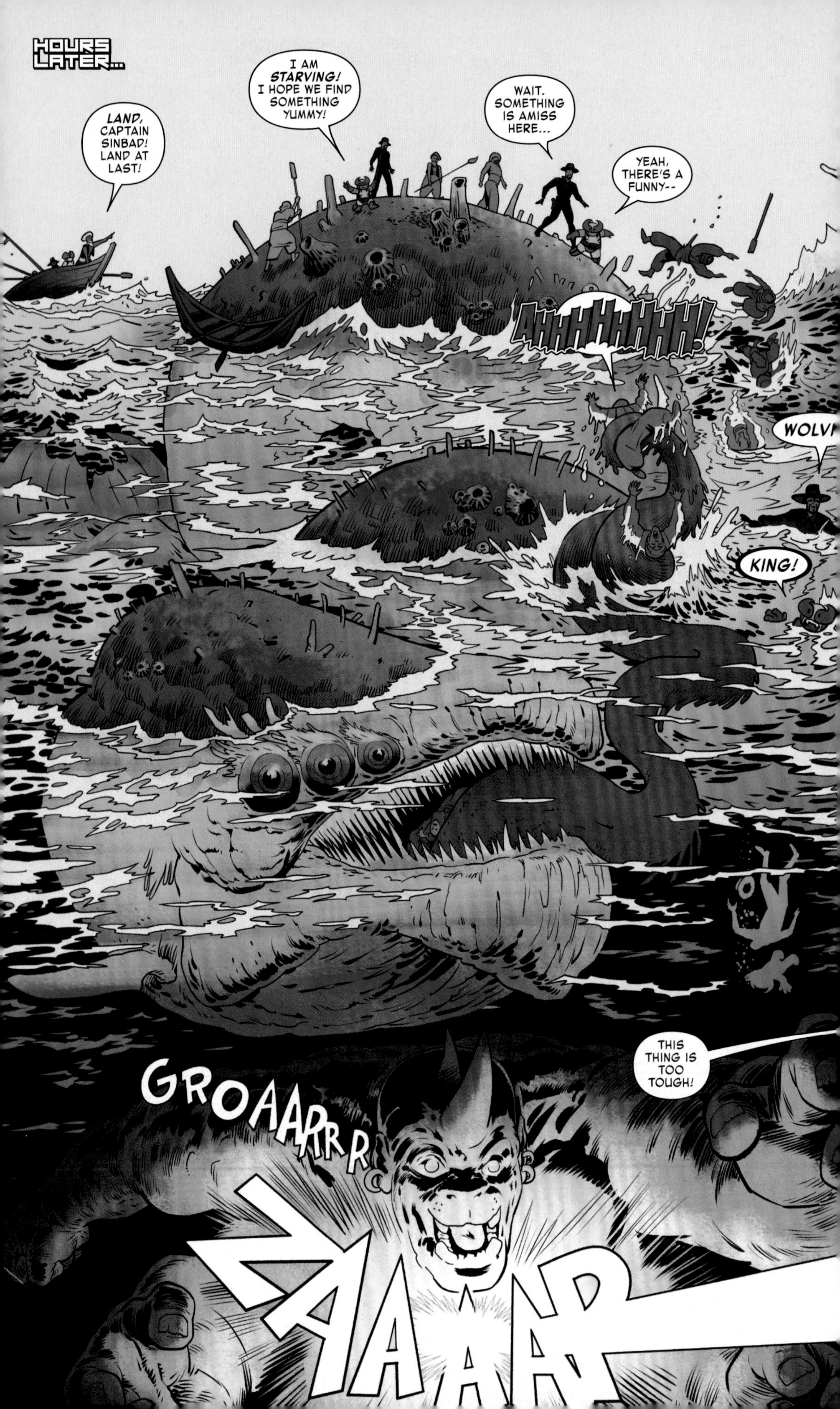
HOURS LATER...
LAND, CAPTAIN SINBAD! LAND AT LAST!
I AM STARVING! I HOPE WE FIND SOMETHING YUMMY!
WAIT. SOMETHING IS AMISS HERE...
YEAH, THERE'S A FUNNY--
AHHHHHHHH!
WOLVI
KING!
THIS THING IS TOO TOUGH!
GROAARRRR
ZAAAR

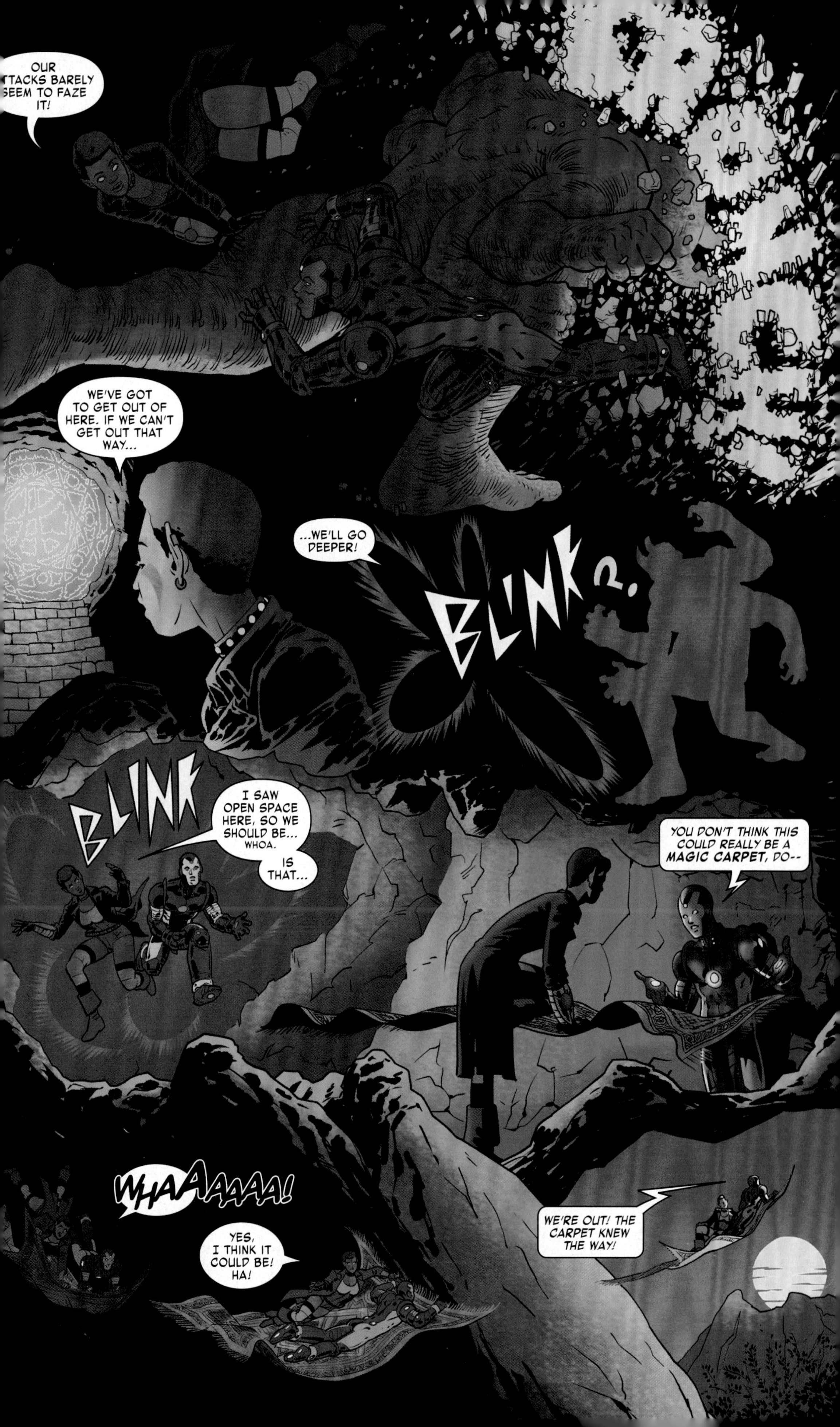
OUR TTACKS BARELY SEEM TO FAZE IT!
WE'VE GOT TO GET OUT OF HERE. IF WE CAN'T GET OUT THAT WAY...
...WE'LL GO DEEPER!
BLINK?
BLINK
I SAW OPEN SPACE HERE, SO WE SHOULD BE... WHOA.
IS THAT...
YOU DON'T THINK THIS COULD REALLY BE A MAGIC CARPET, DO--
WHAAAAAA!
YES, I THINK IT COULD BE! HA!
WE'RE OUT! THE CARPET KNEW THE WAY!

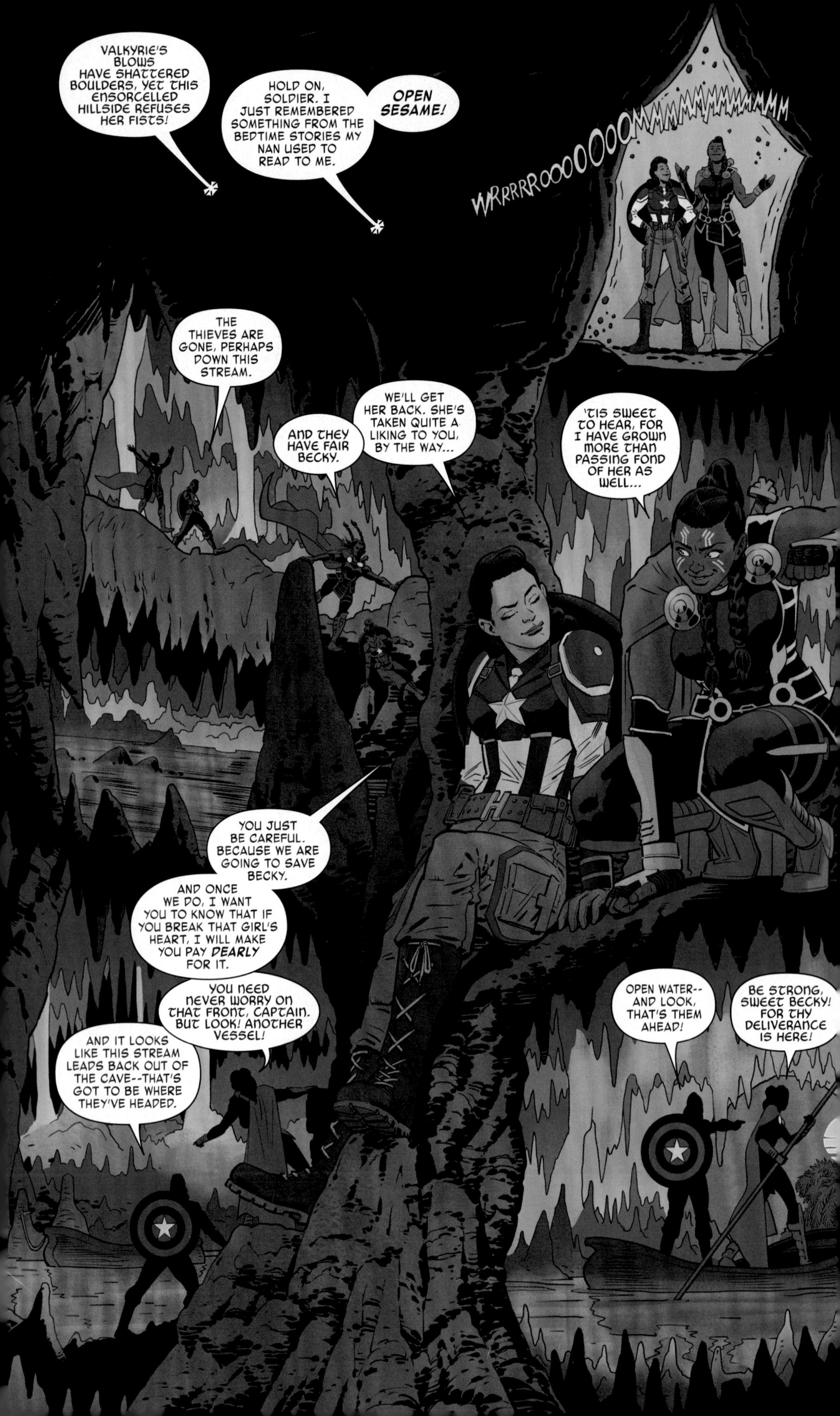
VALKYRIE'S BLOWS HAVE SHATTERED BOULDERS, YET THIS ENSORCELLED HILLSIDE REFUSES HER FISTS!
HOLD ON, SOLDIER. I JUST REMEMBERED SOMETHING FROM THE BEDTIME STORIES MY NAN USED TO READ TO ME.
OPEN SESAME!
WRRRRROOOOOOOMMMMMMMMMMM
THE THIEVES ARE GONE, PERHAPS DOWN THIS STREAM.
AND THEY HAVE FAIR BECKY.
WE'LL GET HER BACK. SHE'S TAKEN QUITE A LIKING TO YOU, BY THE WAY...
'TIS SWEET TO HEAR, FOR I HAVE GROWN MORE THAN PASSING FOND OF HER AS WELL...
YOU JUST BE CAREFUL. BECAUSE WE ARE GOING TO SAVE BECKY.
AND ONCE WE DO, I WANT YOU TO KNOW THAT IF YOU BREAK THAT GIRL'S HEART, I WILL MAKE YOU PAY DEARLY FOR IT.
YOU NEED NEVER WORRY ON THAT FRONT, CAPTAIN. BUT LOOK! ANOTHER VESSEL!
AND IT LOOKS LIKE THIS STREAM LEADS BACK OUT OF THE CAVE--THAT'S GOT TO BE WHERE THEY'VE HEADED.
OPEN WATER--AND LOOK, THAT'S THEM AHEAD!
BE STRONG, SWEET BECKY! FOR THY DELIVERANCE IS HERE!

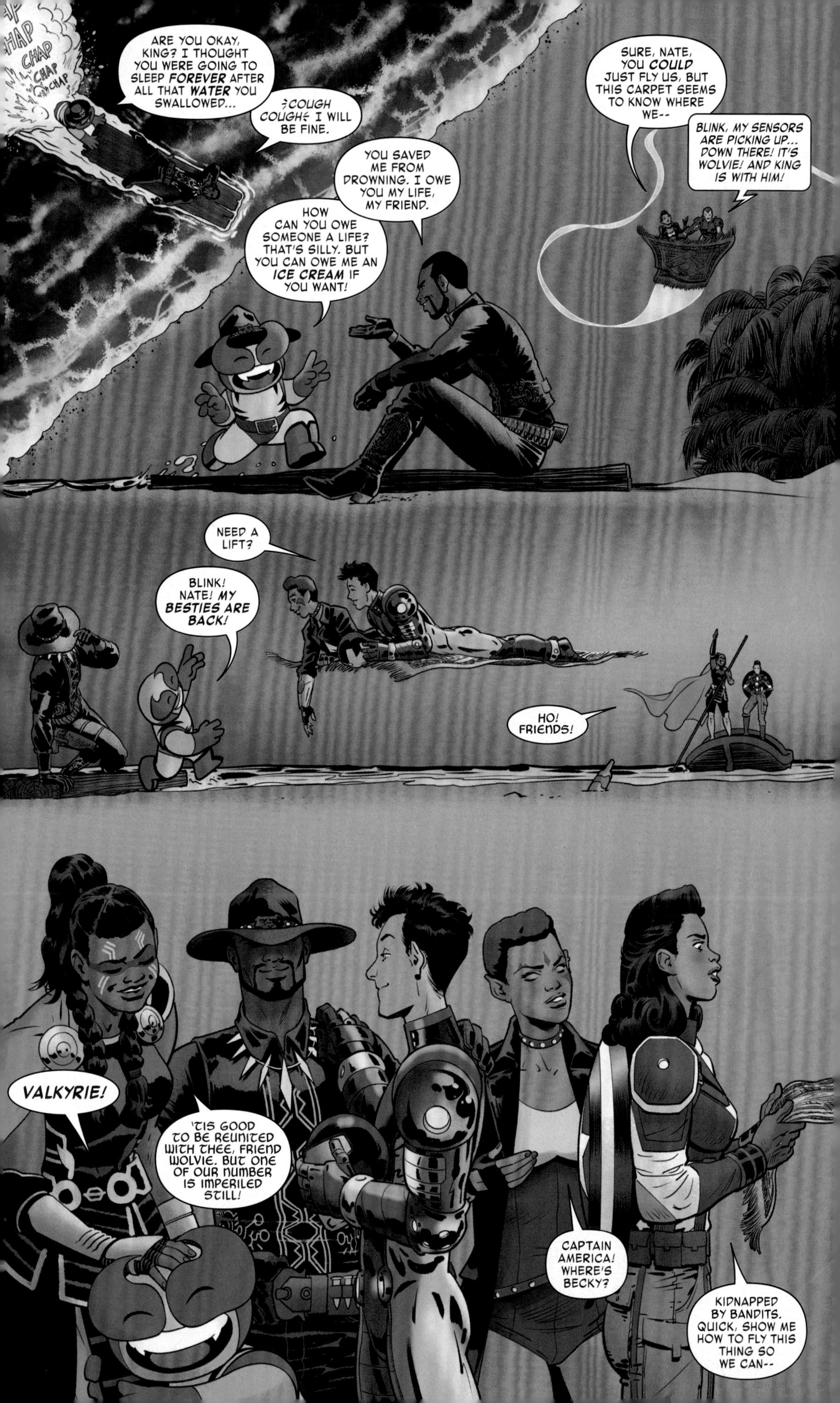
CHAP CHAP CHAP CHAP
ARE YOU OKAY, KING? I THOUGHT YOU WERE GOING TO SLEEP FOREVER AFTER ALL THAT WATER YOU SWALLOWED...
COUGH COUGH I WILL BE FINE.
YOU SAVED ME FROM DROWNING. I OWE YOU MY LIFE, MY FRIEND.
HOW CAN YOU OWE SOMEONE A LIFE? THAT'S SILLY. BUT YOU CAN OWE ME AN ICE CREAM IF YOU WANT!
SURE, NATE, YOU COULD JUST FLY US, BUT THIS CARPET SEEMS TO KNOW WHERE WE--
BLINK, MY SENSORS ARE PICKING UP... DOWN THERE! IT'S WOLVIE! AND KING IS WITH HIM!
NEED A LIFT?
BLINK! NATE! MY BESTIES ARE BACK!
HO! FRIENDS!
VALKYRIE!
'TIS GOOD TO BE REUNITED WITH THEE, FRIEND WOLVIE. BUT ONE OF OUR NUMBER IS IMPERILED STILL!
CAPTAIN AMERICA! WHERE'S BECKY?
KIDNAPPED BY BANDITS. QUICK, SHOW ME HOW TO FLY THIS THING SO WE CAN--

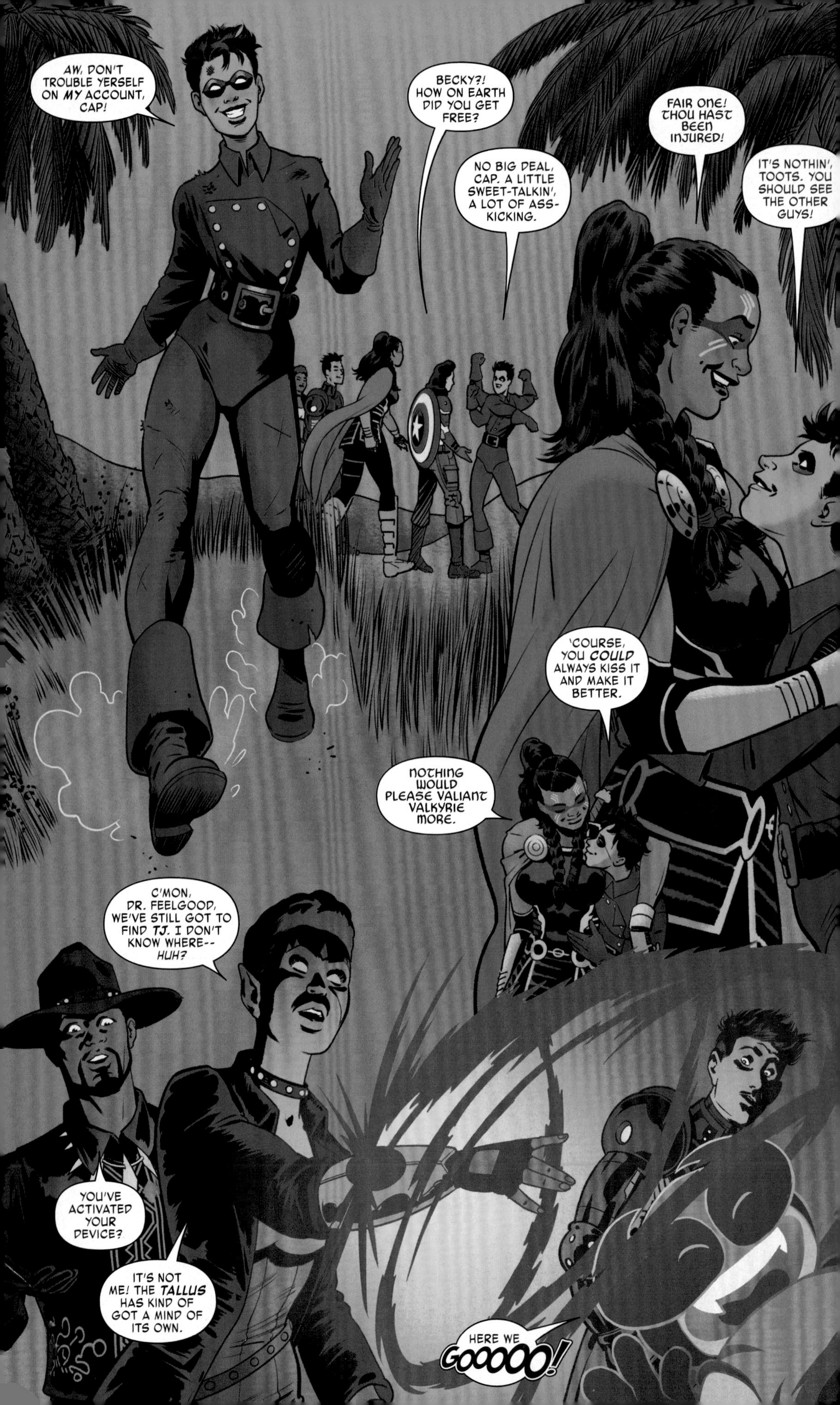
AW, DON'T TROUBLE YERSELF ON MY ACCOUNT, CAP!
BECKY?! HOW ON EARTH DID YOU GET FREE?
NO BIG DEAL, CAP. A LITTLE SWEET-TALKIN', A LOT OF ASS-KICKING.
FAIR ONE! THOU HAST BEEN INJURED!
IT'S NOTHIN', TOOTS. YOU SHOULD SEE THE OTHER GUYS!
'COURSE, YOU COULD ALWAYS KISS IT AND MAKE IT BETTER.
NOTHING WOULD PLEASE VALIANT VALKYRIE MORE.
C'MON, DR. FEELGOOD, WE'VE STILL GOT TO FIND TJ. I DON'T KNOW WHERE-- HUH?
YOU'VE ACTIVATED YOUR DEVICE?
IT'S NOT ME! THE TALLUS HAS KIND OF GOT A MIND OF ITS OWN.
HERE WE GOOOOO!

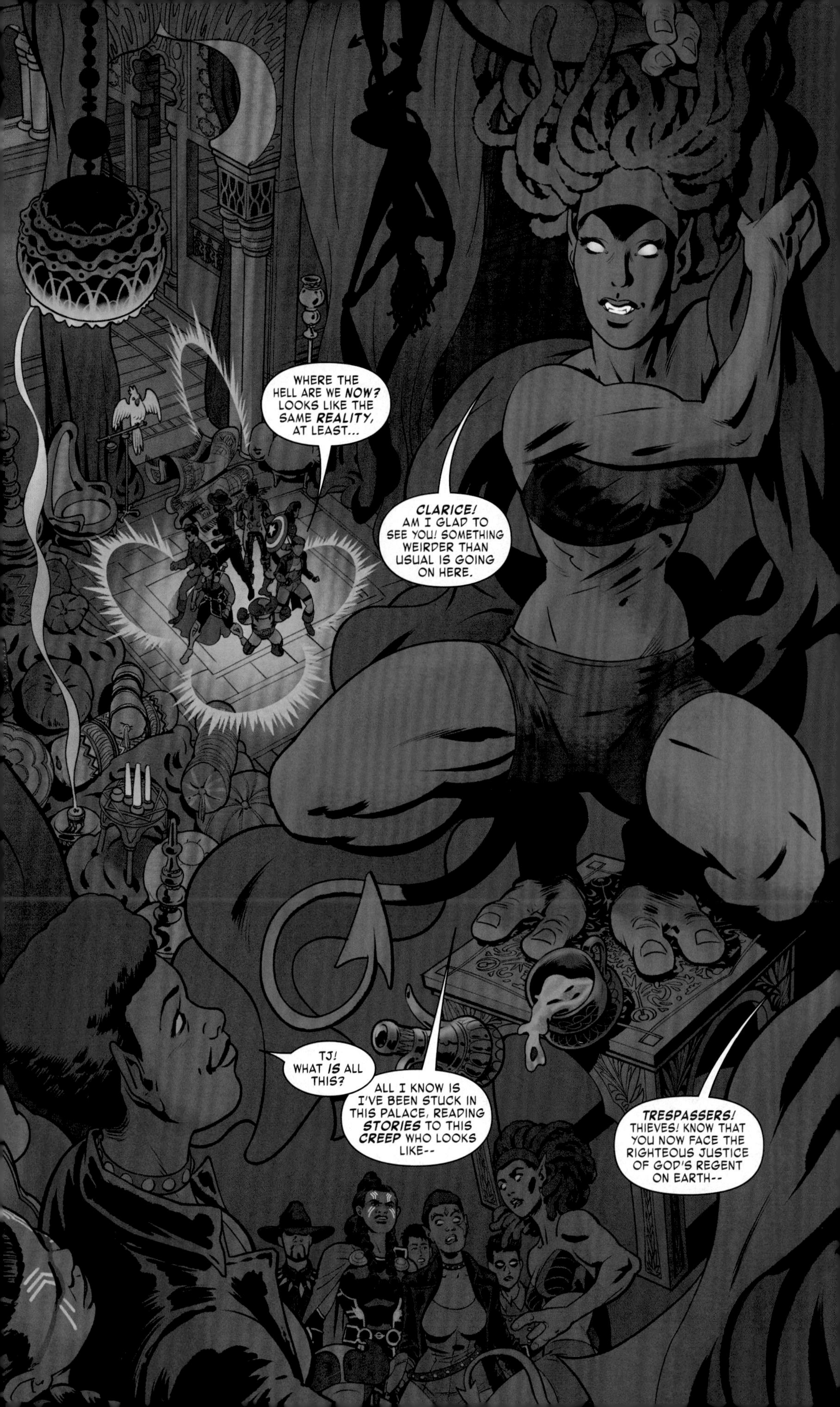
WHERE THE HELL ARE WE NOW? LOOKS LIKE THE SAME REALITY, AT LEAST...
CLARICE! AM I GLAD TO SEE YOU! SOMETHING WEIRDER THAN USUAL IS GOING ON HERE.
TJ! WHAT IS ALL THIS?
ALL I KNOW IS I'VE BEEN STUCK IN THIS PALACE, READING STORIES TO THIS CREEP WHO LOOKS LIKE--
TRESPASSERS! THIEVES! KNOW THAT YOU NOW FACE THE RIGHTEOUS JUSTICE OF GOD'S REGENT ON EARTH--

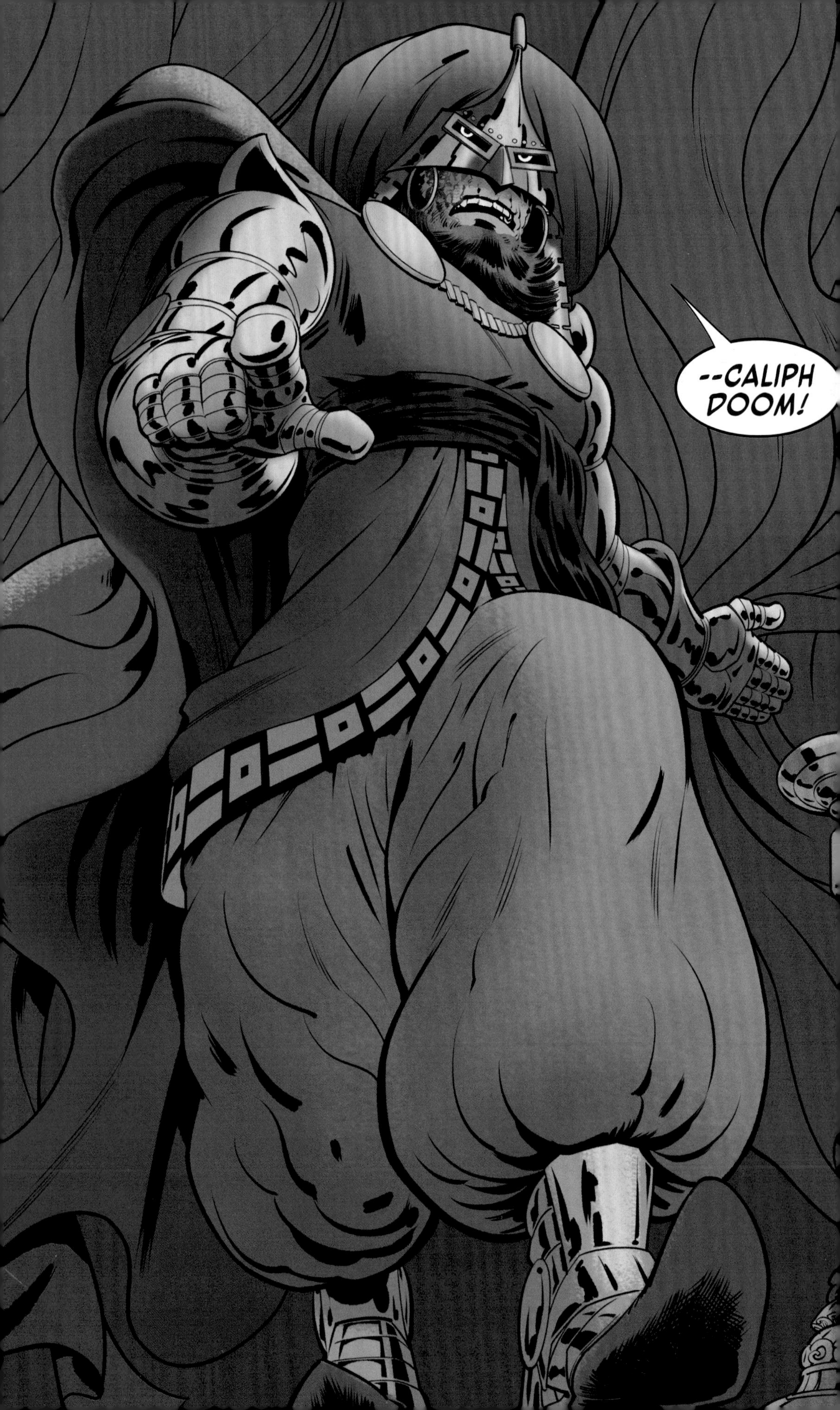
--CALIPH DOOM!

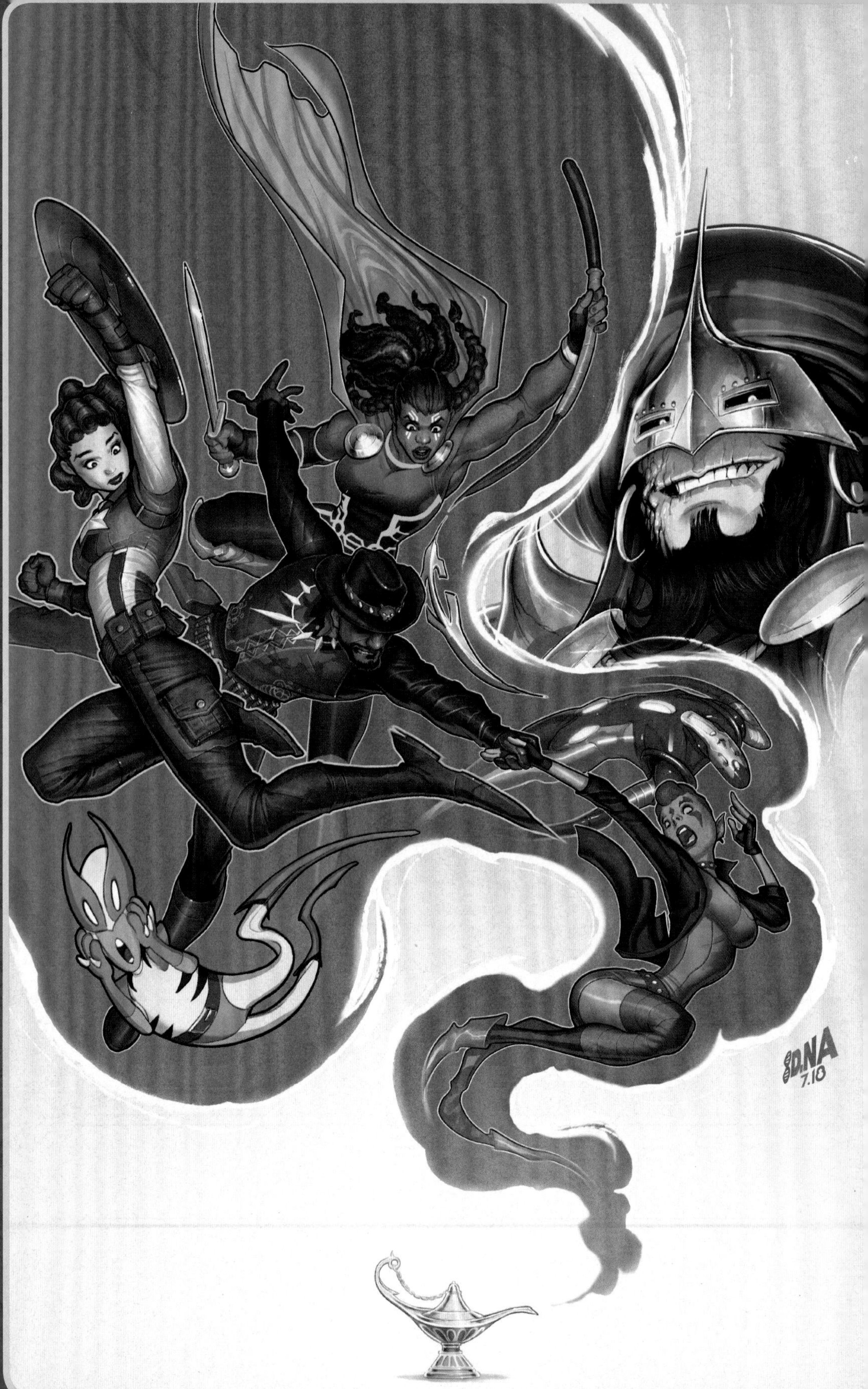
D.NA
7.18

10

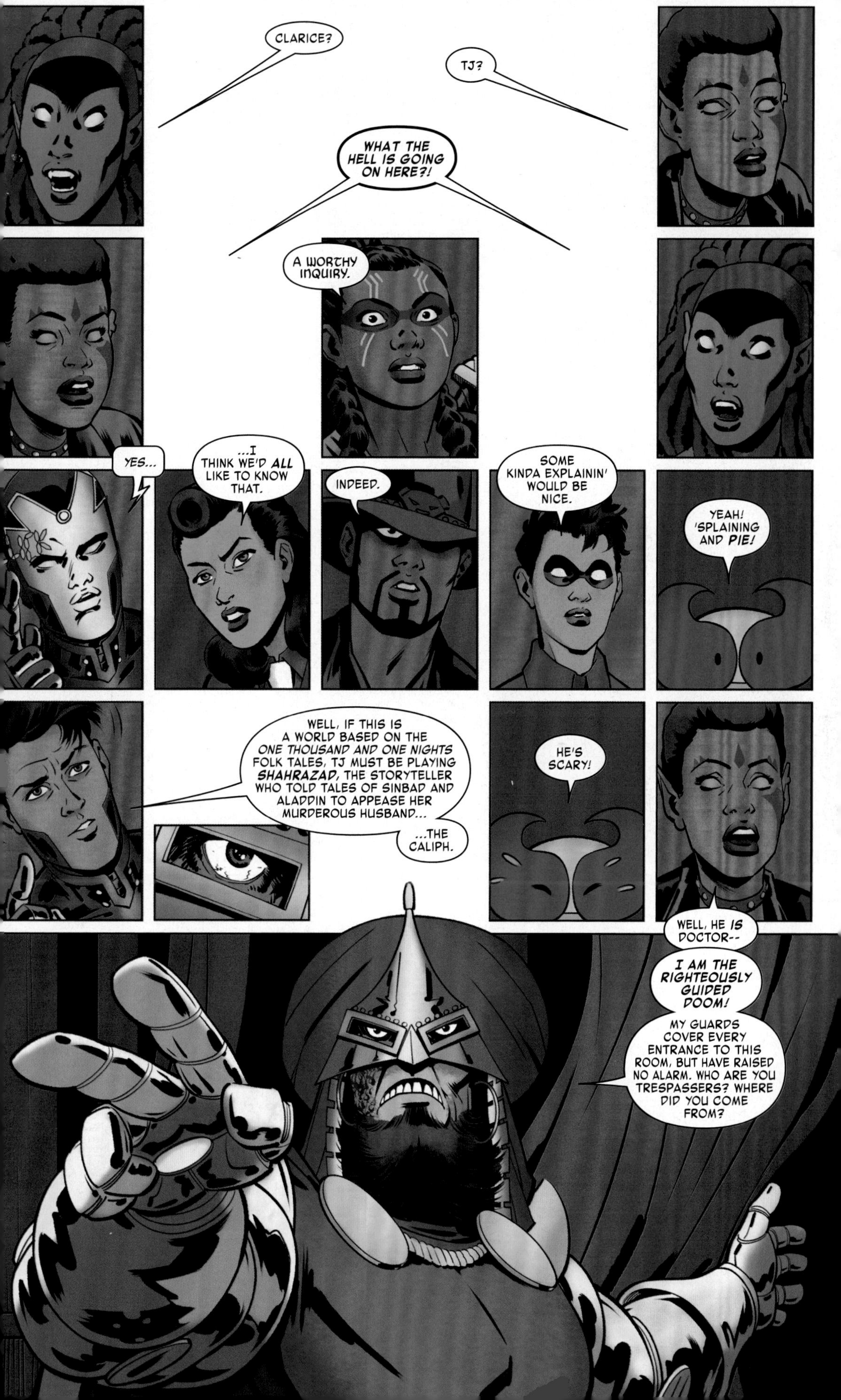
CLARICE?
TJ?
WHAT THE HELL IS GOING ON HERE?!
A WORTHY INQUIRY.
YES...
...I THINK WE'D ALL LIKE TO KNOW THAT.
INDEED.
SOME KINDA EXPLAININ' WOULD BE NICE.
YEAH! 'SPLAINING AND PIE!
WELL, IF THIS IS A WORLD BASED ON THE ONE THOUSAND AND ONE NIGHTS FOLK TALES, TJ MUST BE PLAYING SHAHRAZAD, THE STORYTELLER WHO TOLD TALES OF SINBAD AND ALADDIN TO APPEASE HER MURDEROUS HUSBAND...
...THE CALIPH.
HE'S SCARY!
WELL, HE IS DOCTOR--
I AM THE RIGHTEOUSLY GUIDED DOOM!
MY GUARDS COVER EVERY ENTRANCE TO THIS ROOM, BUT HAVE RAISED NO ALARM. WHO ARE YOU TRESPASSERS? WHERE DID YOU COME FROM?

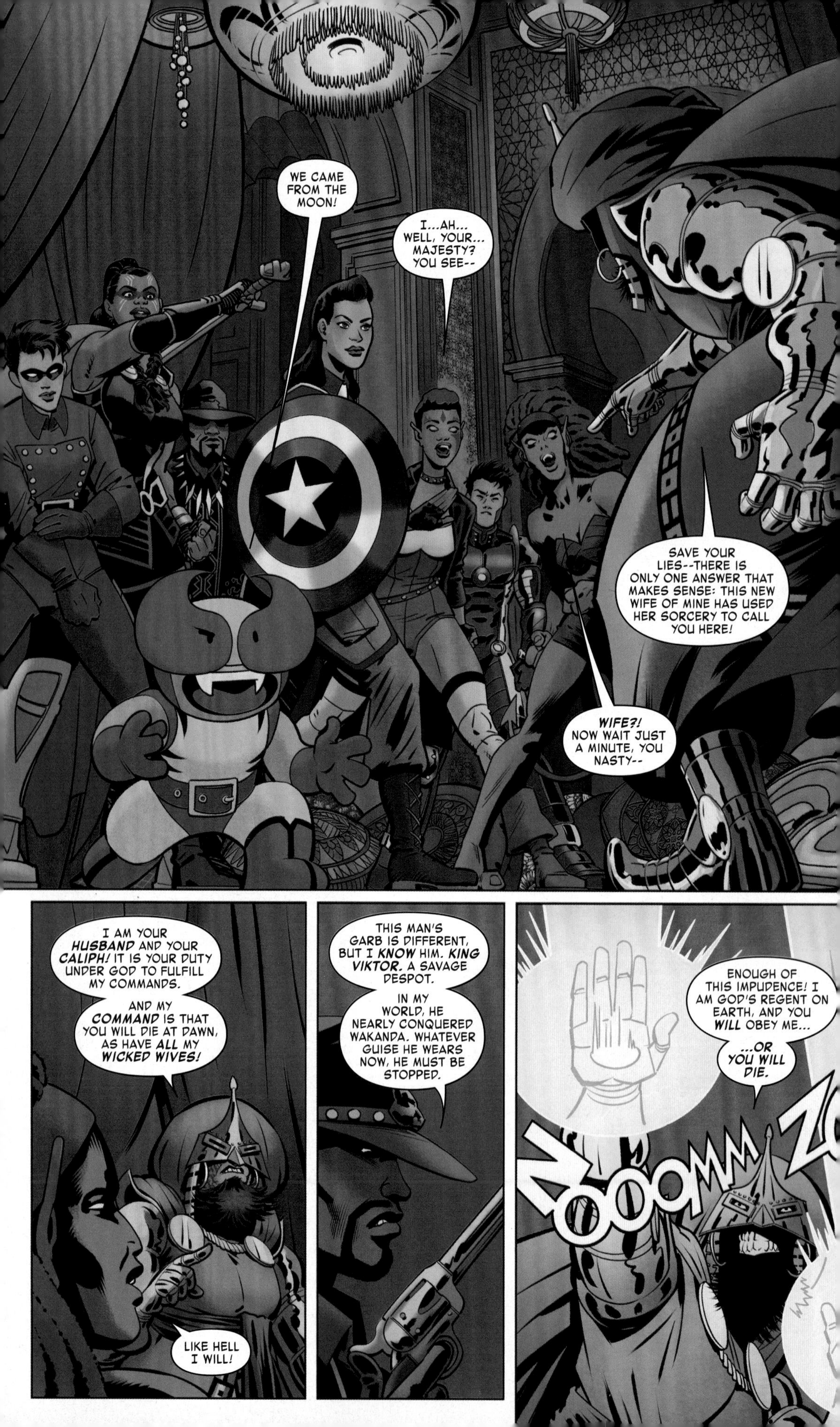
WE CAME FROM THE MOON!
I...AH... WELL, YOUR... MAJESTY? YOU SEE--
SAVE YOUR LIES--THERE IS ONLY ONE ANSWER THAT MAKES SENSE: THIS NEW WIFE OF MINE HAS USED HER SORCERY TO CALL YOU HERE!
WIFE?! NOW WAIT JUST A MINUTE, YOU NASTY--
I AM YOUR HUSBAND AND YOUR CALIPH! IT IS YOUR DUTY UNDER GOD TO FULFILL MY COMMANDS.
AND MY COMMAND IS THAT YOU WILL DIE AT DAWN, AS HAVE ALL MY WICKED WIVES!
LIKE HELL I WILL!
THIS MAN'S GARB IS DIFFERENT, BUT I KNOW HIM. KING VIKTOR. A SAVAGE DESPOT.
IN MY WORLD, HE NEARLY CONQUERED WAKANDA. WHATEVER GUISE HE WEARS NOW, HE MUST BE STOPPED.
ENOUGH OF THIS IMPUDENCE! I AM GOD'S REGENT ON EARTH, AND YOU WILL OBEY ME...
...OR YOU WILL DIE.
ZOOOMM

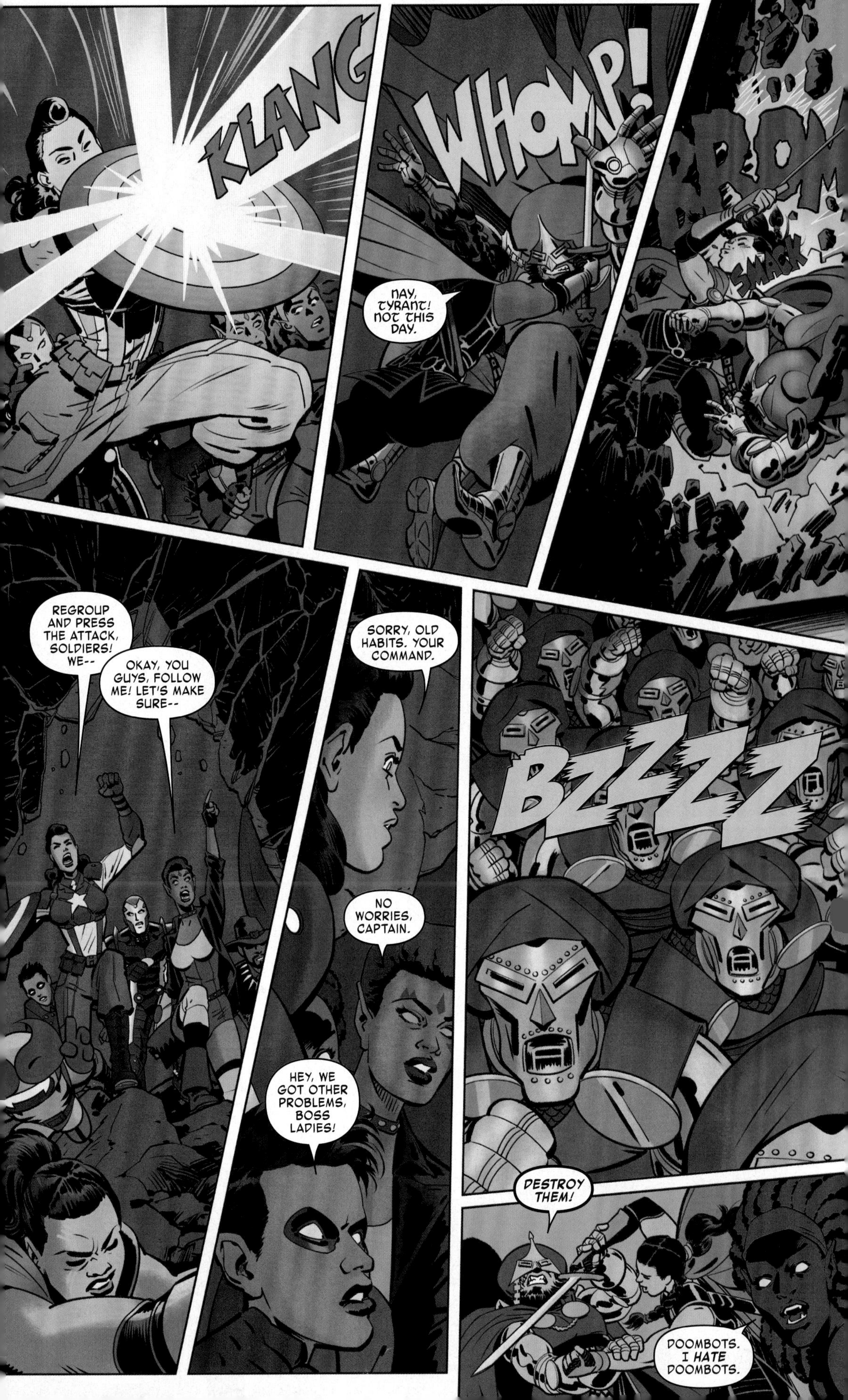
KLANG
WHOMP!
NAY, TYRANT! NOT THIS DAY.
SMACK
REGROUP AND PRESS THE ATTACK, SOLDIERS! WE--
OKAY, YOU GUYS, FOLLOW ME! LET'S MAKE SURE--
SORRY, OLD HABITS. YOUR COMMAND.
NO WORRIES, CAPTAIN.
HEY, WE GOT OTHER PROBLEMS, BOSS LADIES!
BZZZZ
DESTROY THEM!
DOOMBOTS. I HATE DOOMBOTS.

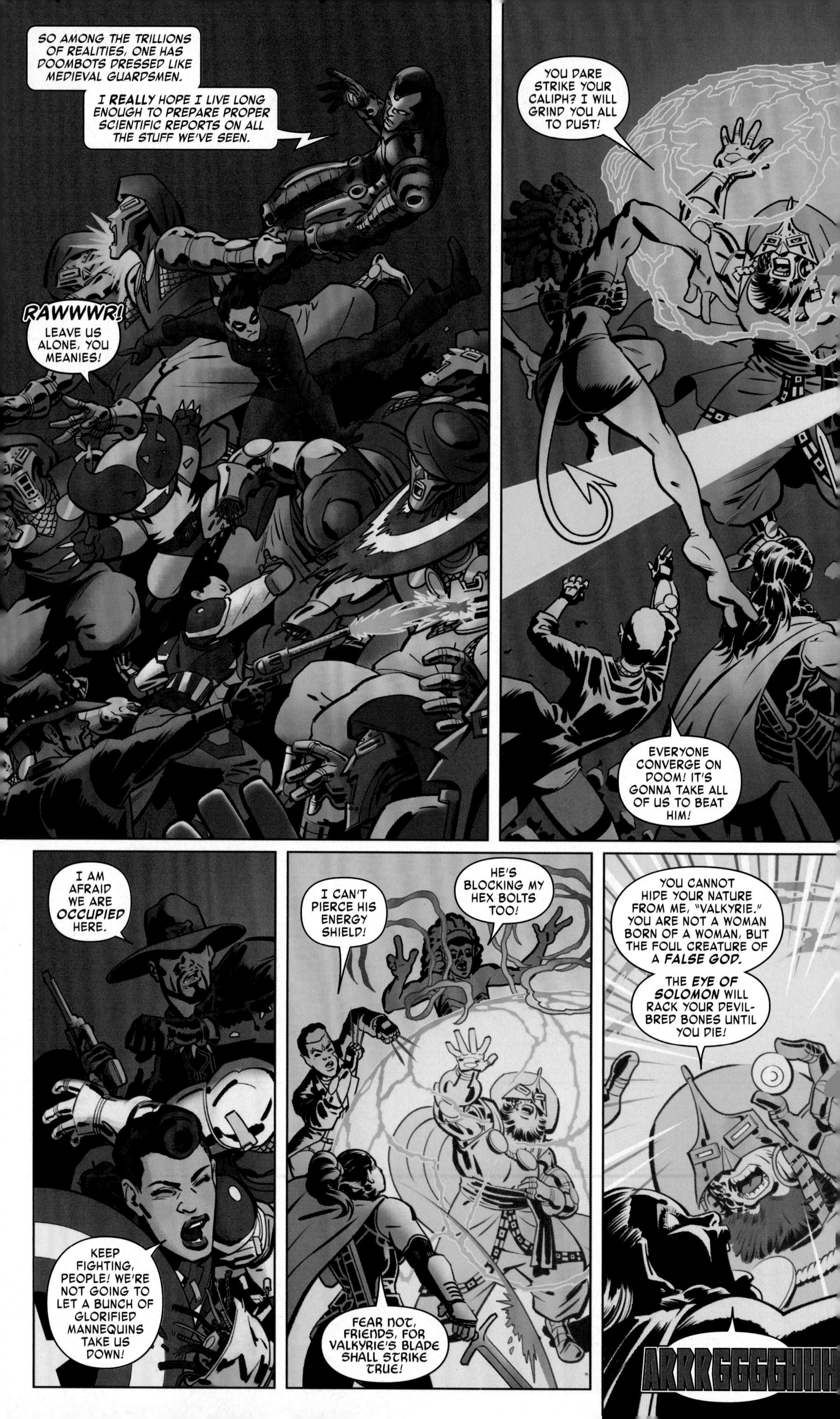
SO AMONG THE TRILLIONS OF REALITIES, ONE HAS DOOMBOTS DRESSED LIKE MEDIEVAL GUARDSMEN.
I REALLY HOPE I LIVE LONG ENOUGH TO PREPARE PROPER SCIENTIFIC REPORTS ON ALL THE STUFF WE'VE SEEN.
RAWWWR! LEAVE US ALONE, YOU MEANIES!
YOU DARE STRIKE YOUR CALIPH? I WILL GRIND YOU ALL TO DUST!
EVERYONE CONVERGE ON DOOM! IT'S GONNA TAKE ALL OF US TO BEAT HIM!
I AM AFRAID WE ARE OCCUPIED HERE.
KEEP FIGHTING, PEOPLE! WE'RE NOT GOING TO LET A BUNCH OF GLORIFIED MANNEQUINS TAKE US DOWN!
I CAN'T PIERCE HIS ENERGY SHIELD!
HE'S BLOCKING MY HEX BOLTS TOO!
FEAR NOT, FRIENDS, FOR VALKYRIE'S BLADE SHALL STRIKE TRUE!
YOU CANNOT HIDE YOUR NATURE FROM ME, "VALKYRIE." YOU ARE NOT A WOMAN BORN OF A WOMAN, BUT THE FOUL CREATURE OF A FALSE GOD.
THE EYE OF SOLOMON WILL RACK YOUR DEVIL-BRED BONES UNTIL YOU DIE!
ARRRGGGGHHH

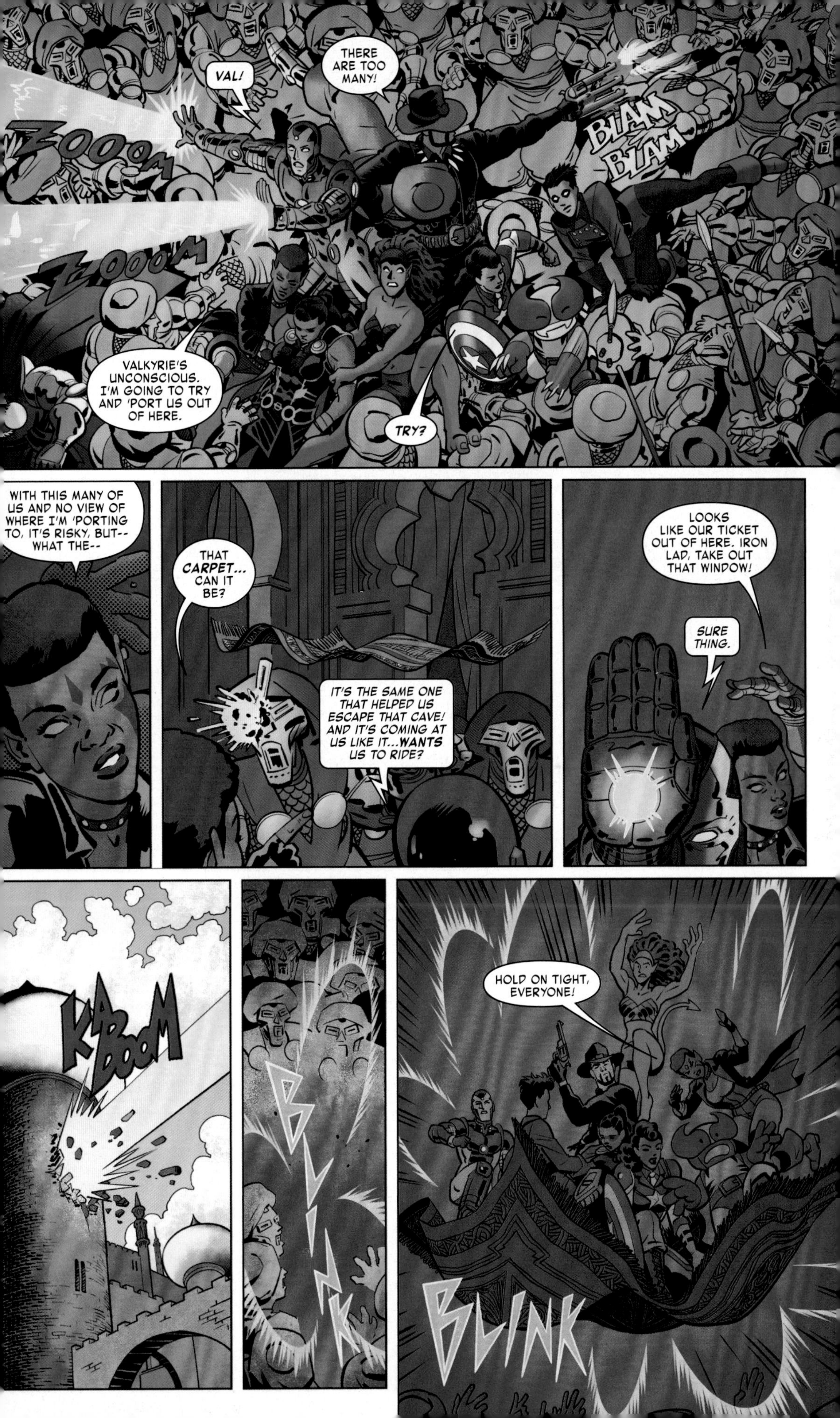

VAL!
THERE ARE TOO MANY!
ZOOOM
ZOOOM
BLAM BLAM
VALKYRIE'S UNCONSCIOUS. I'M GOING TO TRY AND 'PORT US OUT OF HERE.
TRY?
WITH THIS MANY OF US AND NO VIEW OF WHERE I'M 'PORTING TO, IT'S RISKY, BUT-- WHAT THE--
THAT CARPET... CAN IT BE?
IT'S THE SAME ONE THAT HELPED US ESCAPE THAT CAVE! AND IT'S COMING AT US LIKE IT...WANTS US TO RIDE?
LOOKS LIKE OUR TICKET OUT OF HERE. IRON LAD, TAKE OUT THAT WINDOW!
SURE THING.
KABOOM
BLINK
HOLD ON TIGHT, EVERYONE!
BLINK

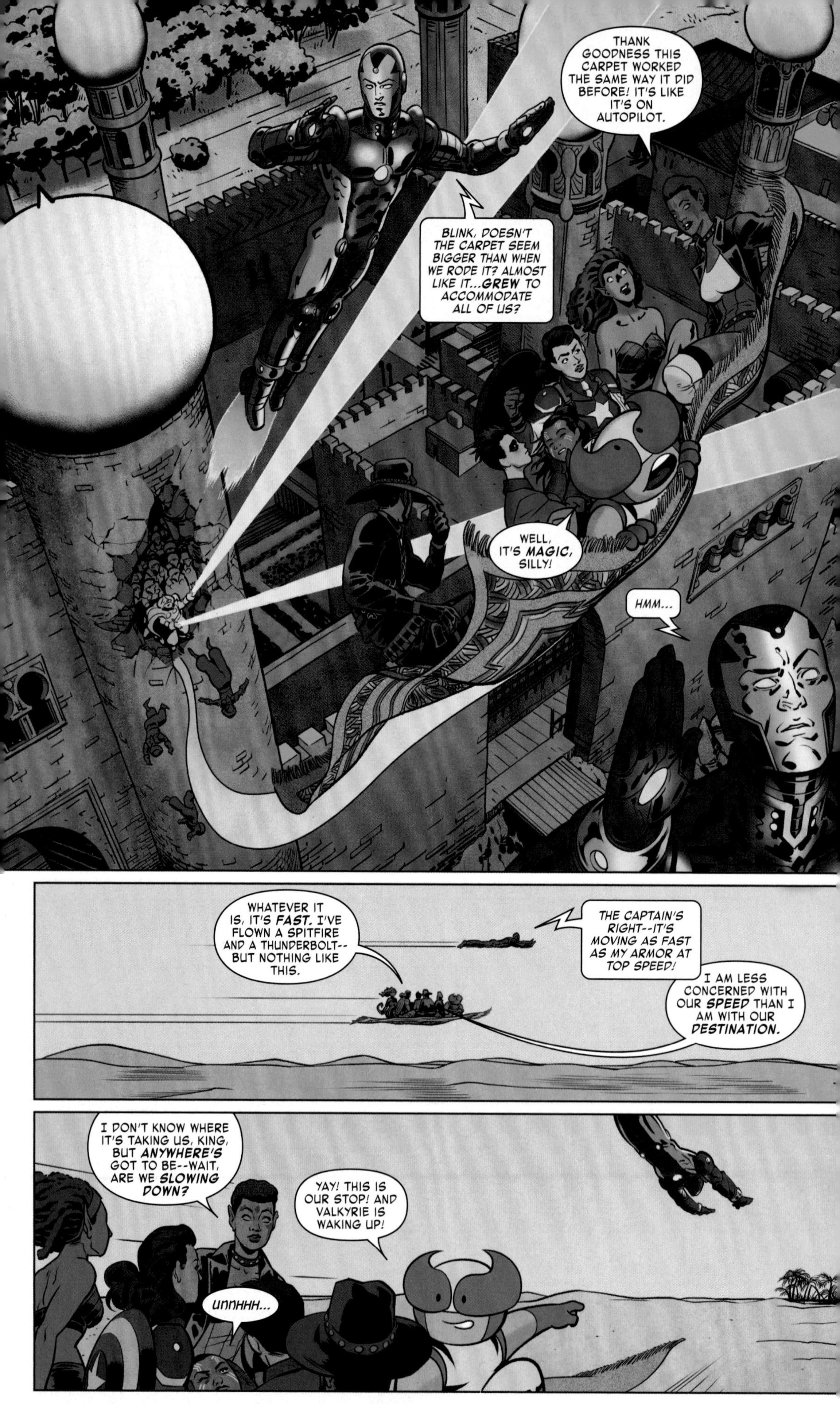
THANK GOODNESS THIS CARPET WORKED THE SAME WAY IT DID BEFORE! IT'S LIKE IT'S ON AUTOPILOT.
BLINK, DOESN'T THE CARPET SEEM BIGGER THAN WHEN WE RODE IT? ALMOST LIKE IT...GREW TO ACCOMMODATE ALL OF US?
WELL, IT'S MAGIC, SILLY!
HMM...
WHATEVER IT IS, IT'S FAST. I'VE FLOWN A SPITFIRE AND A THUNDERBOLT--BUT NOTHING LIKE THIS.
THE CAPTAIN'S RIGHT--IT'S MOVING AS FAST AS MY ARMOR AT TOP SPEED!
I AM LESS CONCERNED WITH OUR SPEED THAN I AM WITH OUR DESTINATION.
I DON'T KNOW WHERE IT'S TAKING US, KING, BUT ANYWHERE'S GOT TO BE--WAIT, ARE WE SLOWING DOWN?
YAY! THIS IS OUR STOP! AND VALKYRIE IS WAKING UP!
UNNHHH...

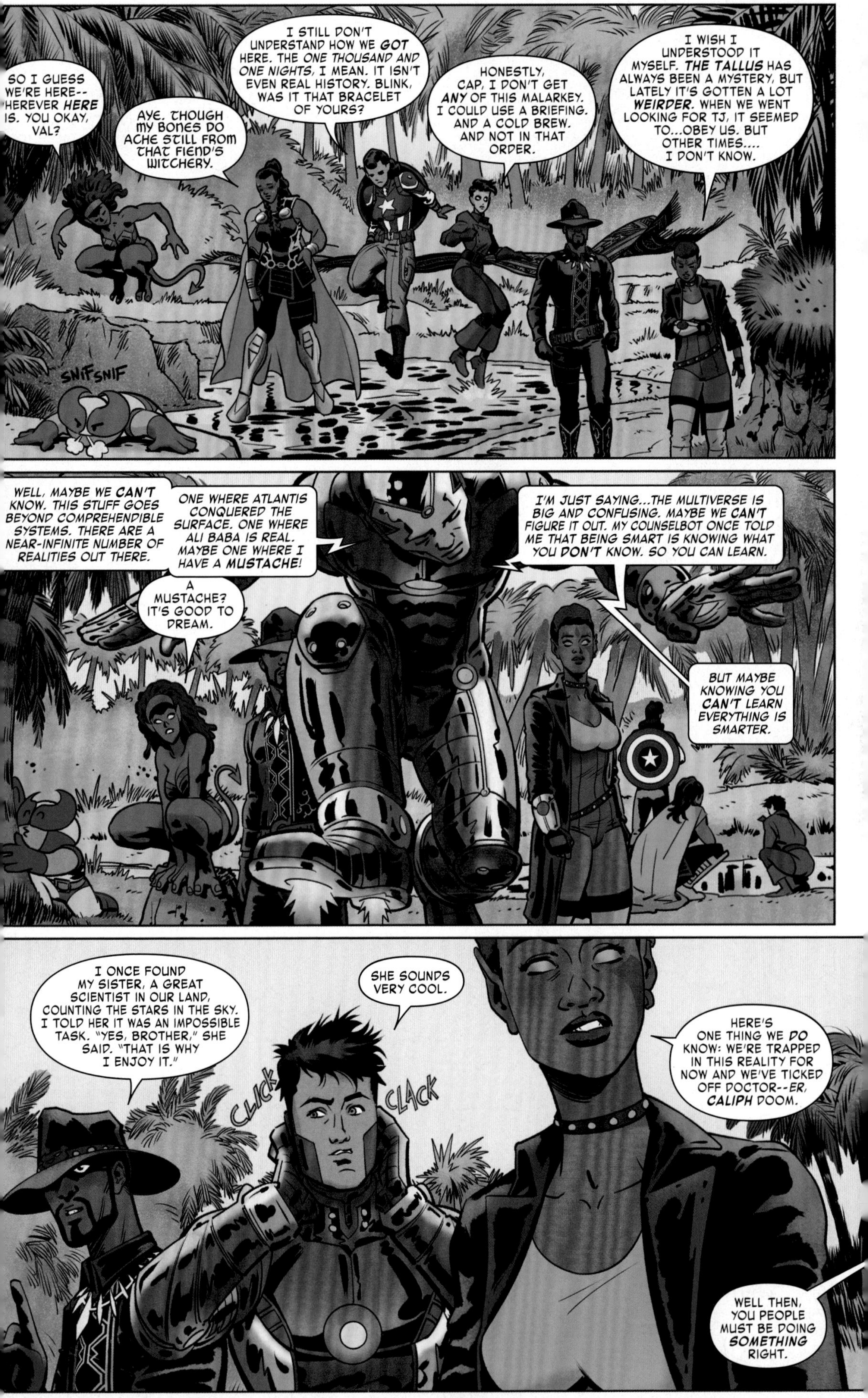

SO I GUESS WE'RE HERE--WHEREVER HERE IS. YOU OKAY, VAL?
AYE. THOUGH MY BONES DO ACHE STILL FROM THAT FIEND'S WITCHERY.
I STILL DON'T UNDERSTAND HOW WE GOT HERE. THE ONE THOUSAND AND ONE NIGHTS, I MEAN. IT ISN'T EVEN REAL HISTORY. BLINK, WAS IT THAT BRACELET OF YOURS?
HONESTLY, CAP, I DON'T GET ANY OF THIS MALARKEY. I COULD USE A BRIEFING. AND A COLD BREW. AND NOT IN THAT ORDER.
I WISH I UNDERSTOOD IT MYSELF. THE TALLUS HAS ALWAYS BEEN A MYSTERY, BUT LATELY IT'S GOTTEN A LOT WEIRDER. WHEN WE WENT LOOKING FOR TJ, IT SEEMED TO...OBEY US. BUT OTHER TIMES.... I DON'T KNOW.
SNIF SNIF
WELL, MAYBE WE CAN'T KNOW. THIS STUFF GOES BEYOND COMPREHENDIBLE SYSTEMS. THERE ARE A NEAR-INFINITE NUMBER OF REALITIES OUT THERE.
ONE WHERE ATLANTIS CONQUERED THE SURFACE. ONE WHERE ALI BABA IS REAL. MAYBE ONE WHERE I HAVE A MUSTACHE!
A MUSTACHE? IT'S GOOD TO DREAM.
I'M JUST SAYING...THE MULTIVERSE IS BIG AND CONFUSING. MAYBE WE CAN'T FIGURE IT OUT. MY COUNSELBOT ONCE TOLD ME THAT BEING SMART IS KNOWING WHAT YOU DON'T KNOW. SO YOU CAN LEARN.
BUT MAYBE KNOWING YOU CAN'T LEARN EVERYTHING IS SMARTER.
I ONCE FOUND MY SISTER, A GREAT SCIENTIST IN OUR LAND, COUNTING THE STARS IN THE SKY. I TOLD HER IT WAS AN IMPOSSIBLE TASK. "YES, BROTHER," SHE SAID. "THAT IS WHY I ENJOY IT."
SHE SOUNDS VERY COOL.
CLICK CLACK
HERE'S ONE THING WE DO KNOW: WE'RE TRAPPED IN THIS REALITY FOR NOW AND WE'VE TICKED OFF DOCTOR--ER, CALIPH DOOM.
WELL THEN, YOU PEOPLE MUST BE DOING SOMETHING RIGHT.

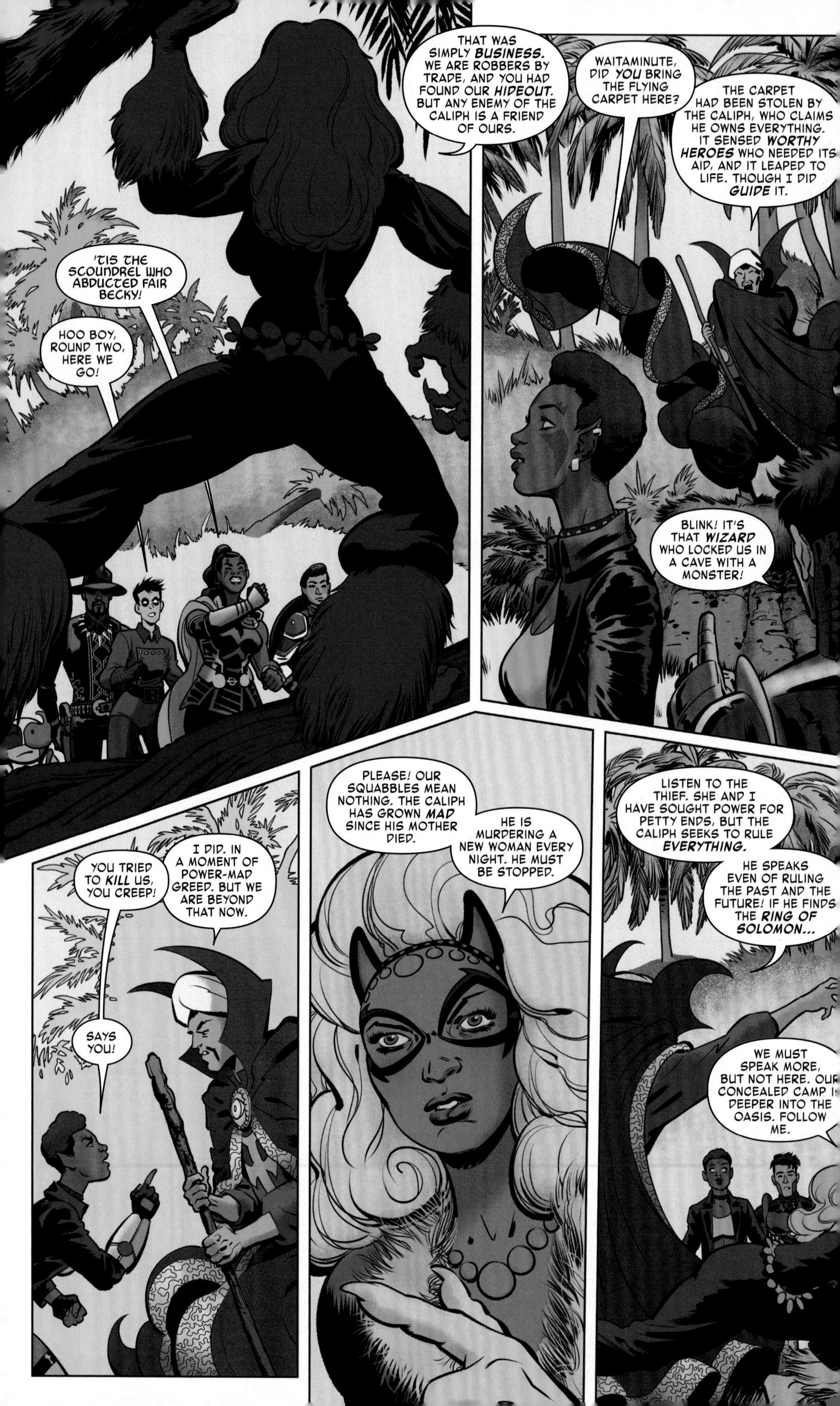
THAT WAS SIMPLY BUSINESS. WE ARE ROBBERS BY TRADE, AND YOU HAD FOUND OUR HIDEOUT. BUT ANY ENEMY OF THE CALIPH IS A FRIEND OF OURS.
'TIS THE SCOUNDREL WHO ABDUCTED FAIR BECKY!
HOO BOY, ROUND TWO, HERE WE GO!
WAITAMINUTE, DID YOU BRING THE FLYING CARPET HERE?
THE CARPET HAD BEEN STOLEN BY THE CALIPH, WHO CLAIMS HE OWNS EVERYTHING. IT SENSED WORTHY HEROES WHO NEEDED ITS AID, AND IT LEAPED TO LIFE. THOUGH I DID GUIDE IT.
BLINK! IT'S THAT WIZARD WHO LOCKED US IN A CAVE WITH A MONSTER!
YOU TRIED TO KILL US, YOU CREEP!
I DID. IN A MOMENT OF POWER-MAD GREED. BUT WE ARE BEYOND THAT NOW.
SAYS YOU!
PLEASE! OUR SQUABBLES MEAN NOTHING. THE CALIPH HAS GROWN MAD SINCE HIS MOTHER DIED.
HE IS MURDERING A NEW WOMAN EVERY NIGHT. HE MUST BE STOPPED.
LISTEN TO THE THIEF. SHE AND I HAVE SOUGHT POWER FOR PETTY ENDS, BUT THE CALIPH SEEKS TO RULE EVERYTHING.
HE SPEAKS EVEN OF RULING THE PAST AND THE FUTURE! IF HE FINDS THE RING OF SOLOMON...
WE MUST SPEAK MORE, BUT NOT HERE. OUR CONCEALED CAMP IS DEEPER INTO THE OASIS. FOLLOW ME.

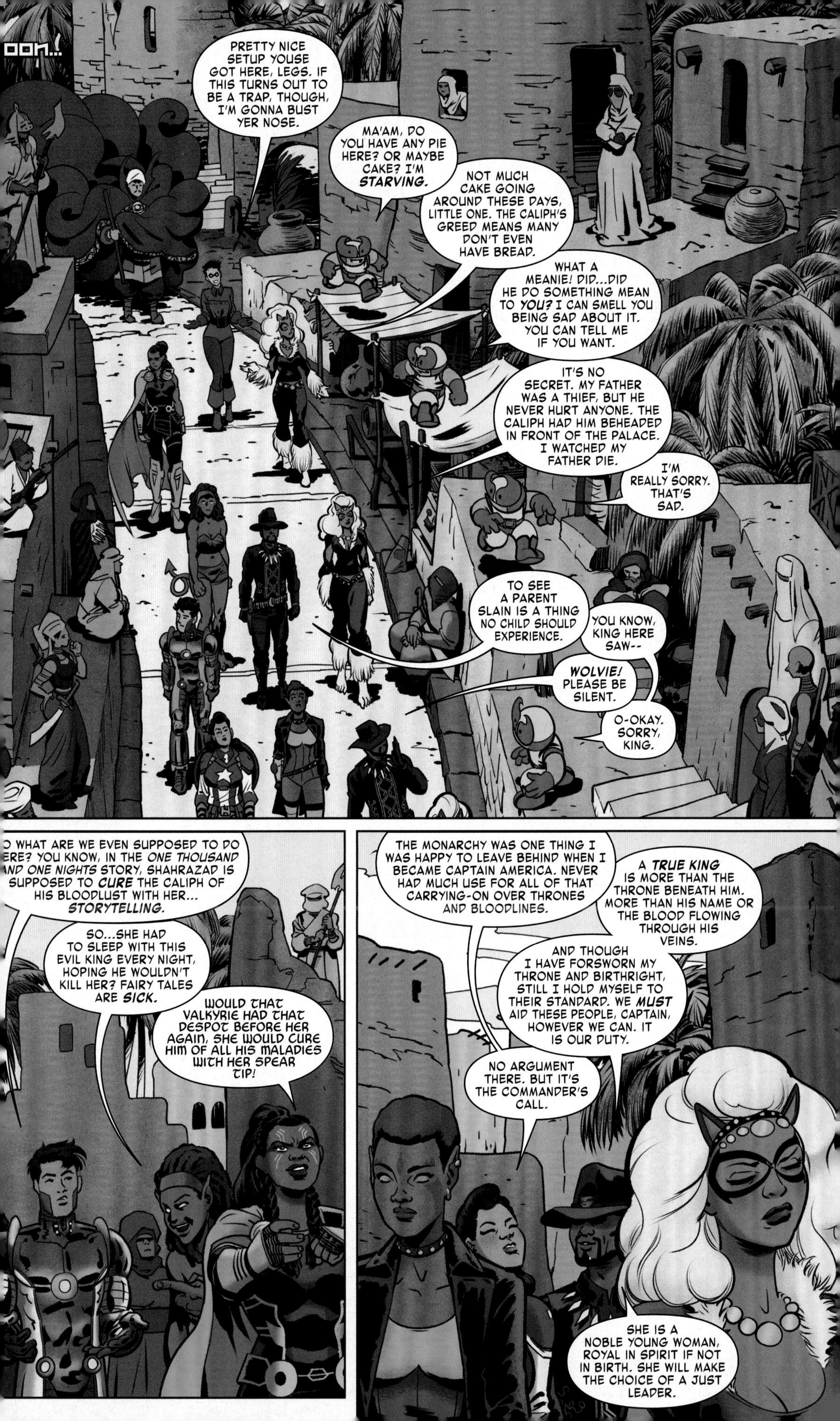
OON..!
PRETTY NICE SETUP YOUSE GOT HERE, LEGS. IF THIS TURNS OUT TO BE A TRAP, THOUGH, I'M GONNA BUST YER NOSE.
MA'AM, DO YOU HAVE ANY PIE HERE? OR MAYBE CAKE? I'M *STARVING.*
NOT MUCH CAKE GOING AROUND THESE DAYS, LITTLE ONE. THE CALIPH'S GREED MEANS MANY DON'T EVEN HAVE BREAD.
WHAT A MEANIE! DID...DID HE DO SOMETHING MEAN TO *YOU?* I CAN SMELL YOU BEING SAD ABOUT IT. YOU CAN TELL ME IF YOU WANT.
IT'S NO SECRET. MY FATHER WAS A THIEF, BUT HE NEVER HURT ANYONE. THE CALIPH HAD HIM BEHEADED IN FRONT OF THE PALACE. I WATCHED MY FATHER DIE.
I'M REALLY SORRY. THAT'S SAD.
TO SEE A PARENT SLAIN IS A THING NO CHILD SHOULD EXPERIENCE.
YOU KNOW, KING HERE SAW--
WOLVIE! PLEASE BE SILENT.
O-OKAY. SORRY, KING.
O WHAT ARE WE EVEN SUPPOSED TO DO ERE? YOU KNOW, IN THE *ONE THOUSAND AND ONE NIGHTS* STORY, SHAHRAZAD IS SUPPOSED TO *CURE* THE CALIPH OF HIS BLOODLUST WITH HER... *STORYTELLING.*
SO...SHE HAD TO SLEEP WITH THIS EVIL KING EVERY NIGHT, HOPING HE WOULDN'T KILL HER? FAIRY TALES ARE *SICK.*
WOULD THAT VALKYRIE HAD THAT DESPOT BEFORE HER AGAIN, SHE WOULD CURE HIM OF ALL HIS MALADIES WITH HER SPEAR TIP!
THE MONARCHY WAS ONE THING I WAS HAPPY TO LEAVE BEHIND WHEN I BECAME CAPTAIN AMERICA. NEVER HAD MUCH USE FOR ALL OF THAT CARRYING-ON OVER THRONES AND BLOODLINES.
A *TRUE KING* IS MORE THAN THE THRONE BENEATH HIM. MORE THAN HIS NAME OR THE BLOOD FLOWING THROUGH HIS VEINS.
AND THOUGH I HAVE FORSWORN MY THRONE AND BIRTHRIGHT, STILL I HOLD MYSELF TO THEIR STANDARD. WE *MUST* AID THESE PEOPLE, CAPTAIN, HOWEVER WE CAN. IT IS OUR DUTY.
NO ARGUMENT THERE. BUT IT'S THE COMMANDER'S CALL.
SHE IS A NOBLE YOUNG WOMAN, ROYAL IN SPIRIT IF NOT IN BIRTH. SHE WILL MAKE THE CHOICE OF A JUST LEADER.

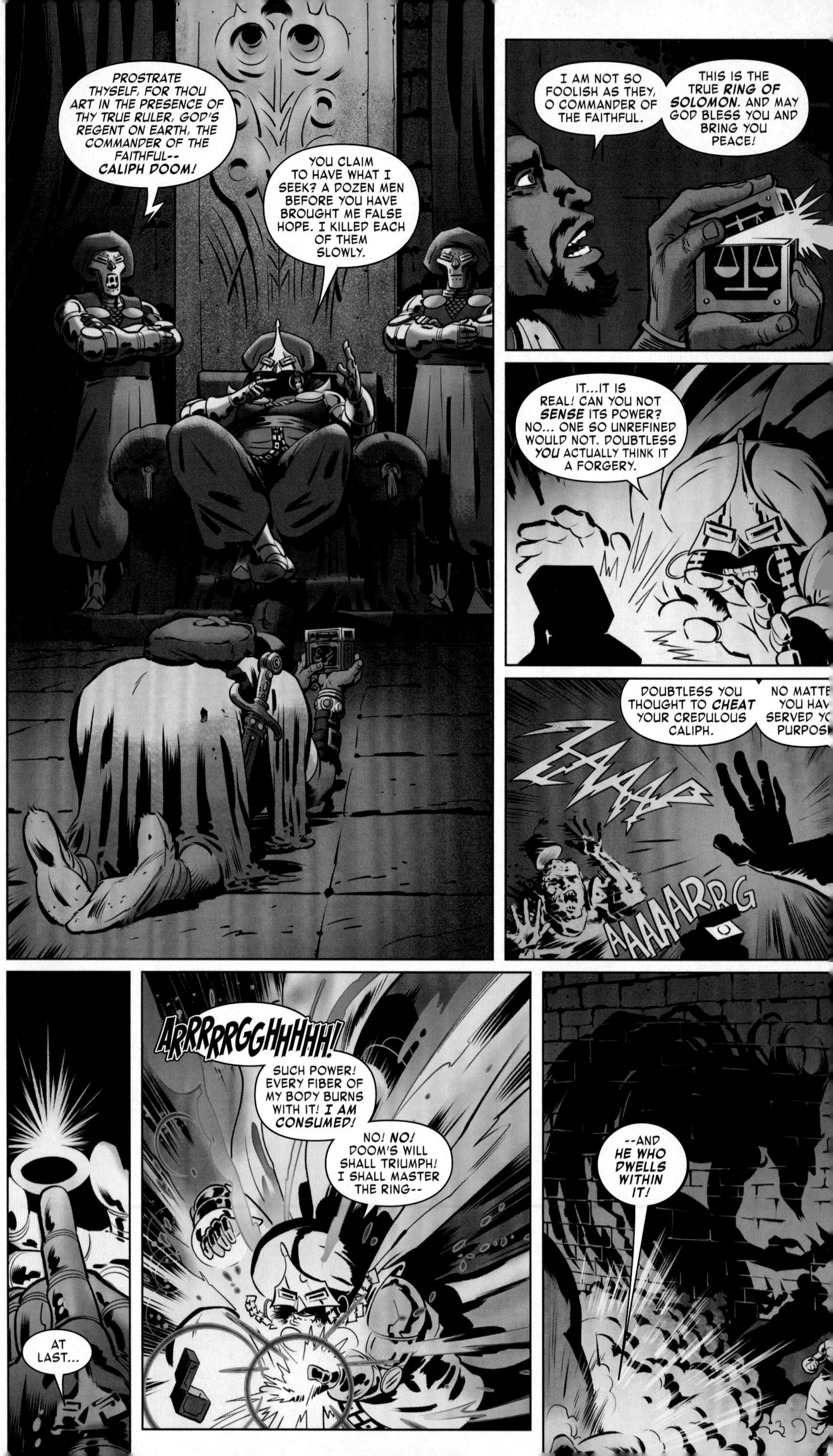
PROSTRATE THYSELF, FOR THOU ART IN THE PRESENCE OF THY TRUE RULER, GOD'S REGENT ON EARTH, THE COMMANDER OF THE FAITHFUL-- CALIPH DOOM!
YOU CLAIM TO HAVE WHAT I SEEK? A DOZEN MEN BEFORE YOU HAVE BROUGHT ME FALSE HOPE. I KILLED EACH OF THEM SLOWLY.
I AM NOT SO FOOLISH AS THEY, O COMMANDER OF THE FAITHFUL.
THIS IS THE TRUE RING OF SOLOMON. AND MAY GOD BLESS YOU AND BRING YOU PEACE!
IT...IT IS REAL! CAN YOU NOT SENSE ITS POWER? NO... ONE SO UNREFINED WOULD NOT. DOUBTLESS YOU ACTUALLY THINK IT A FORGERY.
DOUBTLESS YOU THOUGHT TO CHEAT YOUR CREDULOUS CALIPH.
ZAAAP
AAAAARRG
AT LAST...
ARRRRRGGHHHHH!
SUCH POWER! EVERY FIBER OF MY BODY BURNS WITH IT! I AM CONSUMED!
NO! NO! DOOM'S WILL SHALL TRIUMPH! I SHALL MASTER THE RING--
--AND HE WHO DWELLS WITHIN IT!

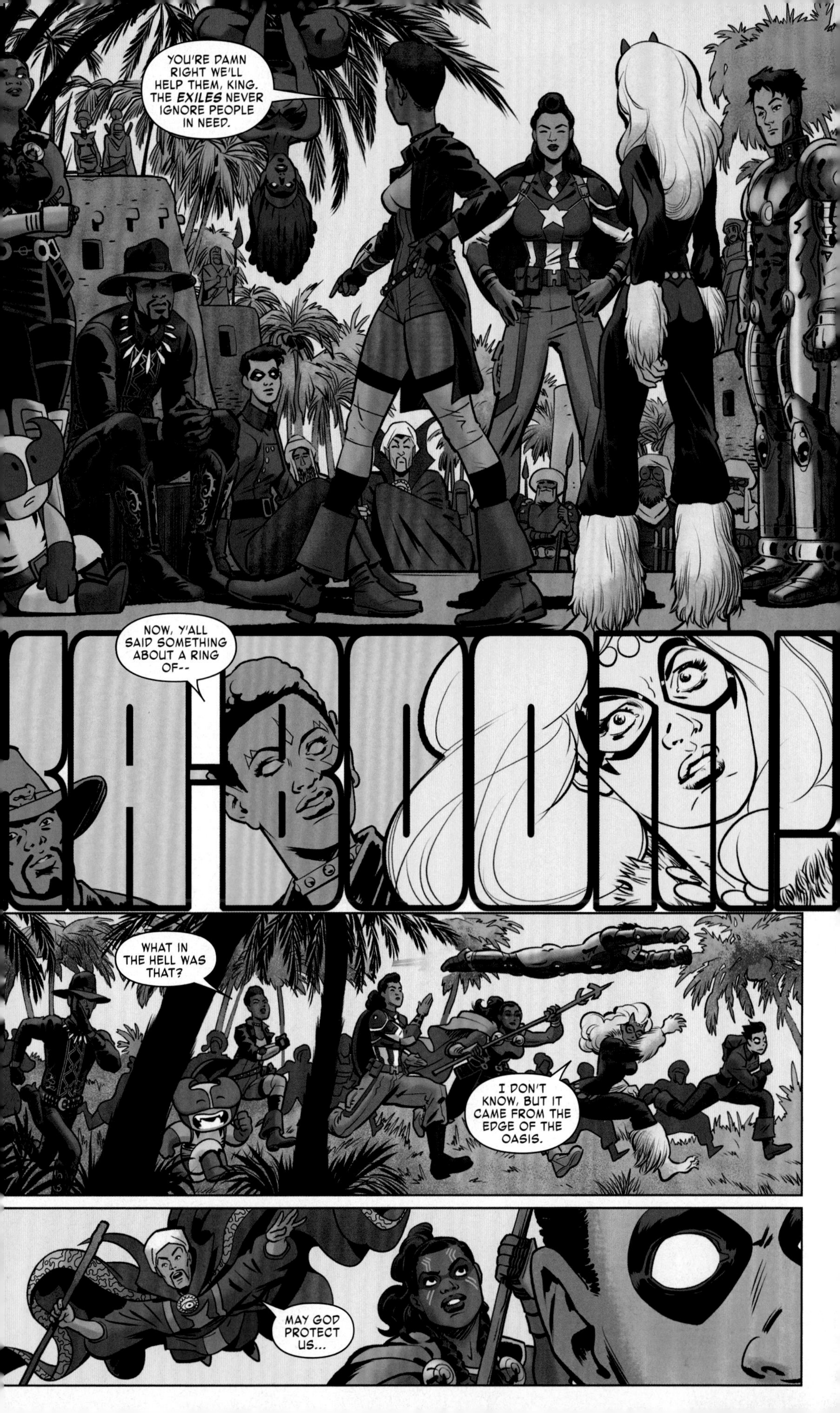

YOU'RE DAMN RIGHT WE'LL HELP THEM, KING. THE *EXILES* NEVER IGNORE PEOPLE IN NEED.
NOW, Y'ALL SAID SOMETHING ABOUT A RING OF--
KABOOM!
WHAT IN THE HELL WAS THAT?
I DON'T KNOW, BUT IT CAME FROM THE EDGE OF THE OASIS.
MAY GOD PROTECT US...

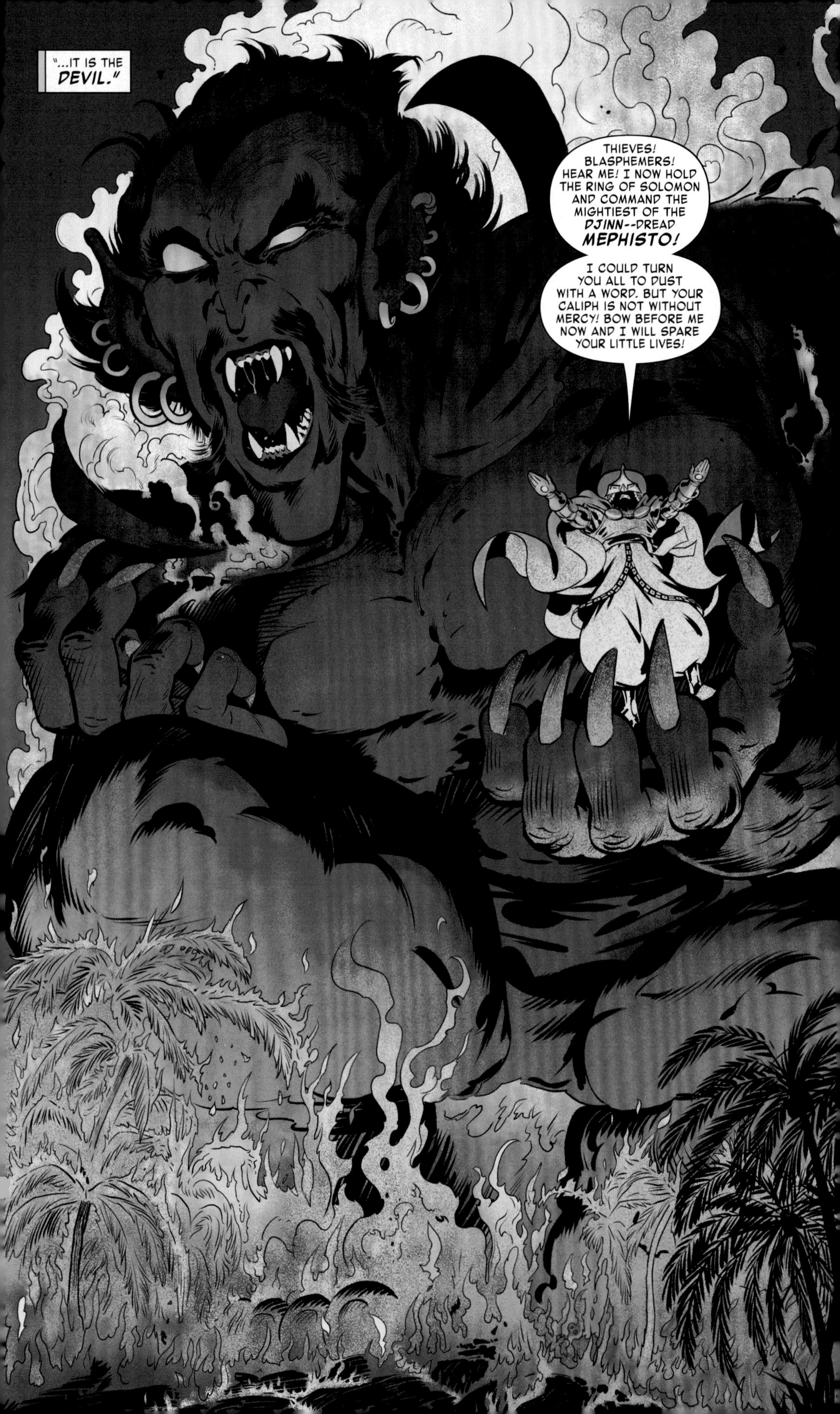
"...IT IS THE DEVIL."
THIEVES! BLASPHEMERS! HEAR ME! I NOW HOLD THE RING OF SOLOMON AND COMMAND THE MIGHTIEST OF THE DJINN--DREAD MEPHISTO!
I COULD TURN YOU ALL TO DUST WITH A WORD. BUT YOUR CALIPH IS NOT WITHOUT MERCY! BOW BEFORE ME NOW AND I WILL SPARE YOUR LITTLE LIVES!

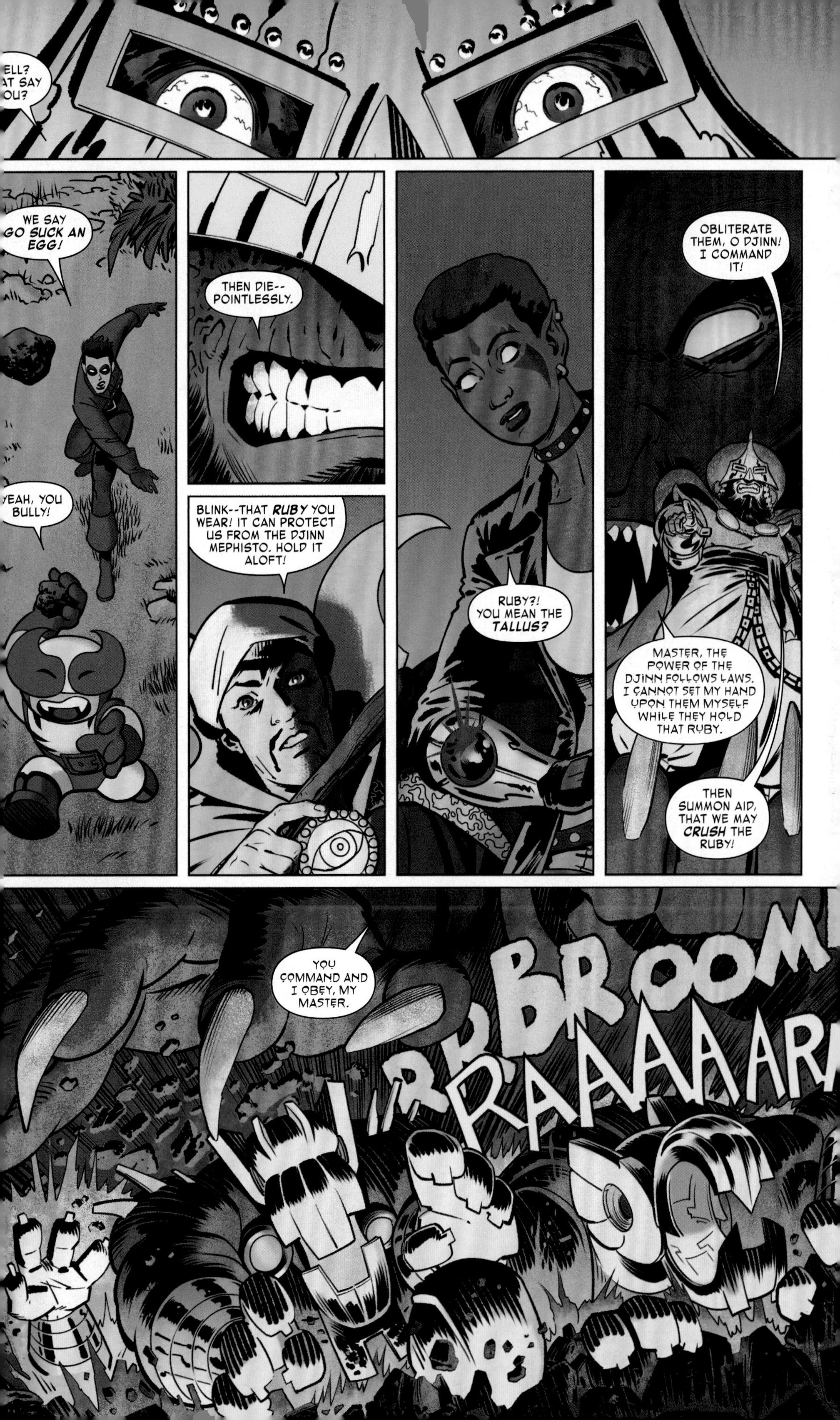

ELL? AT SAY OU?
WE SAY GO SUCK AN EGG!
YEAH, YOU BULLY!
THEN DIE-- POINTLESSLY.
BLINK--THAT RUBY YOU WEAR! IT CAN PROTECT US FROM THE DJINN MEPHISTO. HOLD IT ALOFT!
RUBY?! YOU MEAN THE TALLUS?
OBLITERATE THEM, O DJINN! I COMMAND IT!
MASTER, THE POWER OF THE DJINN FOLLOWS LAWS. I CANNOT SET MY HAND UPON THEM MYSELF WHILE THEY HOLD THAT RUBY.
THEN SUMMON AID, THAT WE MAY CRUSH THE RUBY!
YOU COMMAND AND I OBEY, MY MASTER.
BROOM
RAAAAAR

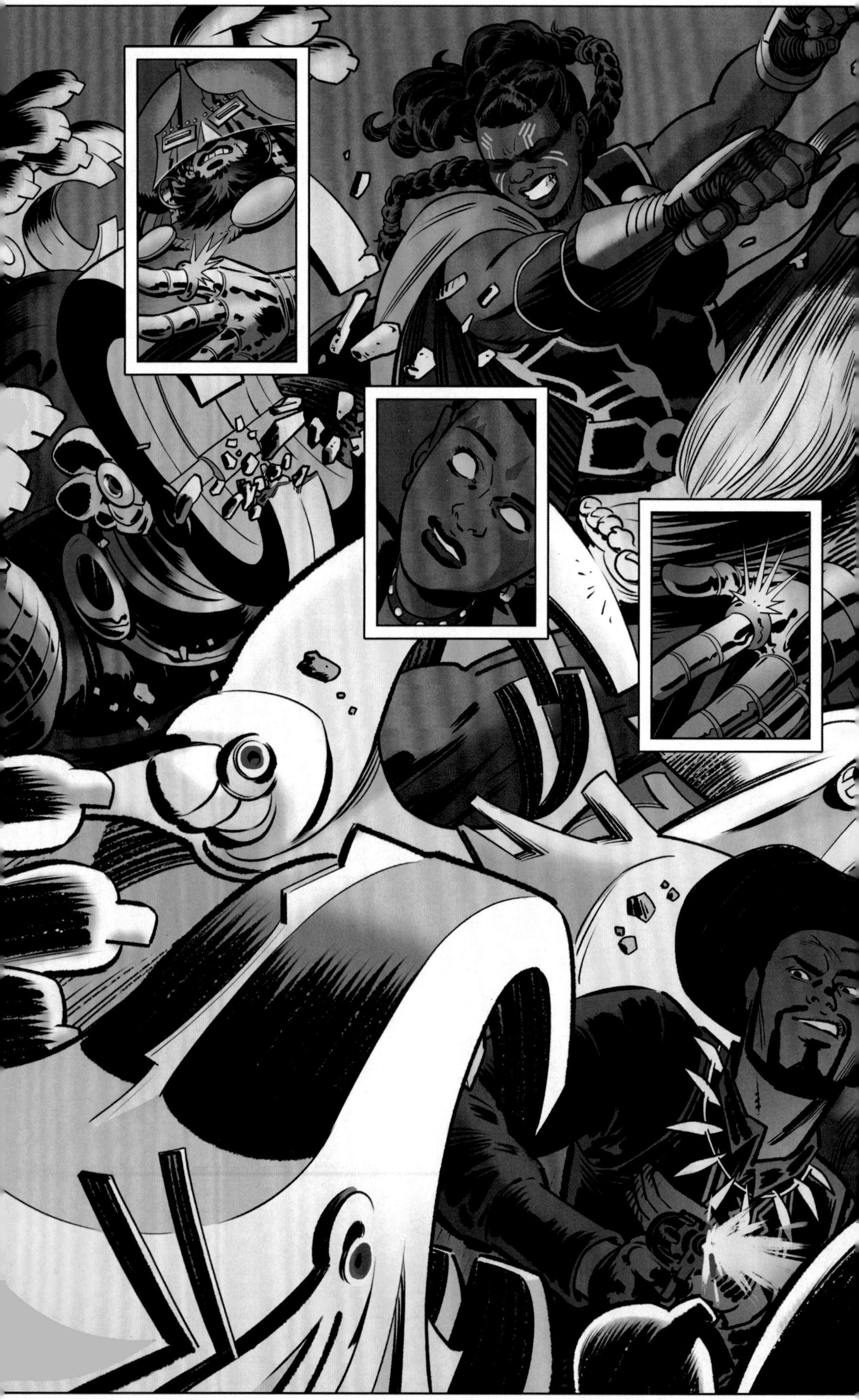

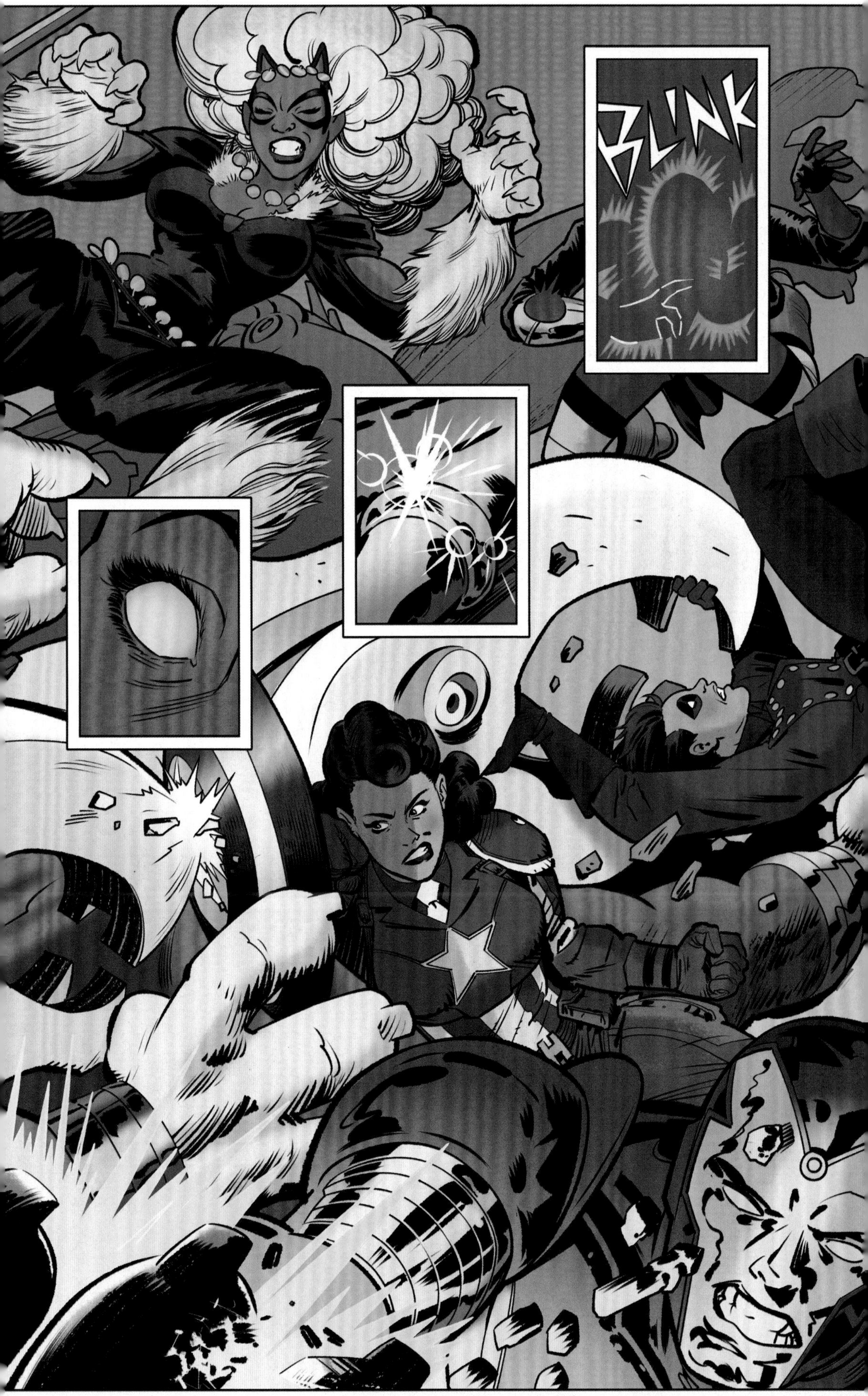
BLINK

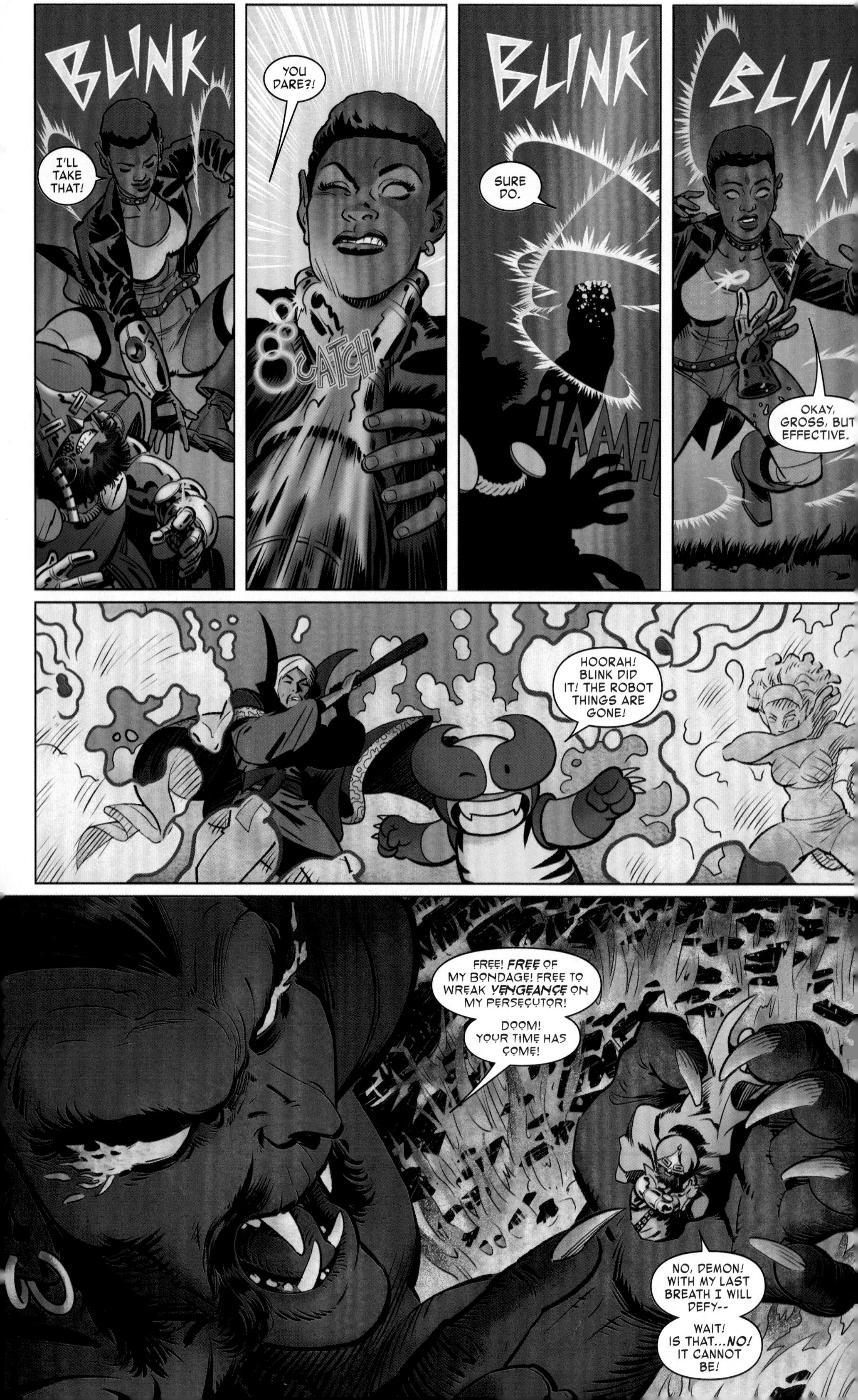
BLINK
I'LL TAKE THAT!
YOU DARE?!
CATCH
BLINK
SURE DO.
¡¡AAAH!
BLINK
OKAY, GROSS, BUT EFFECTIVE.
HOORAH! BLINK DID IT! THE ROBOT THINGS ARE GONE!
FREE! FREE OF MY BONDAGE! FREE TO WREAK VENGEANCE ON MY PERSECUTOR!
DOOM! YOUR TIME HAS COME!
NO, DEMON! WITH MY LAST BREATH I WILL DEFY--
WAIT! IS THAT...NO! IT CANNOT BE!

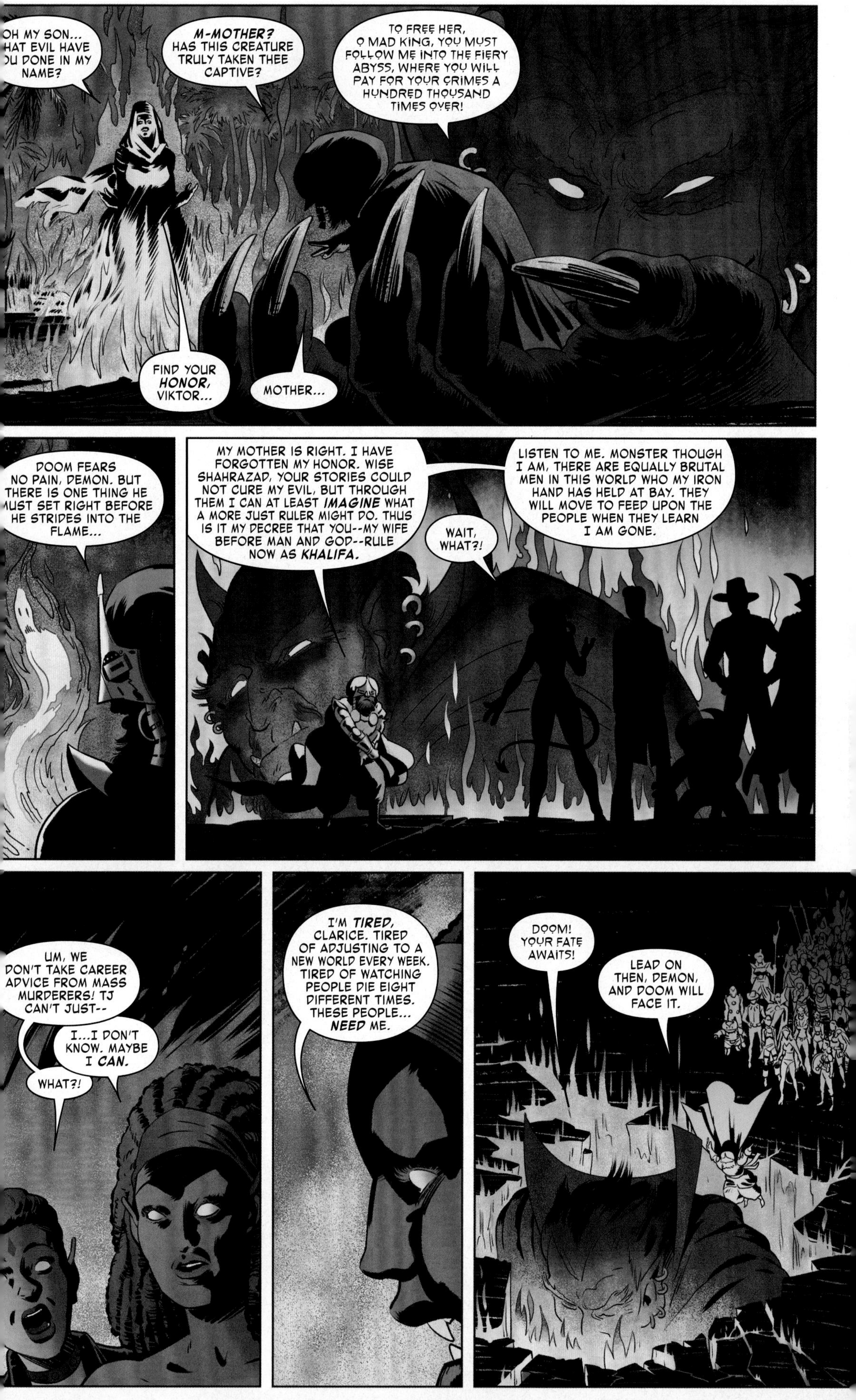

OH MY SON... HAT EVIL HAVE OU DONE IN MY NAME?
M-MOTHER? HAS THIS CREATURE TRULY TAKEN THEE CAPTIVE?
TO FREE HER, O MAD KING, YOU MUST FOLLOW ME INTO THE FIERY ABYSS, WHERE YOU WILL PAY FOR YOUR CRIMES A HUNDRED THOUSAND TIMES OVER!
FIND YOUR HONOR, VIKTOR...
MOTHER...
DOOM FEARS NO PAIN, DEMON. BUT THERE IS ONE THING HE MUST SET RIGHT BEFORE HE STRIDES INTO THE FLAME...
MY MOTHER IS RIGHT. I HAVE FORGOTTEN MY HONOR. WISE SHAHRAZAD, YOUR STORIES COULD NOT CURE MY EVIL, BUT THROUGH THEM I CAN AT LEAST IMAGINE WHAT A MORE JUST RULER MIGHT DO. THUS IS IT MY DECREE THAT YOU--MY WIFE BEFORE MAN AND GOD--RULE NOW AS KHALIFA.
WAIT, WHAT?!
LISTEN TO ME. MONSTER THOUGH I AM, THERE ARE EQUALLY BRUTAL MEN IN THIS WORLD WHO MY IRON HAND HAS HELD AT BAY. THEY WILL MOVE TO FEED UPON THE PEOPLE WHEN THEY LEARN I AM GONE.
UM, WE DON'T TAKE CAREER ADVICE FROM MASS MURDERERS! TJ CAN'T JUST--
I...I DON'T KNOW. MAYBE I CAN.
WHAT?!
I'M TIRED, CLARICE. TIRED OF ADJUSTING TO A NEW WORLD EVERY WEEK. TIRED OF WATCHING PEOPLE DIE EIGHT DIFFERENT TIMES. THESE PEOPLE... NEED ME.
DOOM! YOUR FATE AWAITS!
LEAD ON THEN, DEMON, AND DOOM WILL FACE IT.

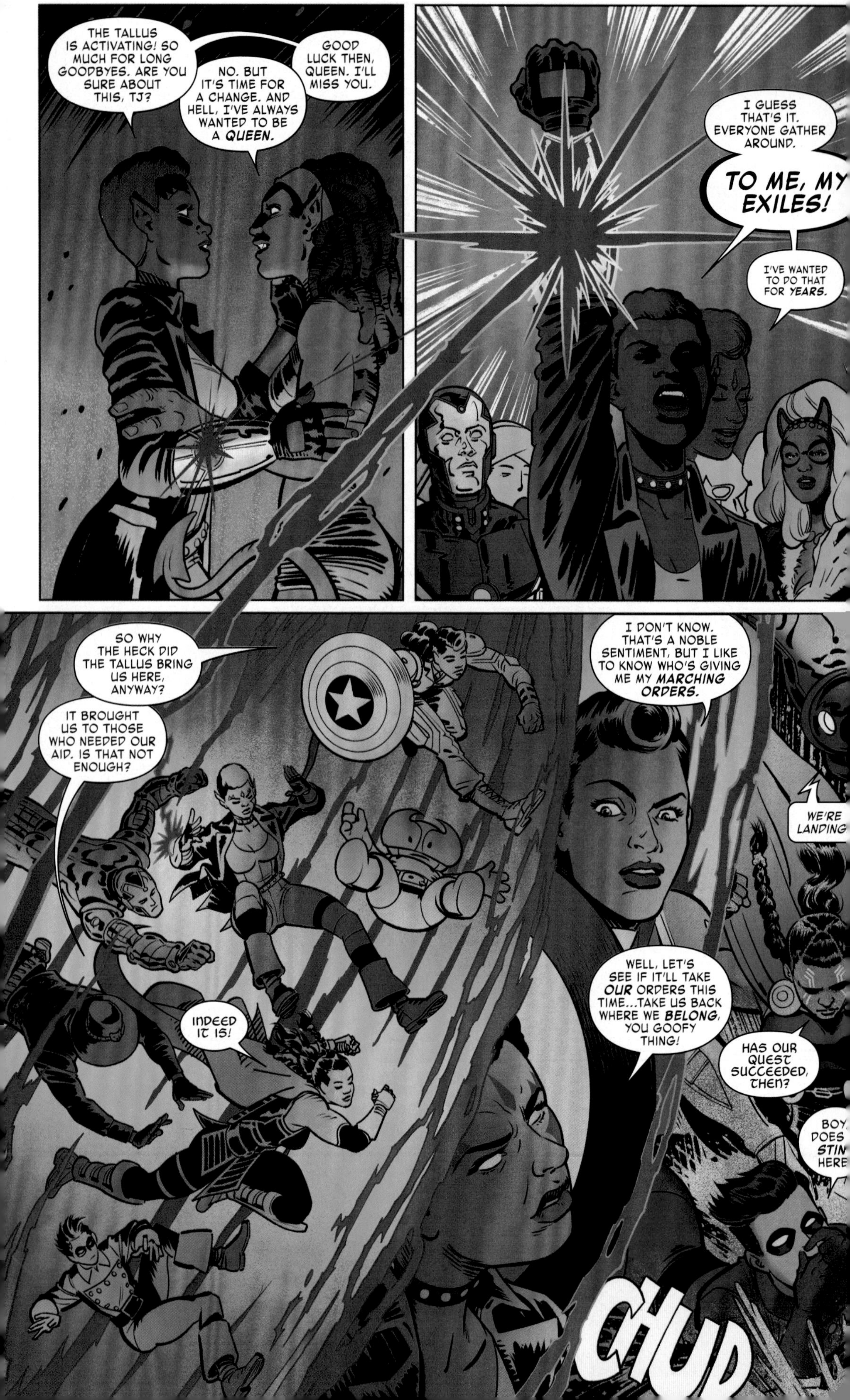
THE TALLUS IS ACTIVATING! SO MUCH FOR LONG GOODBYES. ARE YOU SURE ABOUT THIS, TJ?
NO. BUT IT'S TIME FOR A CHANGE. AND HELL, I'VE ALWAYS WANTED TO BE A QUEEN.
GOOD LUCK THEN, QUEEN. I'LL MISS YOU.
I GUESS THAT'S IT. EVERYONE GATHER AROUND.
TO ME, MY EXILES!
I'VE WANTED TO DO THAT FOR YEARS.
SO WHY THE HECK DID THE TALLUS BRING US HERE, ANYWAY?
IT BROUGHT US TO THOSE WHO NEEDED OUR AID. IS THAT NOT ENOUGH?
I DON'T KNOW. THAT'S A NOBLE SENTIMENT, BUT I LIKE TO KNOW WHO'S GIVING ME MY MARCHING ORDERS.
WE'RE LANDING
INDEED IT IS!
WELL, LET'S SEE IF IT'LL TAKE OUR ORDERS THIS TIME...TAKE US BACK WHERE WE BELONG, YOU GOOFY THING!
HAS OUR QUEST SUCCEEDED, THEN?
BOY, DOES STIN HERE
CHUD

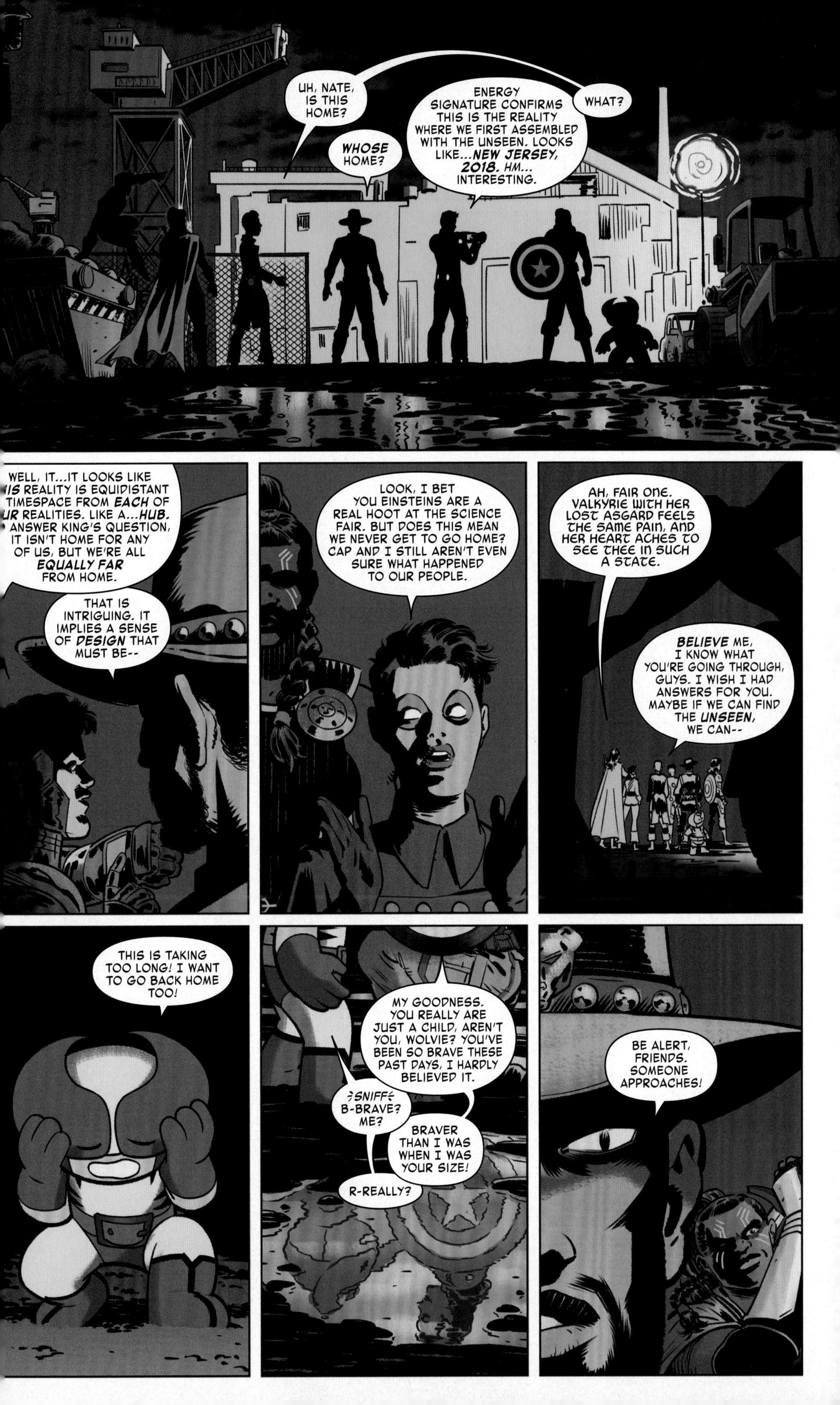

UH, NATE, IS THIS HOME?
WHOSE HOME?
ENERGY SIGNATURE CONFIRMS THIS IS THE REALITY WHERE WE FIRST ASSEMBLED WITH THE UNSEEN. LOOKS LIKE...NEW JERSEY, 2018. HM... INTERESTING.
WHAT?
WELL, IT...IT LOOKS LIKE IS REALITY IS EQUIDISTANT TIMESPACE FROM EACH OF UR REALITIES. LIKE A...HUB. ANSWER KING'S QUESTION, IT ISN'T HOME FOR ANY OF US, BUT WE'RE ALL EQUALLY FAR FROM HOME.
THAT IS INTRIGUING. IT IMPLIES A SENSE OF DESIGN THAT MUST BE--
LOOK, I BET YOU EINSTEINS ARE A REAL HOOT AT THE SCIENCE FAIR. BUT DOES THIS MEAN WE NEVER GET TO GO HOME? CAP AND I STILL AREN'T EVEN SURE WHAT HAPPENED TO OUR PEOPLE.
AH, FAIR ONE. VALKYRIE WITH HER LOST ASGARD FEELS THE SAME PAIN, AND HER HEART ACHES TO SEE THEE IN SUCH A STATE.
BELIEVE ME, I KNOW WHAT YOU'RE GOING THROUGH, GUYS. I WISH I HAD ANSWERS FOR YOU. MAYBE IF WE CAN FIND THE UNSEEN, WE CAN--
THIS IS TAKING TOO LONG! I WANT TO GO BACK HOME TOO!
MY GOODNESS. YOU REALLY ARE JUST A CHILD, AREN'T YOU, WOLVIE? YOU'VE BEEN SO BRAVE THESE PAST DAYS, I HARDLY BELIEVED IT.
SNIFF B-BRAVE? ME?
BRAVER THAN I WAS WHEN I WAS YOUR SIZE!
R-REALLY?
BE ALERT, FRIENDS. SOMEONE APPROACHES!

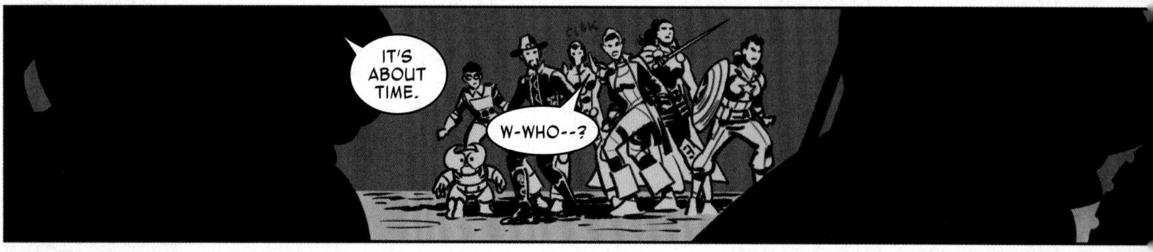
IT'S ABOUT TIME.
W-WHO--?

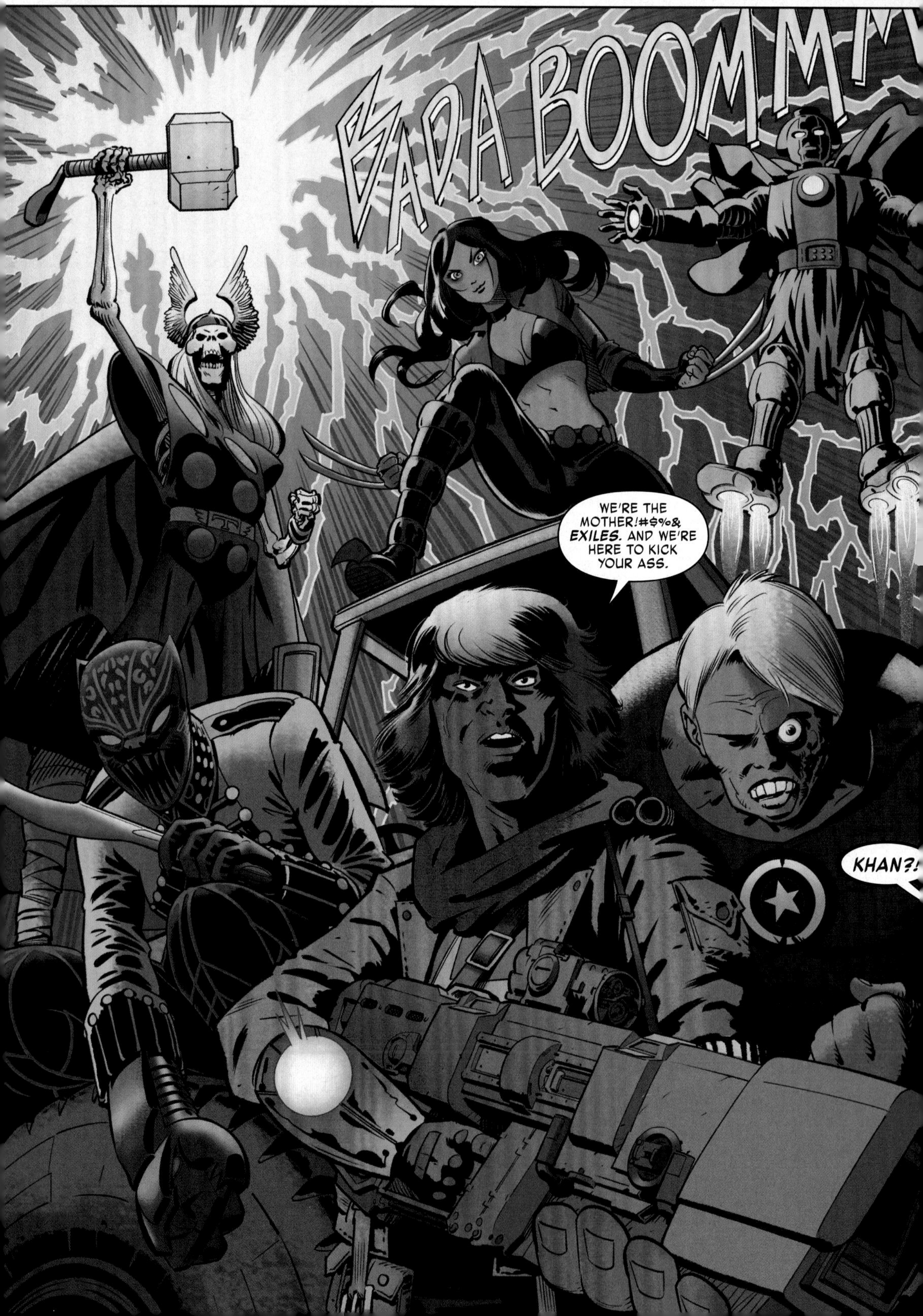
BADA BOOMMM
WE'RE THE MOTHER!#$%& EXILES. AND WE'RE HERE TO KICK YOUR ASS.
KHAN?!

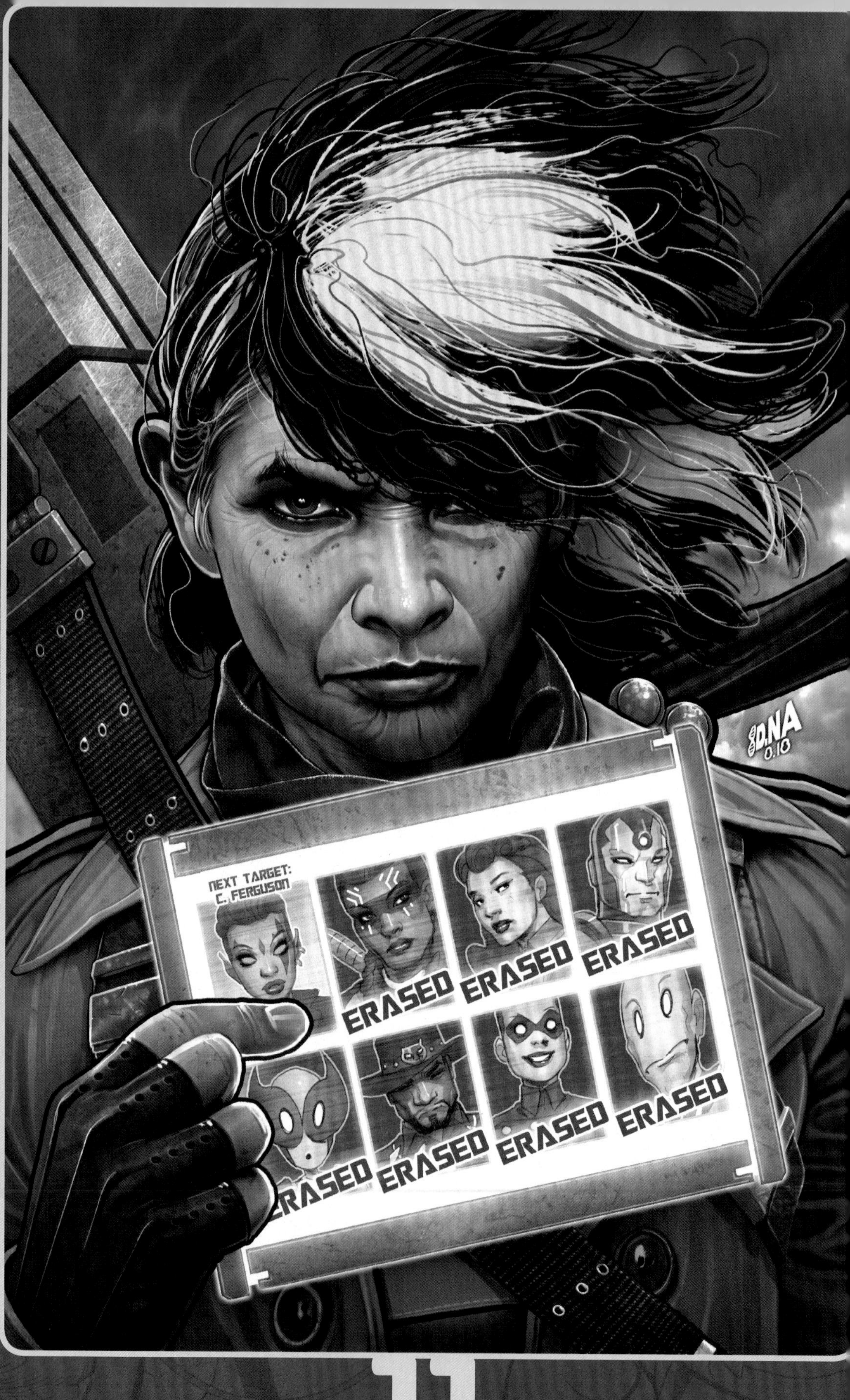

NEXT TARGET:
C. FERGUSON
ERASED
ERASED
ERASED
ERASED
ERASED
ERASED
ERASED
D.NA
0.18

11

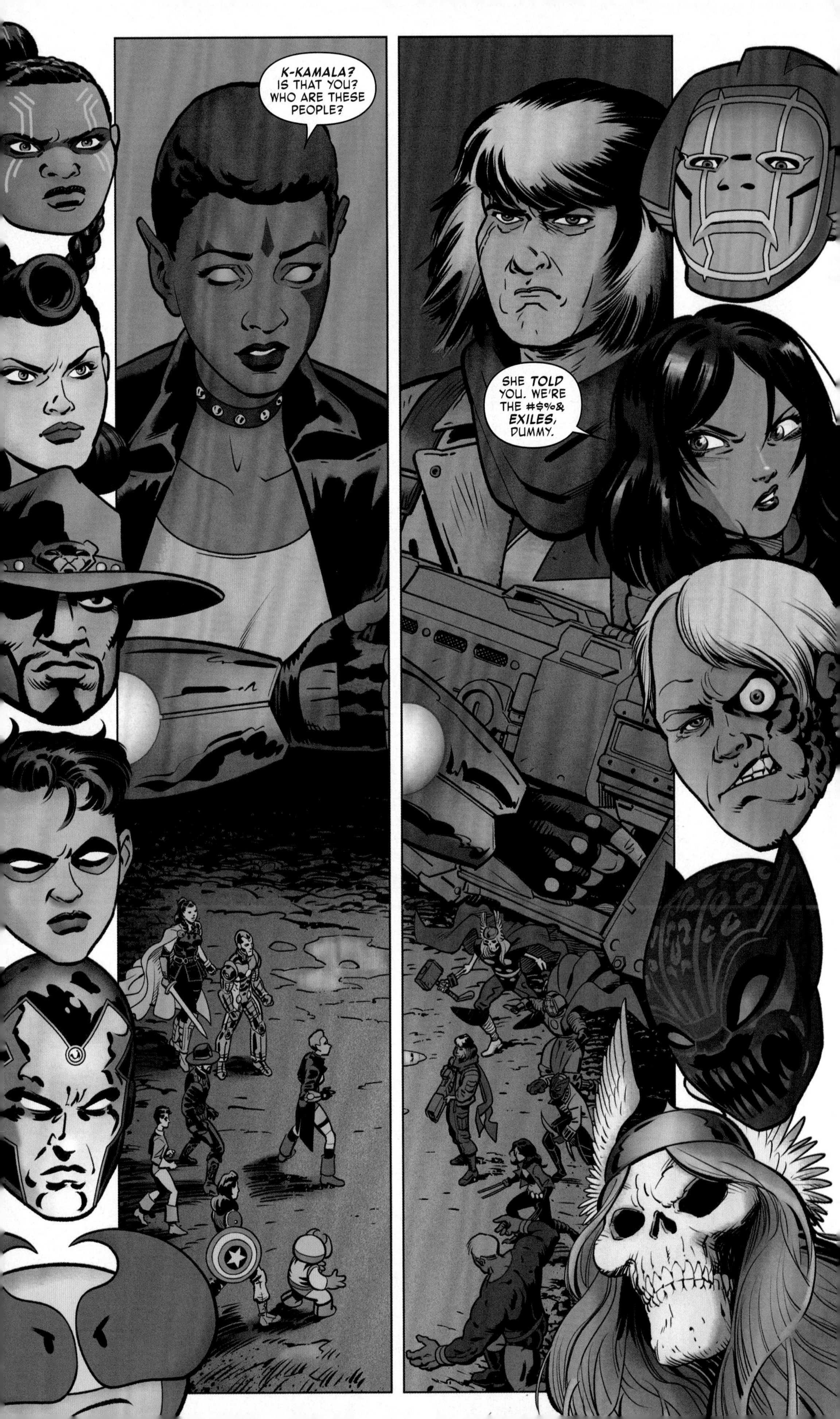
K-KAMALA? IS THAT YOU? WHO ARE THESE PEOPLE?
SHE TOLD YOU. WE'RE THE #$%& EXILES, DUMMY.

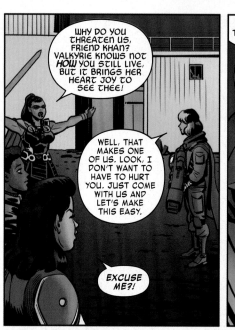

WHY DO YOU THREATEN US, FRIEND KHAN? VALKYRIE KNOWS NOT *HOW* YOU STILL LIVE, BUT IT BRINGS HER HEART JOY TO SEE THEE!

WELL, THAT MAKES ONE OF US. LOOK, I DON'T WANT TO HAVE TO HURT YOU. JUST COME WITH US AND LET'S MAKE THIS EASY.

EXCUSE ME?!

WHY'S SHE BLABBERING WITH THESE INSECTS, *KILLMONGER?* LET'S JUST TAKE THEM.

I AM INCLINED TO AGREE WITH YOU, *IRON PRINCE.* BUT THIS MISSION REQUIRES WORKING TOGETHER--LET US GIVE HER A MOMENT.

LISTEN, KHAN. *KAMALA.* I DON'T KNOW WHAT'S GOING ON HERE, BUT--

I'M GOING TO GET MY *FAMILY* BACK. THAT'S WHAT'S GOING ON.

ENOUGH TALKING TAKE THE DOWN!

KA-BOOM

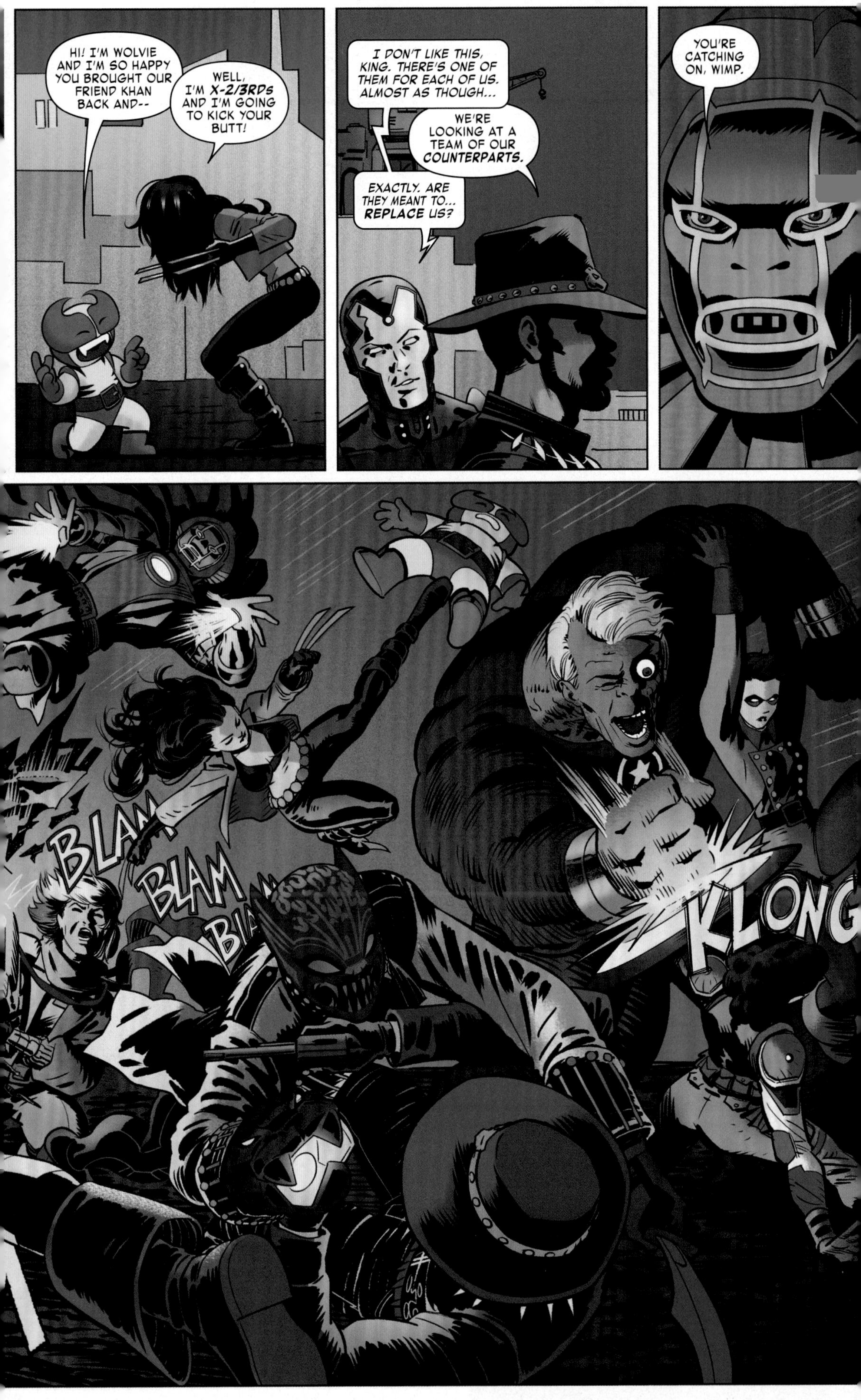

HI! I'M WOLVIE AND I'M SO HAPPY YOU BROUGHT OUR FRIEND KHAN BACK AND--
WELL, I'M X-2/3RDs AND I'M GOING TO KICK YOUR BUTT!
I DON'T LIKE THIS, KING. THERE'S ONE OF THEM FOR EACH OF US. ALMOST AS THOUGH...
WE'RE LOOKING AT A TEAM OF OUR COUNTERPARTS.
EXACTLY. ARE THEY MEANT TO... REPLACE US?
YOU'RE CATCHING ON, WIMP.
BLAM
BLAM
KLONG

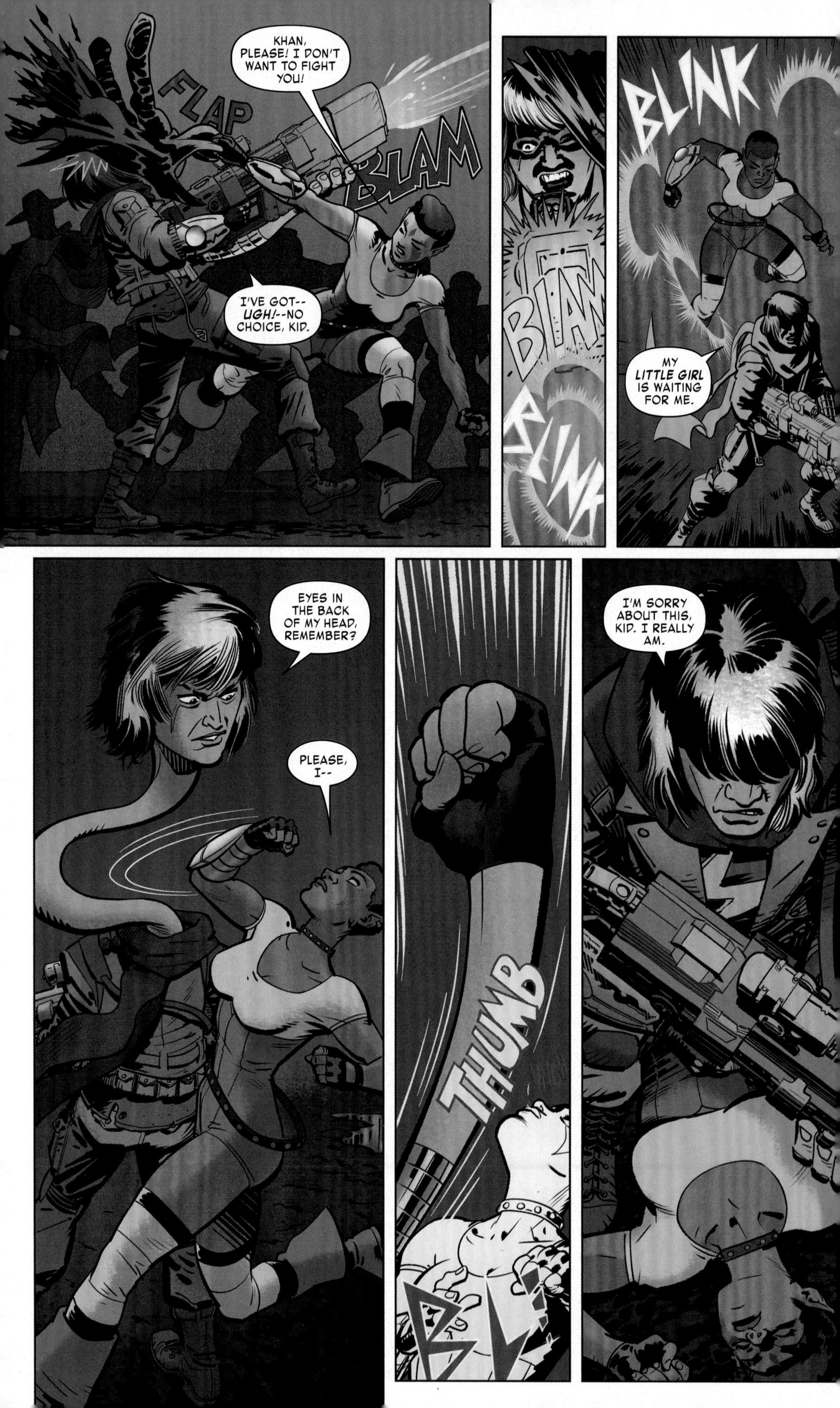
FLAP
KHAN, PLEASE! I DON'T WANT TO FIGHT YOU!
BLAM
I'VE GOT-- UGH!--NO CHOICE, KID.
BLAM
BLINK
BLINK
MY LITTLE GIRL IS WAITING FOR ME.
EYES IN THE BACK OF MY HEAD, REMEMBER?
PLEASE, I--
THUMB
I'M SORRY ABOUT THIS, KID. I REALLY AM.

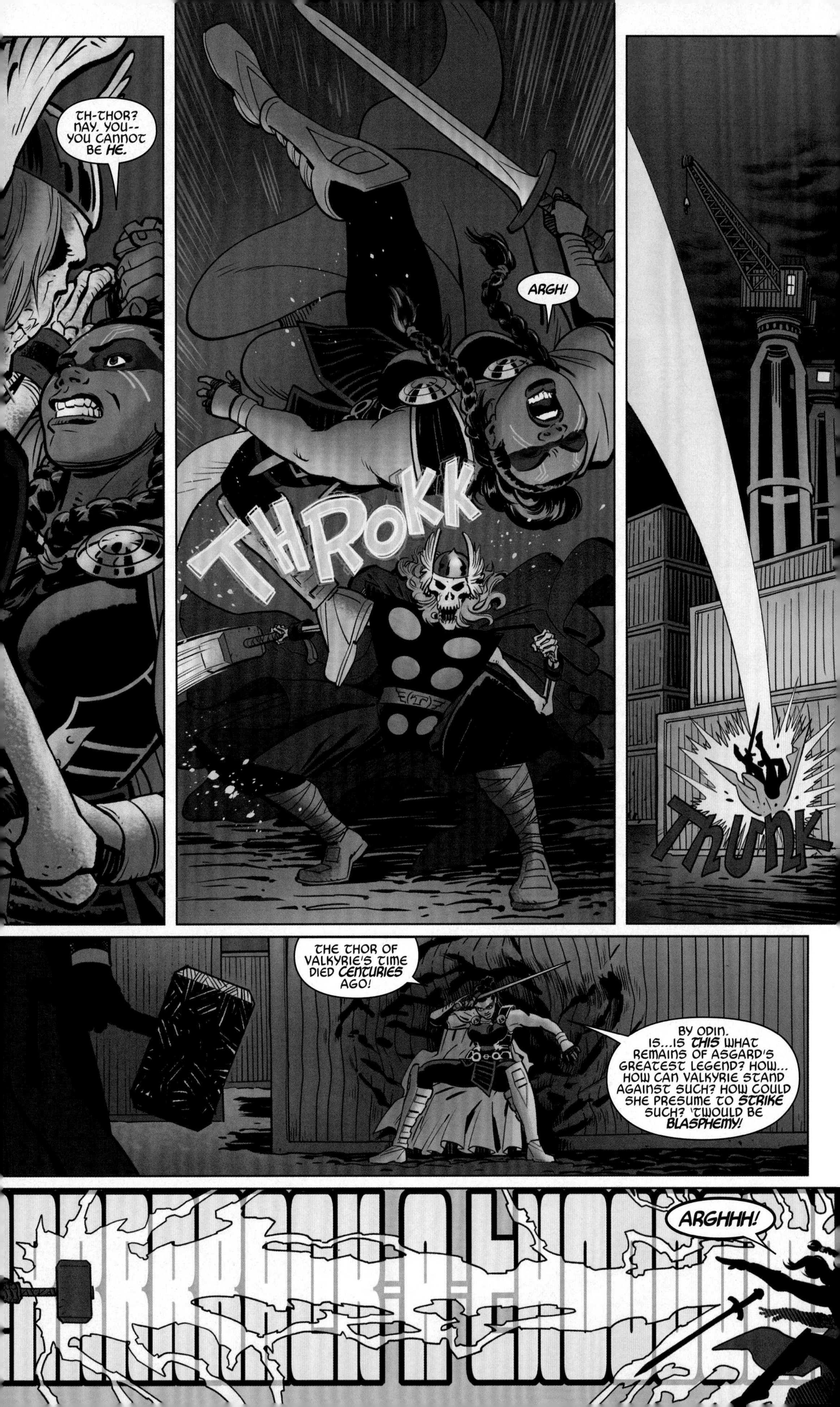
TH-THOR? NAY. YOU-- YOU CANNOT BE HE.
ARGH!
THROKK
THUNK
THE THOR OF VALKYRIE'S TIME DIED CENTURIES AGO!
BY ODIN. IS...IS THIS WHAT REMAINS OF ASGARD'S GREATEST LEGEND? HOW... HOW CAN VALKYRIE STAND AGAINST SUCH? HOW COULD SHE PRESUME TO STRIKE SUCH? 'TWOULD BE BLASPHEMY!
ARGHHH!

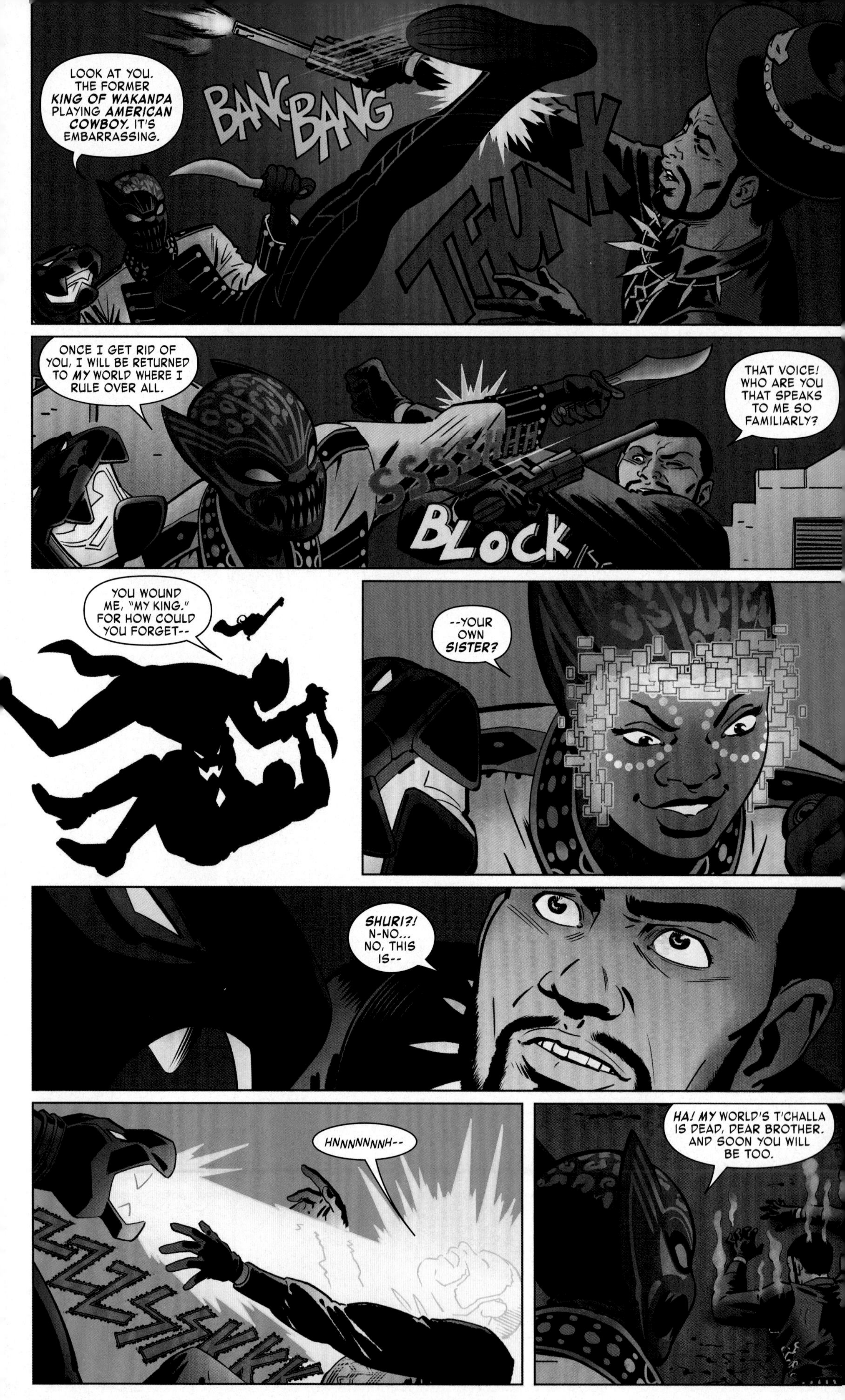
LOOK AT YOU. THE FORMER KING OF WAKANDA PLAYING AMERICAN COWBOY. IT'S EMBARRASSING.
BANG BANG
THUNK
ONCE I GET RID OF YOU, I WILL BE RETURNED TO MY WORLD WHERE I RULE OVER ALL.
THAT VOICE! WHO ARE YOU THAT SPEAKS TO ME SO FAMILIARLY?
SSSSHHH
BLOCK
YOU WOUND ME, "MY KING." FOR HOW COULD YOU FORGET--
--YOUR OWN SISTER?
SHURI?! N-NO... NO, THIS IS--
HNNNNNNNH--
ZZZSSVKK
HA! MY WORLD'S T'CHALLA IS DEAD, DEAR BROTHER. AND SOON YOU WILL BE TOO.

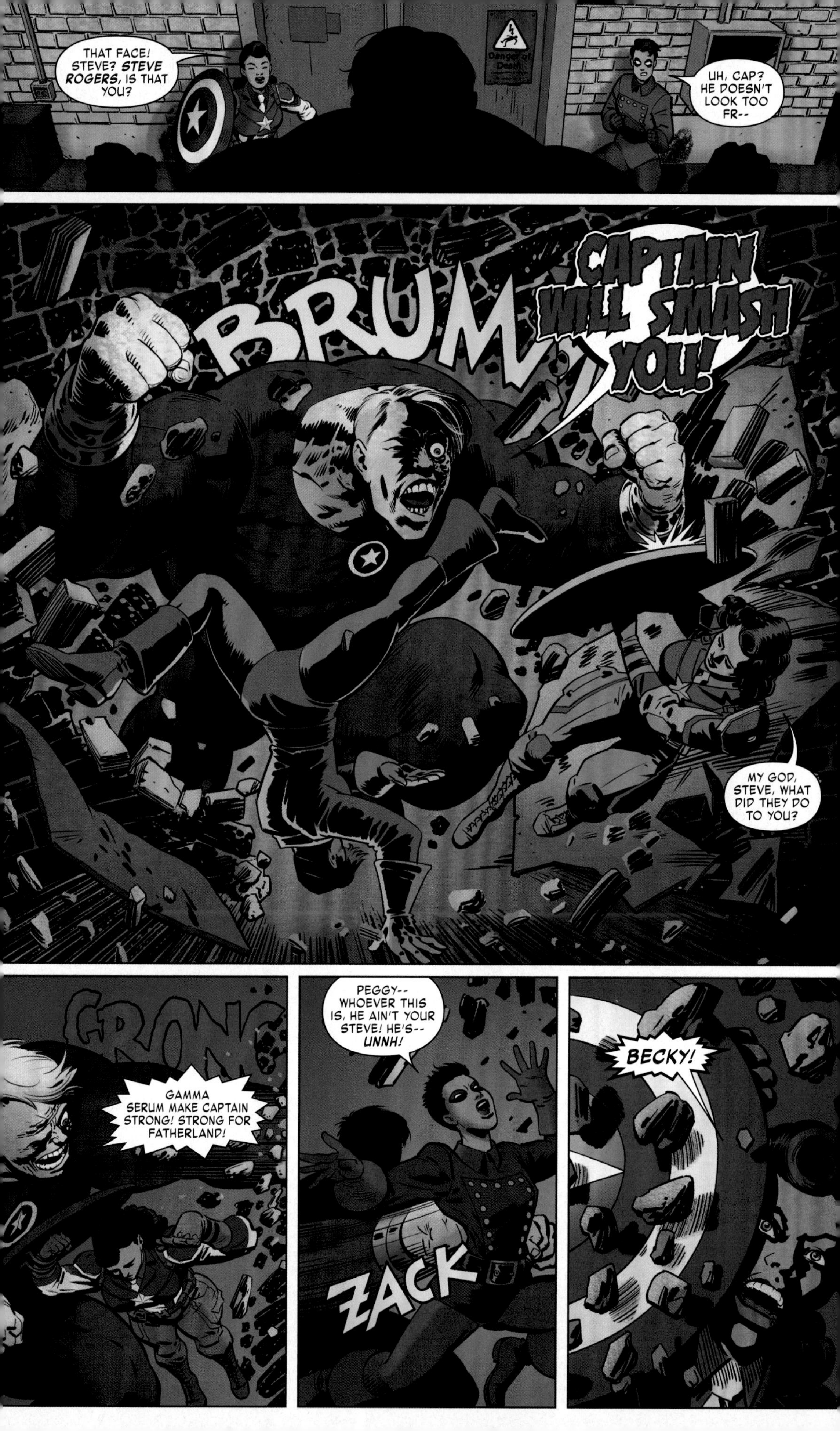
THAT FACE! STEVE? STEVE ROGERS, IS THAT YOU?
Danger of Death!
UH, CAP? HE DOESN'T LOOK TOO FR--
BRUM
CAPTAIN WILL SMASH YOU!
MY GOD, STEVE, WHAT DID THEY DO TO YOU?
GRONG
GAMMA SERUM MAKE CAPTAIN STRONG! STRONG FOR FATHERLAND!
PEGGY-- WHOEVER THIS IS, HE AIN'T YOUR STEVE! HE'S-- UNNH!
ZACK
BECKY!

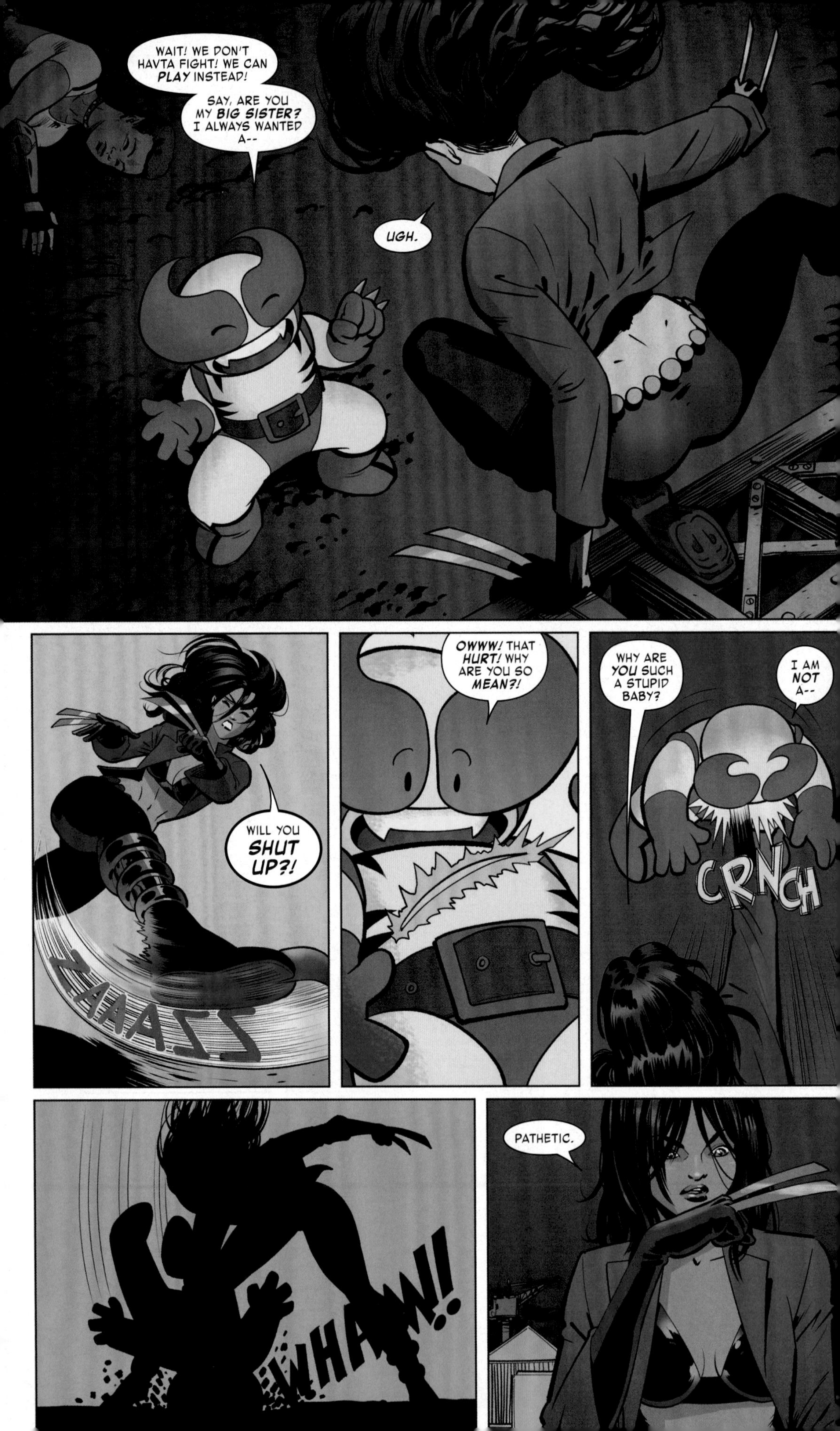
WAIT! WE DON'T HAVTA FIGHT! WE CAN PLAY INSTEAD!
SAY, ARE YOU MY BIG SISTER? I ALWAYS WANTED A--
UGH.
WILL YOU SHUT UP?!
ZAAAZZ
OWWW! THAT HURT! WHY ARE YOU SO MEAN?!
WHY ARE YOU SUCH A STUPID BABY?
I AM NOT A--
CRNCH
WHAM!!
PATHETIC.

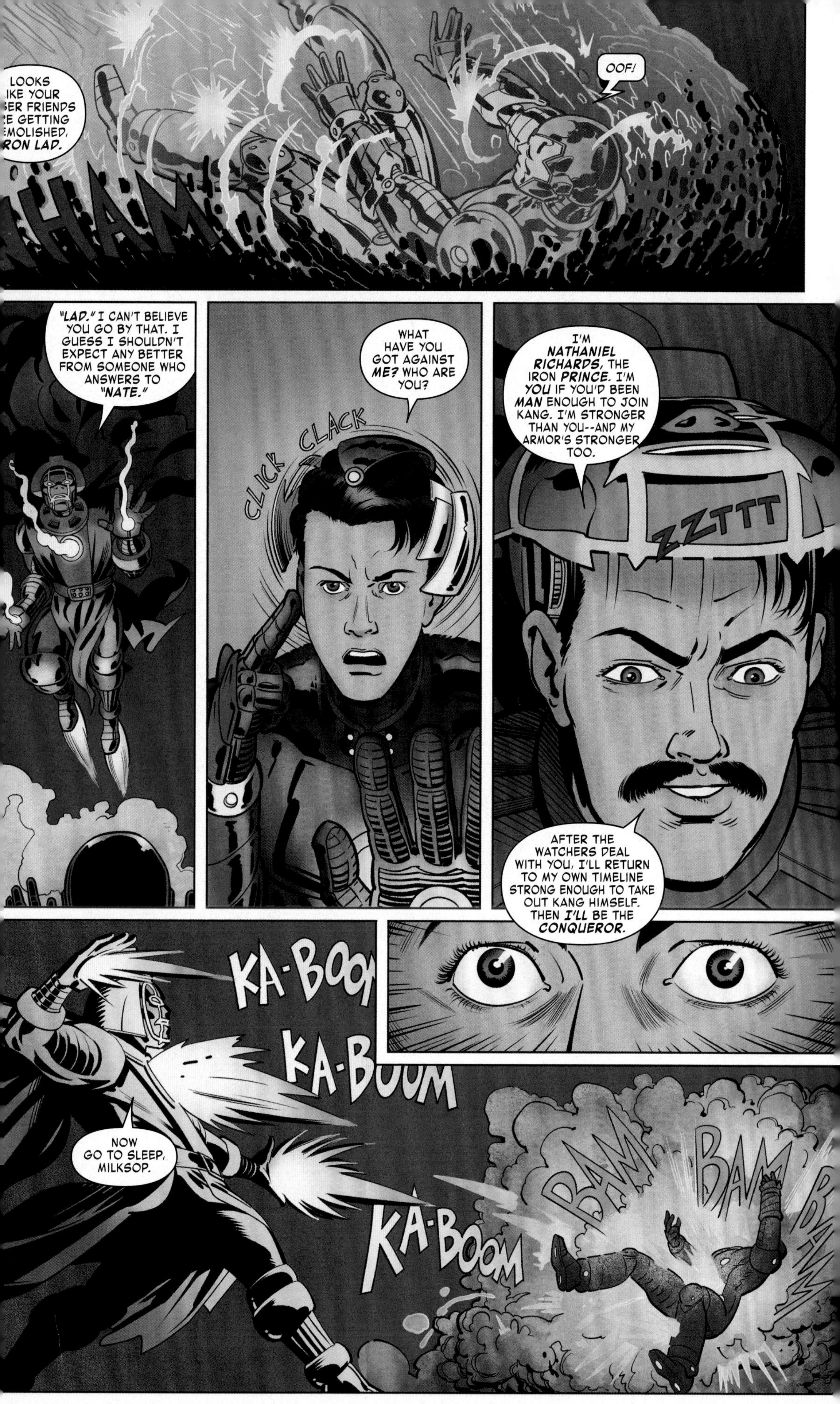
LOOKS
IKE YOUR
ER FRIENDS
E GETTING
EMOLISHED,
RON LAD.
HAM
OOF!
"LAD." I CAN'T BELIEVE YOU GO BY THAT. I GUESS I SHOULDN'T EXPECT ANY BETTER FROM SOMEONE WHO ANSWERS TO "NATE."
WHAT HAVE YOU GOT AGAINST ME? WHO ARE YOU?
CLICK CLACK
I'M NATHANIEL RICHARDS, THE IRON PRINCE. I'M YOU IF YOU'D BEEN MAN ENOUGH TO JOIN KANG. I'M STRONGER THAN YOU--AND MY ARMOR'S STRONGER TOO.
ZZTTT
AFTER THE WATCHERS DEAL WITH YOU, I'LL RETURN TO MY OWN TIMELINE STRONG ENOUGH TO TAKE OUT KANG HIMSELF. THEN I'LL BE THE CONQUEROR.
KA-BOOM
KA-BOOM
NOW GO TO SLEEP, MILKSOP.
KA-BOOM
BAM
BAM

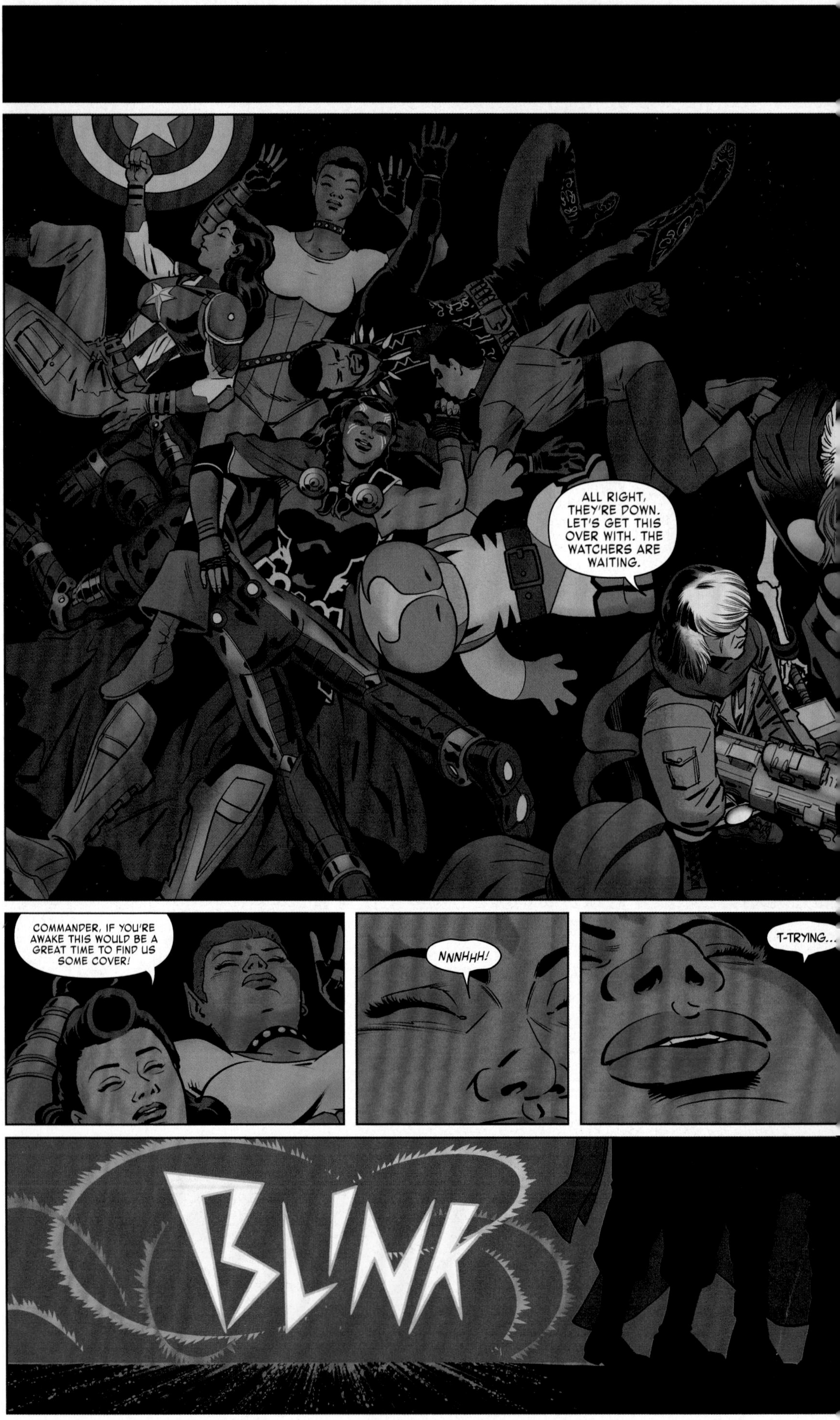
ALL RIGHT, THEY'RE DOWN. LET'S GET THIS OVER WITH. THE WATCHERS ARE WAITING.
COMMANDER, IF YOU'RE AWAKE THIS WOULD BE A GREAT TIME TO FIND US SOME COVER!
NNNHHH!
T-TRYING...
BLINK

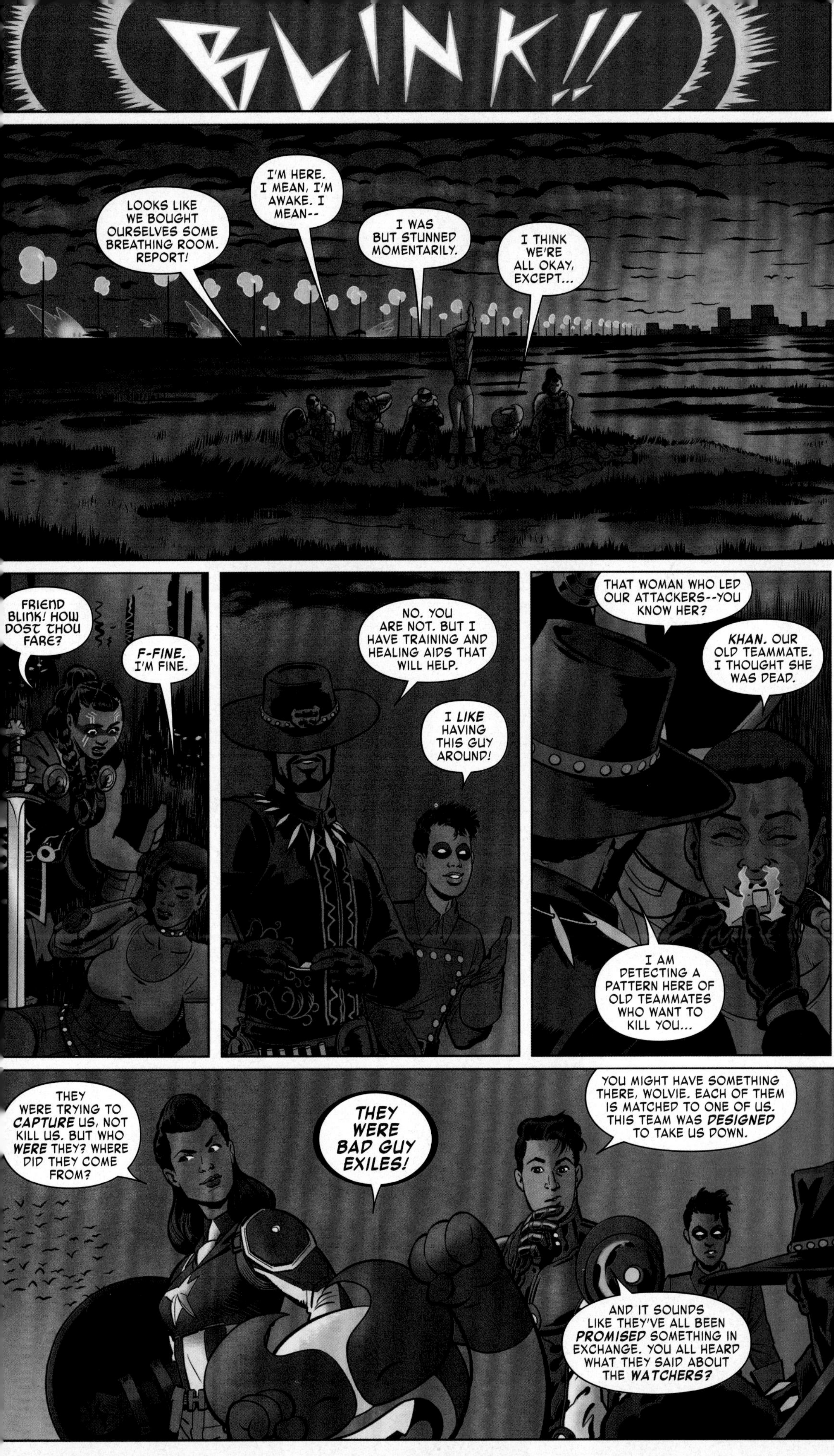
BLINK!!
LOOKS LIKE WE BOUGHT OURSELVES SOME BREATHING ROOM. REPORT!
I'M HERE. I MEAN, I'M AWAKE. I MEAN--
I WAS BUT STUNNED MOMENTARILY.
I THINK WE'RE ALL OKAY, EXCEPT...
FRIEND BLINK! HOW DOST THOU FARE?
F-FINE. I'M FINE.
NO. YOU ARE NOT. BUT I HAVE TRAINING AND HEALING AIDS THAT WILL HELP.
I LIKE HAVING THIS GUY AROUND!
THAT WOMAN WHO LED OUR ATTACKERS--YOU KNOW HER?
KHAN. OUR OLD TEAMMATE. I THOUGHT SHE WAS DEAD.
I AM DETECTING A PATTERN HERE OF OLD TEAMMATES WHO WANT TO KILL YOU...
THEY WERE TRYING TO CAPTURE US, NOT KILL US. BUT WHO WERE THEY? WHERE DID THEY COME FROM?
THEY WERE BAD GUY EXILES!
YOU MIGHT HAVE SOMETHING THERE, WOLVIE. EACH OF THEM IS MATCHED TO ONE OF US. THIS TEAM WAS DESIGNED TO TAKE US DOWN.
AND IT SOUNDS LIKE THEY'VE ALL BEEN PROMISED SOMETHING IN EXCHANGE. YOU ALL HEARD WHAT THEY SAID ABOUT THE WATCHERS?

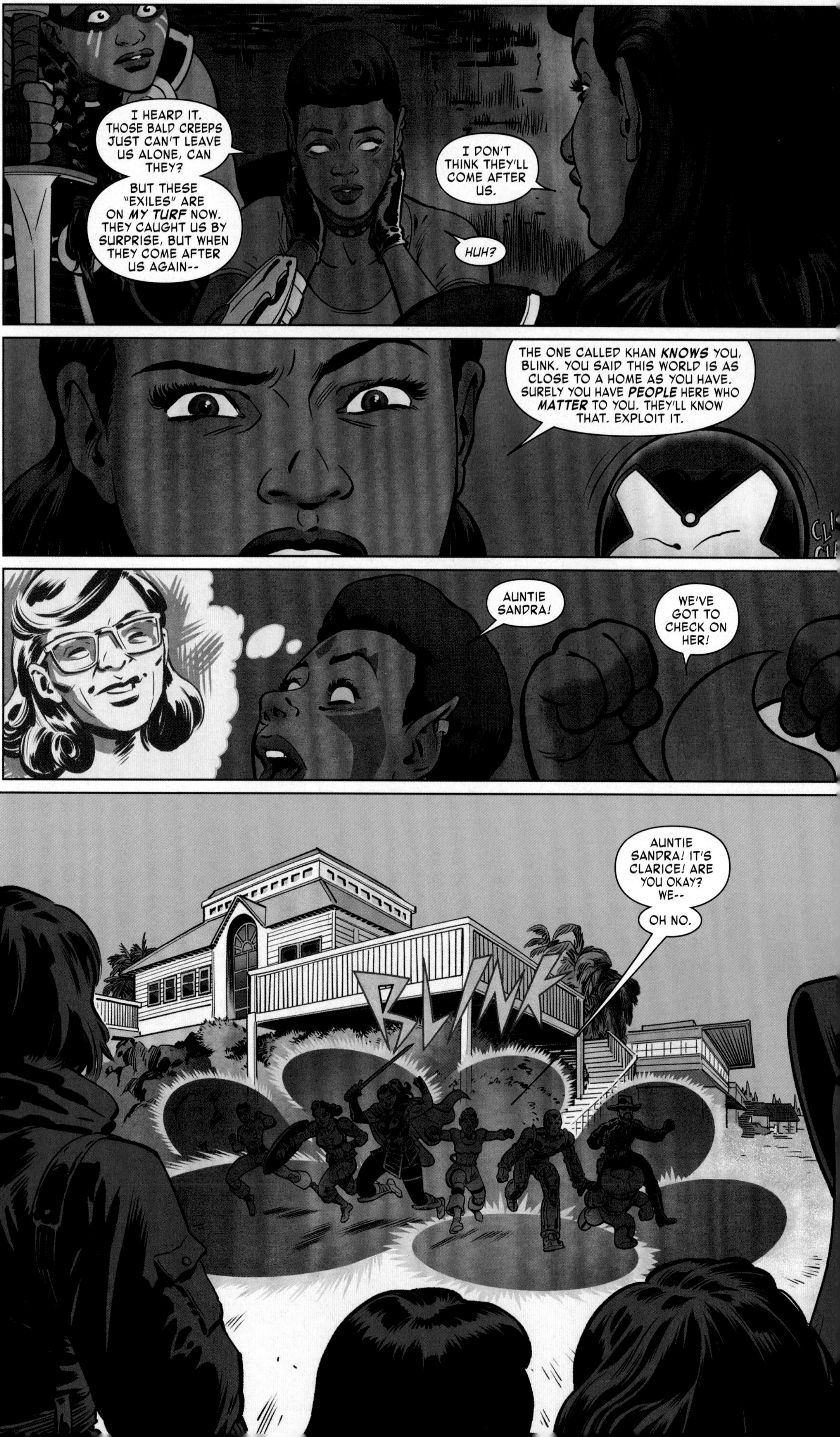
I HEARD IT. THOSE BALD CREEPS JUST CAN'T LEAVE US ALONE, CAN THEY?
BUT THESE "EXILES" ARE ON *MY TURF* NOW. THEY CAUGHT US BY SURPRISE, BUT WHEN THEY COME AFTER US AGAIN--
I DON'T THINK THEY'LL COME AFTER US.
HUH?
THE ONE CALLED KHAN *KNOWS* YOU, BLINK. YOU SAID THIS WORLD IS AS CLOSE TO A HOME AS YOU HAVE. SURELY YOU HAVE *PEOPLE* HERE WHO *MATTER* TO YOU. THEY'LL KNOW THAT. EXPLOIT IT.
AUNTIE SANDRA!
WE'VE GOT TO CHECK ON HER!
AUNTIE SANDRA! IT'S CLARICE! ARE YOU OKAY? WE--
OH NO.
BLINK

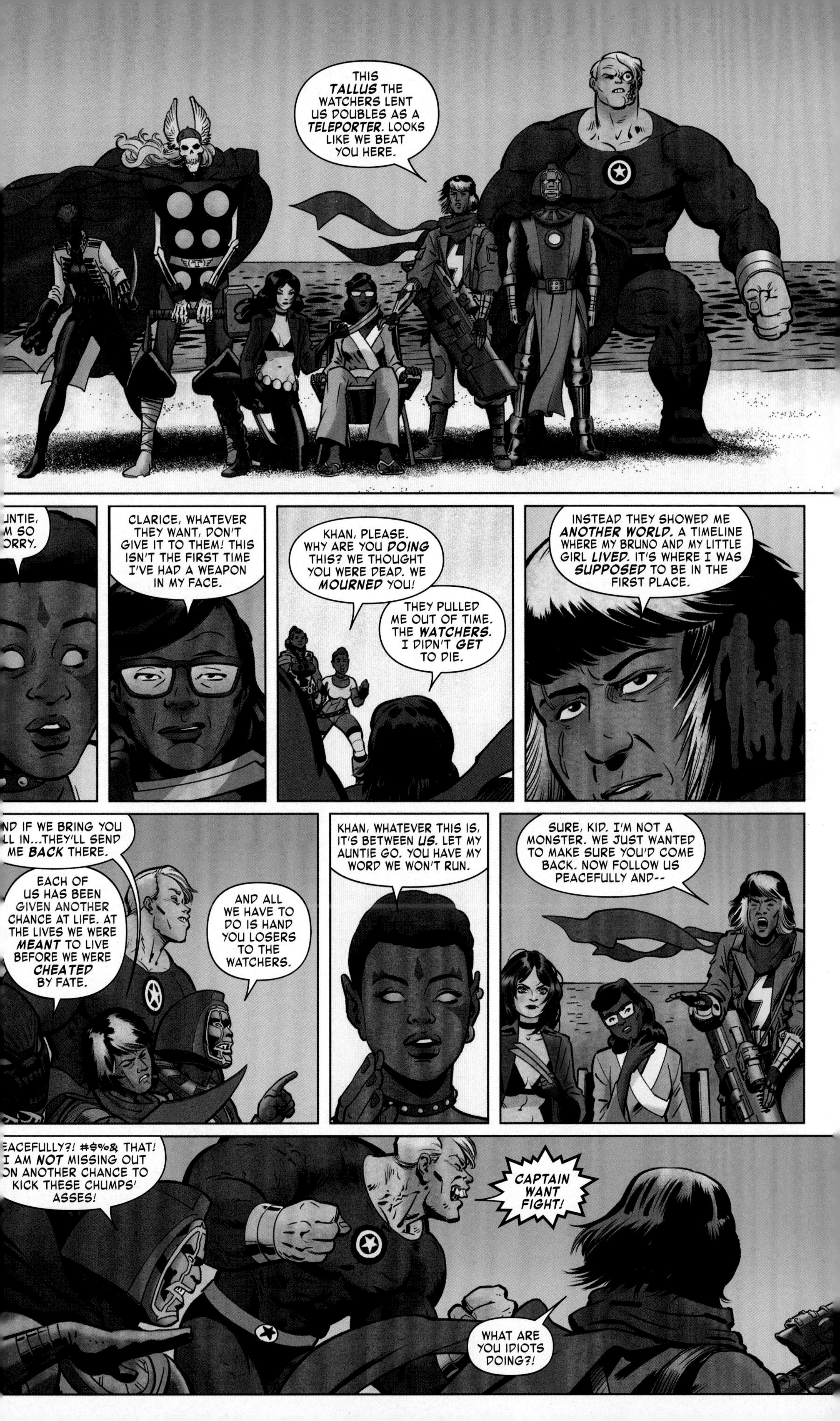

THIS TALLUS THE WATCHERS LENT US DOUBLES AS A TELEPORTER. LOOKS LIKE WE BEAT YOU HERE.
UNTIE, M SO ORRY.
CLARICE, WHATEVER THEY WANT, DON'T GIVE IT TO THEM! THIS ISN'T THE FIRST TIME I'VE HAD A WEAPON IN MY FACE.
KHAN, PLEASE. WHY ARE YOU DOING THIS? WE THOUGHT YOU WERE DEAD. WE MOURNED YOU!
THEY PULLED ME OUT OF TIME. THE WATCHERS. I DIDN'T GET TO DIE.
INSTEAD THEY SHOWED ME ANOTHER WORLD. A TIMELINE WHERE MY BRUNO AND MY LITTLE GIRL LIVED. IT'S WHERE I WAS SUPPOSED TO BE IN THE FIRST PLACE.
ND IF WE BRING YOU LL IN...THEY'LL SEND ME BACK THERE.
EACH OF US HAS BEEN GIVEN ANOTHER CHANCE AT LIFE. AT THE LIVES WE WERE MEANT TO LIVE BEFORE WE WERE CHEATED BY FATE.
AND ALL WE HAVE TO DO IS HAND YOU LOSERS TO THE WATCHERS.
KHAN, WHATEVER THIS IS, IT'S BETWEEN US. LET MY AUNTIE GO. YOU HAVE MY WORD WE WON'T RUN.
SURE, KID. I'M NOT A MONSTER. WE JUST WANTED TO MAKE SURE YOU'D COME BACK. NOW FOLLOW US PEACEFULLY AND--
EACEFULLY?! #$%& THAT! I AM NOT MISSING OUT ON ANOTHER CHANCE TO KICK THESE CHUMPS' ASSES!
CAPTAIN WANT FIGHT!
WHAT ARE YOU IDIOTS DOING?!

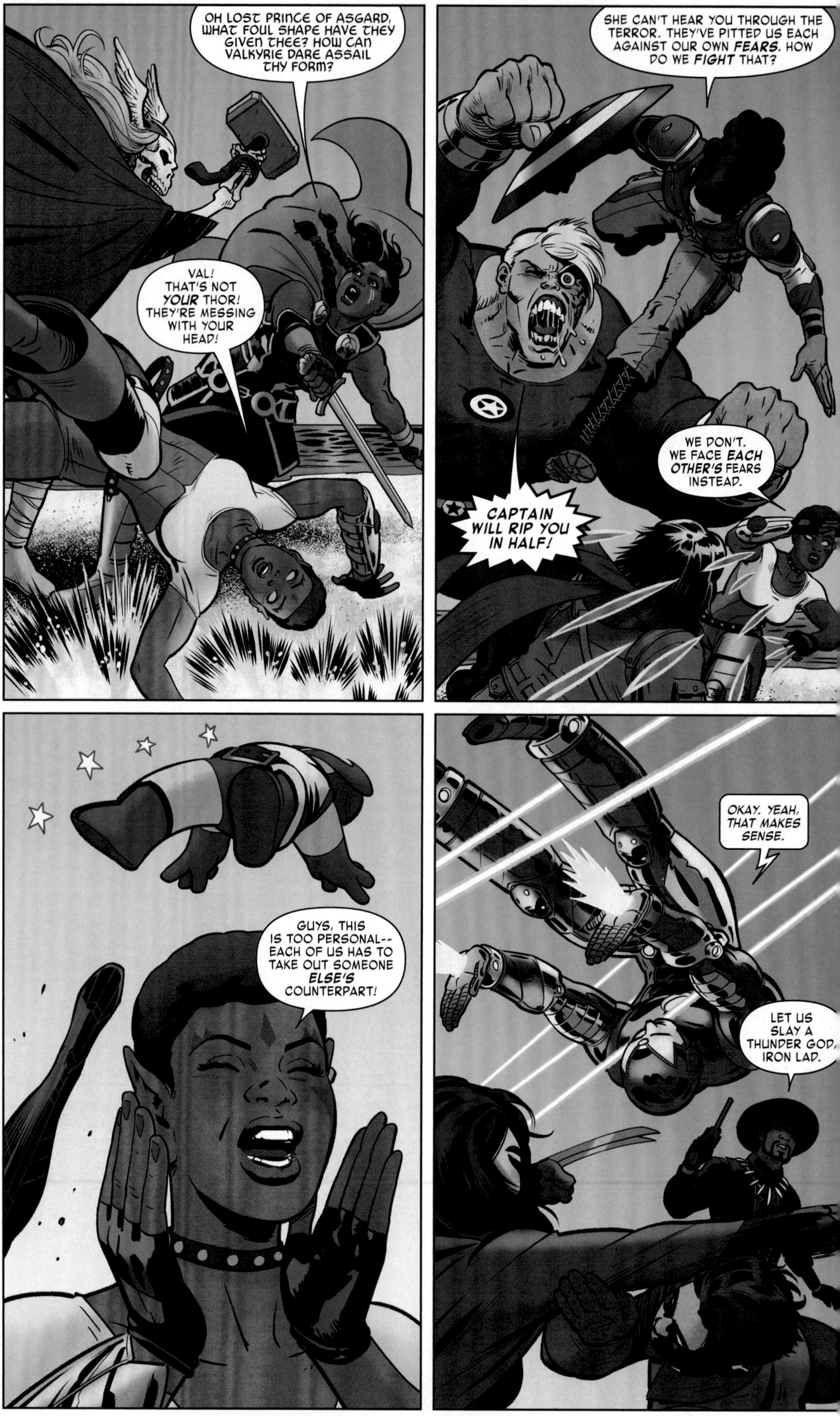
OH LOST PRINCE OF ASGARD, WHAT FOUL SHAPE HAVE THEY GIVEN THEE? HOW CAN VALKYRIE DARE ASSAIL THY FORM?
VAL! THAT'S NOT YOUR THOR! THEY'RE MESSING WITH YOUR HEAD!
SHE CAN'T HEAR YOU THROUGH THE TERROR. THEY'VE PITTED US EACH AGAINST OUR OWN FEARS. HOW DO WE FIGHT THAT?
CAPTAIN WILL RIP YOU IN HALF!
WE DON'T. WE FACE EACH OTHER'S FEARS INSTEAD.
GUYS, THIS IS TOO PERSONAL-- EACH OF US HAS TO TAKE OUT SOMEONE ELSE'S COUNTERPART!
OKAY. YEAH, THAT MAKES SENSE.
LET US SLAY A THUNDER GOD, IRON LAD.

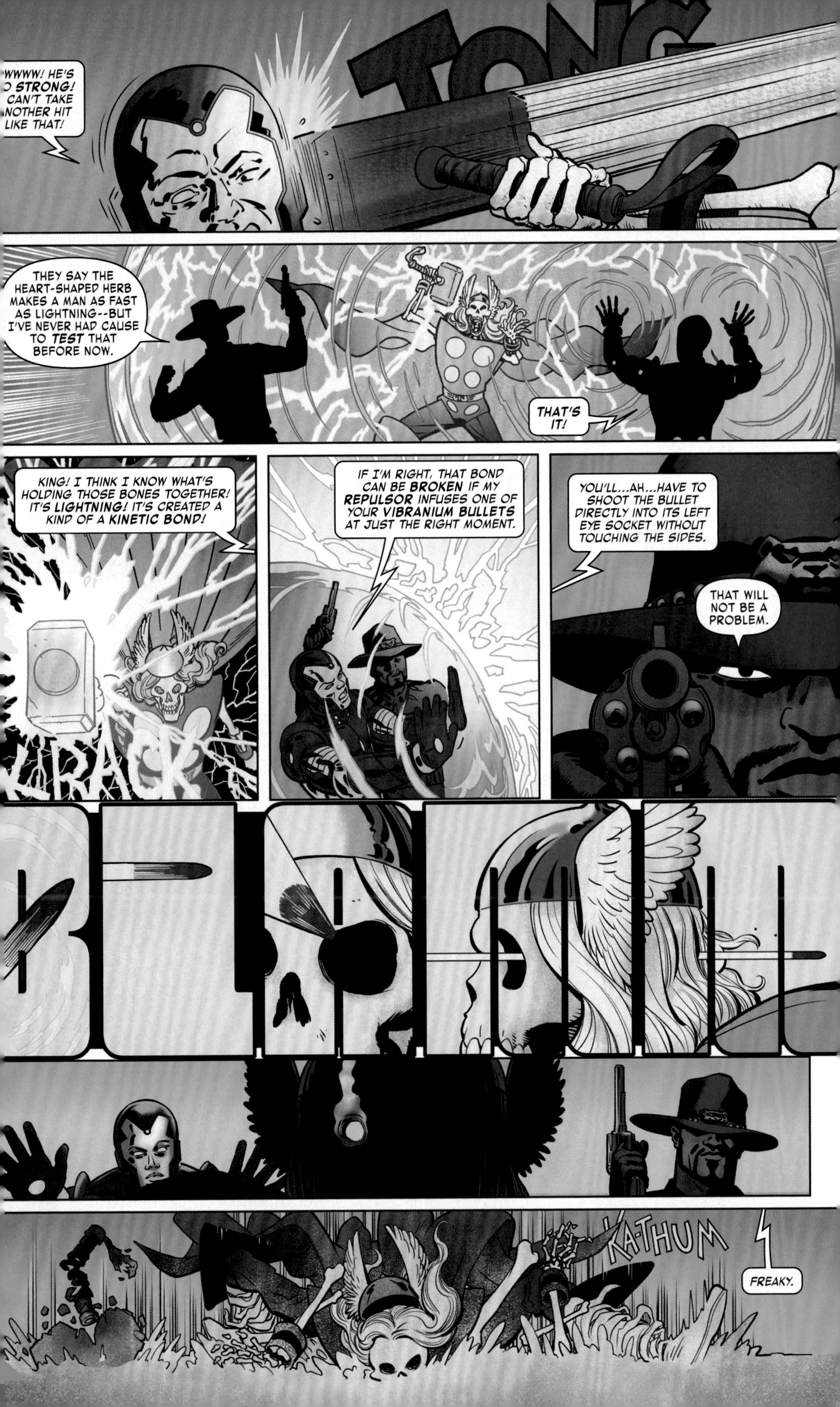

WWWW! HE'S
O STRONG!
CAN'T TAKE
NOTHER HIT
LIKE THAT!
TONG
THEY SAY THE HEART-SHAPED HERB MAKES A MAN AS FAST AS LIGHTNING--BUT I'VE NEVER HAD CAUSE TO TEST THAT BEFORE NOW.
THAT'S IT!
KING! I THINK I KNOW WHAT'S HOLDING THOSE BONES TOGETHER! IT'S LIGHTNING! IT'S CREATED A KIND OF A KINETIC BOND!
KRACK
IF I'M RIGHT, THAT BOND CAN BE BROKEN IF MY REPULSOR INFUSES ONE OF YOUR VIBRANIUM BULLETS AT JUST THE RIGHT MOMENT.
YOU'LL...AH...HAVE TO SHOOT THE BULLET DIRECTLY INTO ITS LEFT EYE SOCKET WITHOUT TOUCHING THE SIDES.
THAT WILL NOT BE A PROBLEM.
KA-THUM
FREAKY.

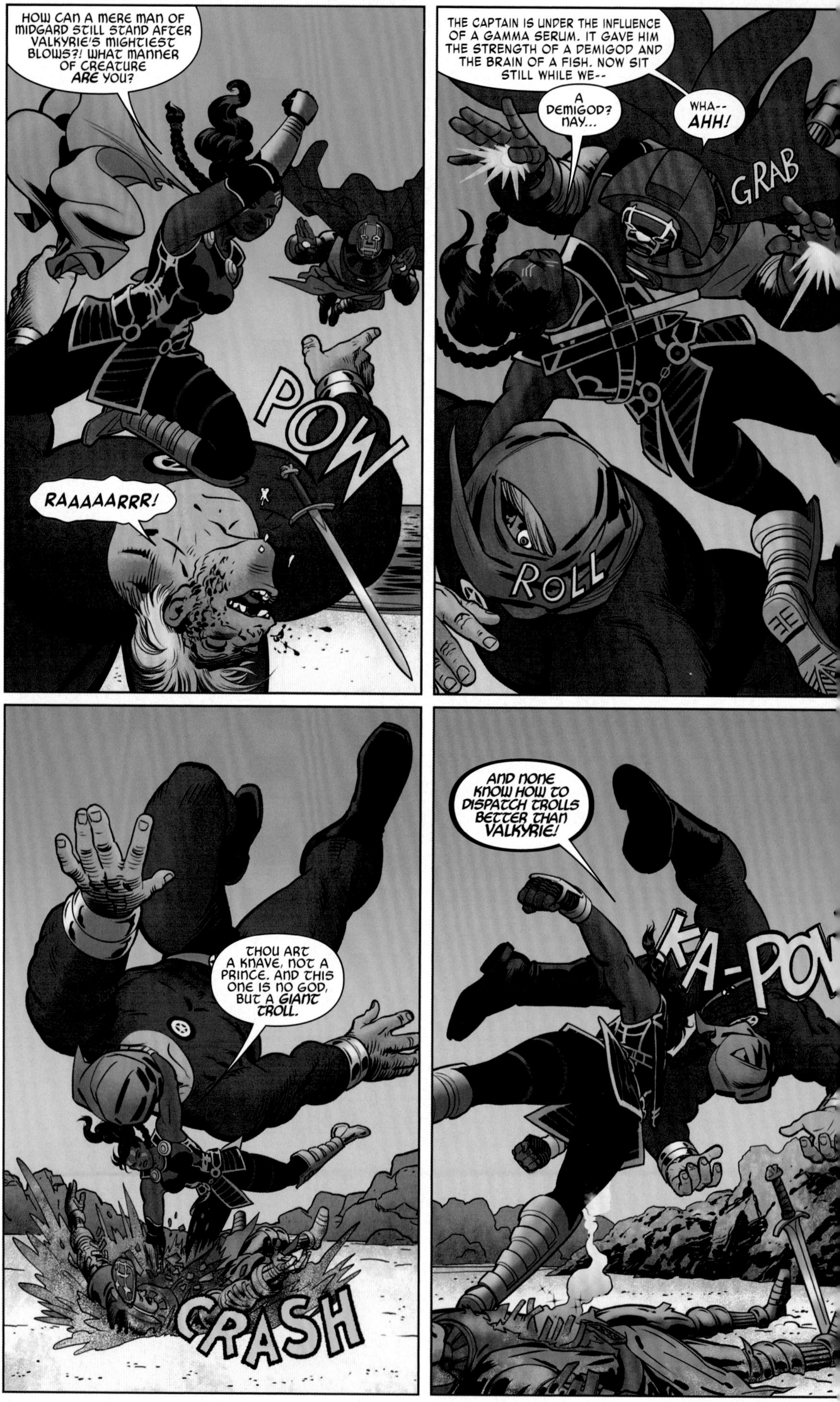
HOW CAN A MERE MAN OF MIDGARD STILL STAND AFTER VALKYRIE'S MIGHTIEST BLOWS?! WHAT MANNER OF CREATURE ARE YOU?
POW
RAAAAARRR!
THE CAPTAIN IS UNDER THE INFLUENCE OF A GAMMA SERUM. IT GAVE HIM THE STRENGTH OF A DEMIGOD AND THE BRAIN OF A FISH. NOW SIT STILL WHILE WE--
A DEMIGOD? NAY...
WHA-- AHH!
GRAB
ROLL
THOU ART A KNAVE, NOT A PRINCE. AND THIS ONE IS NO GOD, BUT A GIANT TROLL.
CRASH
AND NONE KNOW HOW TO DISPATCH TROLLS BETTER THAN VALKYRIE!
KA-POW

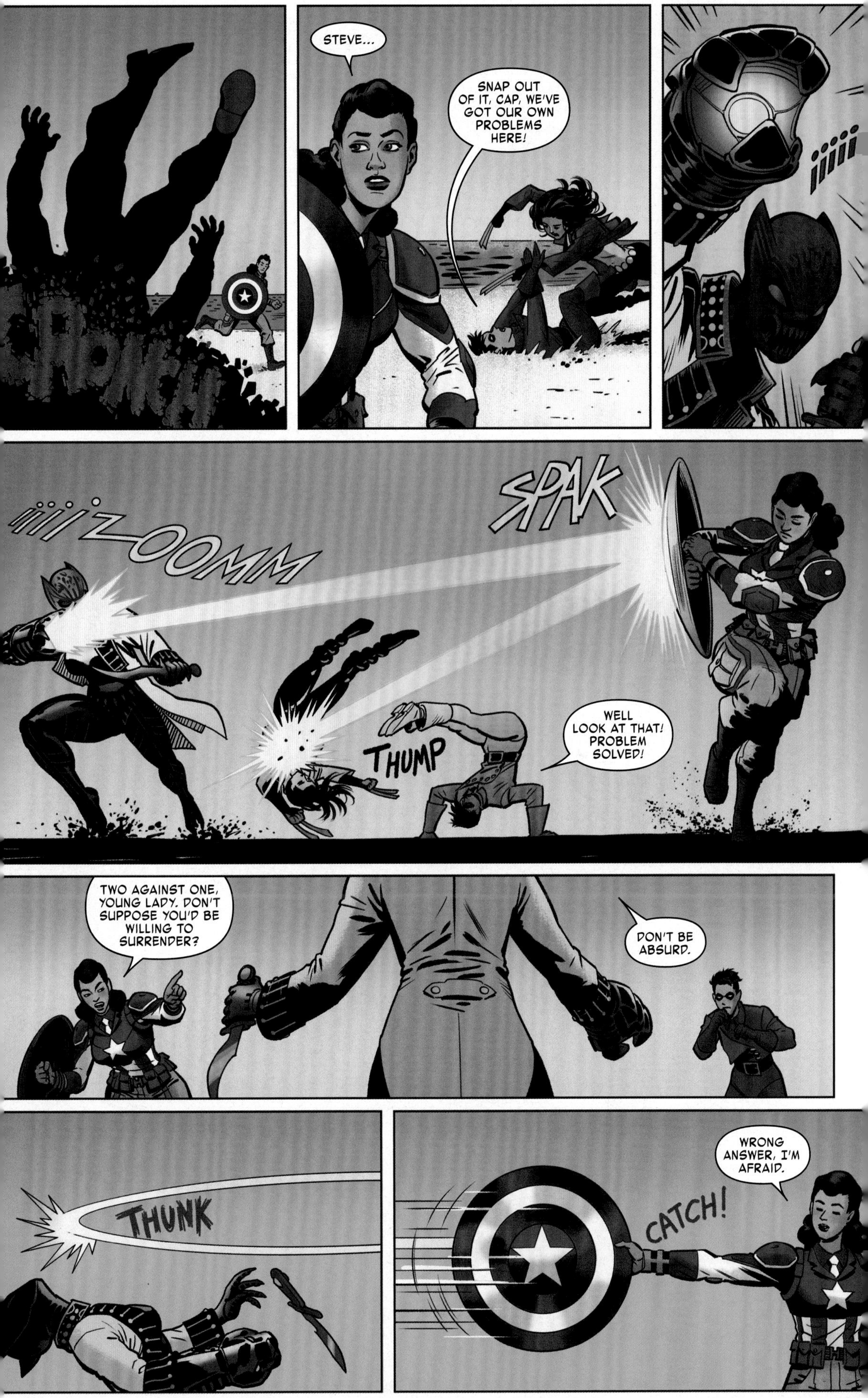

KRONCH
STEVE...
SNAP OUT OF IT, CAP, WE'VE GOT OUR OWN PROBLEMS HERE!
iiiiii
iiiiZOOMM
SPAK
THUMP
WELL LOOK AT THAT! PROBLEM SOLVED!
TWO AGAINST ONE, YOUNG LADY. DON'T SUPPOSE YOU'D BE WILLING TO SURRENDER?
DON'T BE ABSURD.
THUNK
CATCH!
WRONG ANSWER, I'M AFRAID.

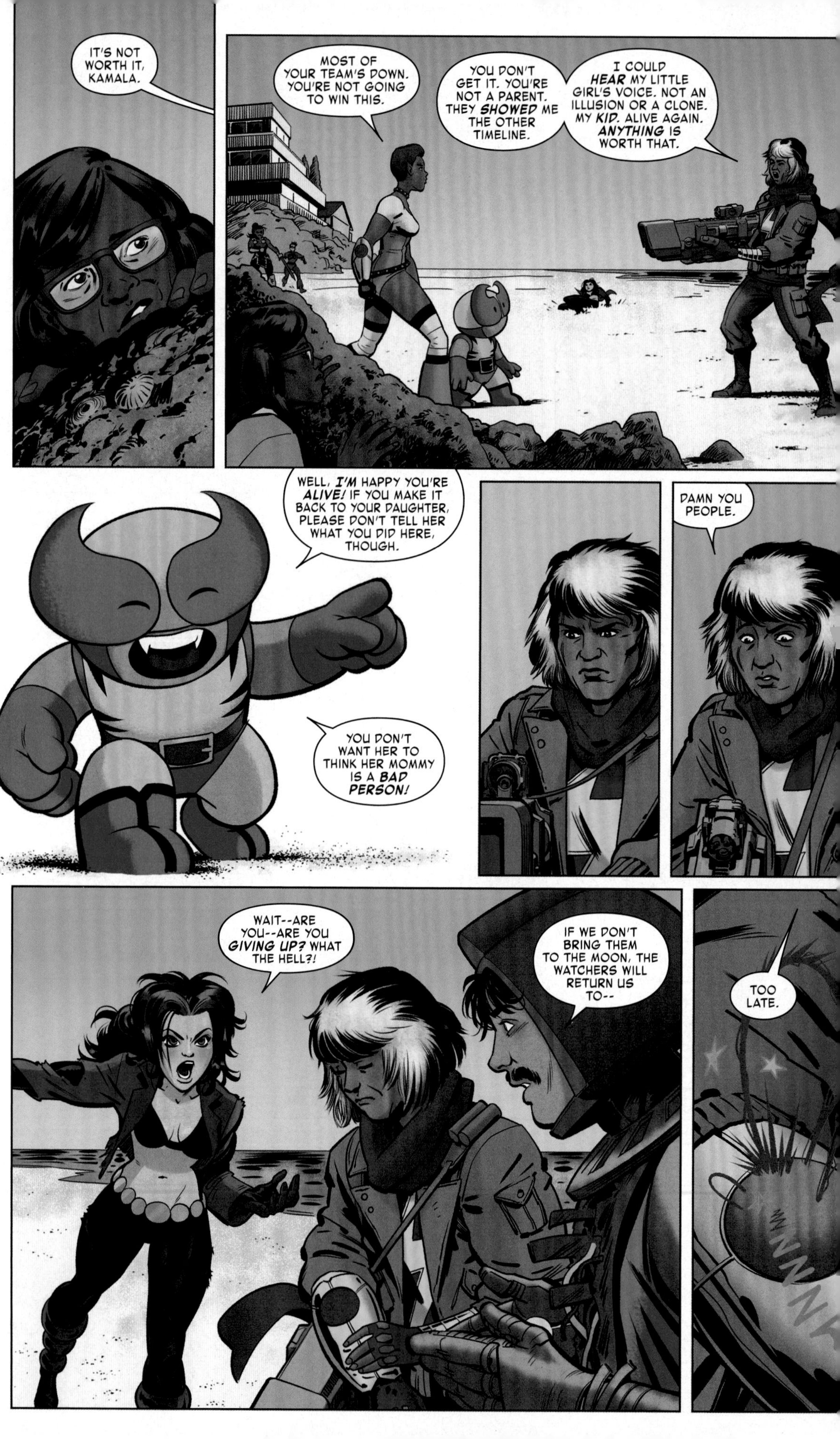
IT'S NOT WORTH IT, KAMALA.
MOST OF YOUR TEAM'S DOWN. YOU'RE NOT GOING TO WIN THIS.
YOU DON'T GET IT. YOU'RE NOT A PARENT. THEY SHOWED ME THE OTHER TIMELINE.
I COULD HEAR MY LITTLE GIRL'S VOICE. NOT AN ILLUSION OR A CLONE. MY KID. ALIVE AGAIN. ANYTHING IS WORTH THAT.
WELL, I'M HAPPY YOU'RE ALIVE! IF YOU MAKE IT BACK TO YOUR DAUGHTER, PLEASE DON'T TELL HER WHAT YOU DID HERE, THOUGH.
YOU DON'T WANT HER TO THINK HER MOMMY IS A BAD PERSON!
DAMN YOU PEOPLE.
WAIT--ARE YOU--ARE YOU GIVING UP? WHAT THE HELL?!
IF WE DON'T BRING THEM TO THE MOON, THE WATCHERS WILL RETURN US TO--
TOO LATE.

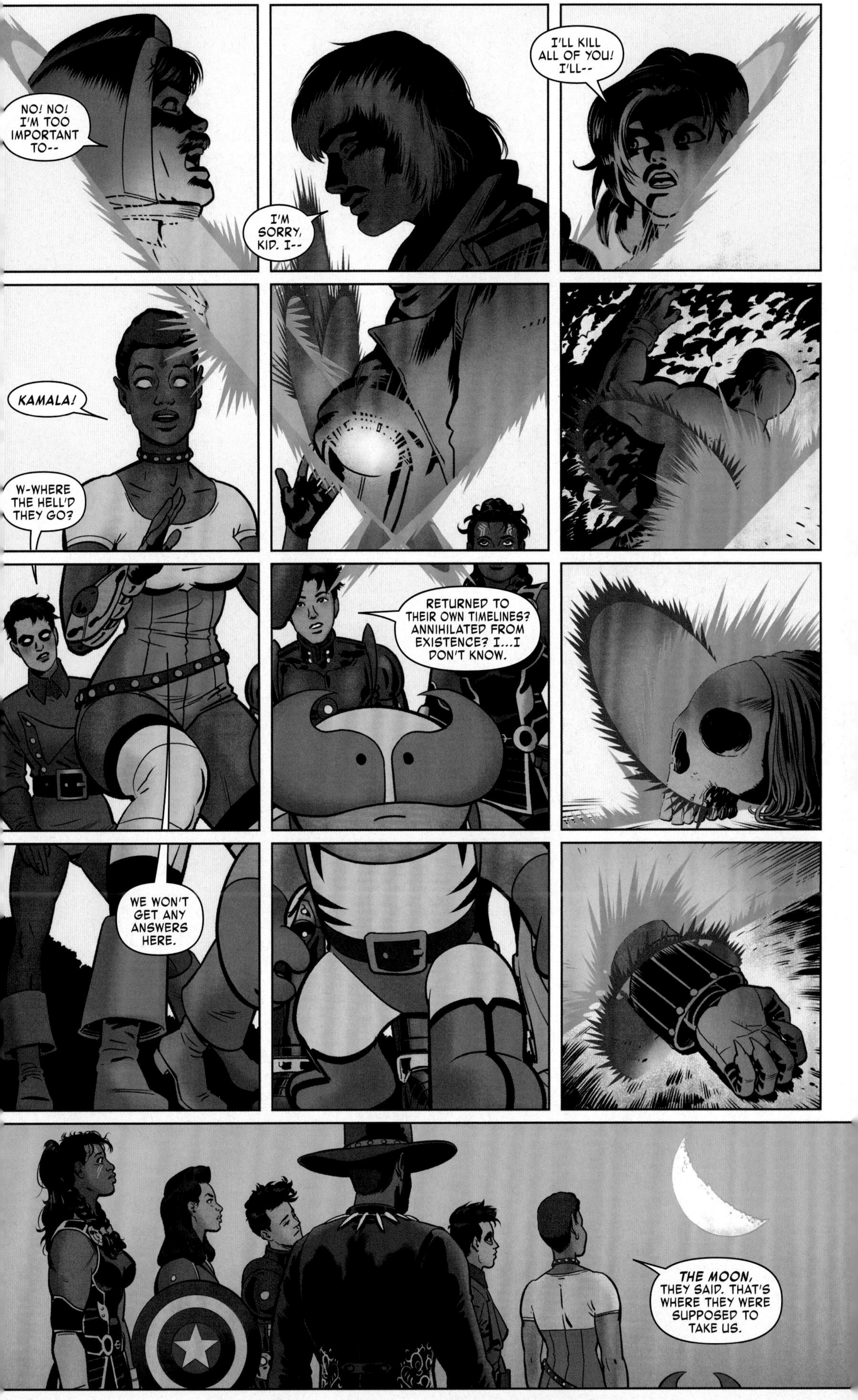
NO! NO! I'M TOO IMPORTANT TO--
I'M SORRY, KID. I--
I'LL KILL ALL OF YOU! I'LL--
KAMALA!
W-WHERE THE HELL'D THEY GO?
RETURNED TO THEIR OWN TIMELINES? ANNIHILATED FROM EXISTENCE? I...I DON'T KNOW.
WE WON'T GET ANY ANSWERS HERE.
THE MOON, THEY SAID. THAT'S WHERE THEY WERE SUPPOSED TO TAKE US.

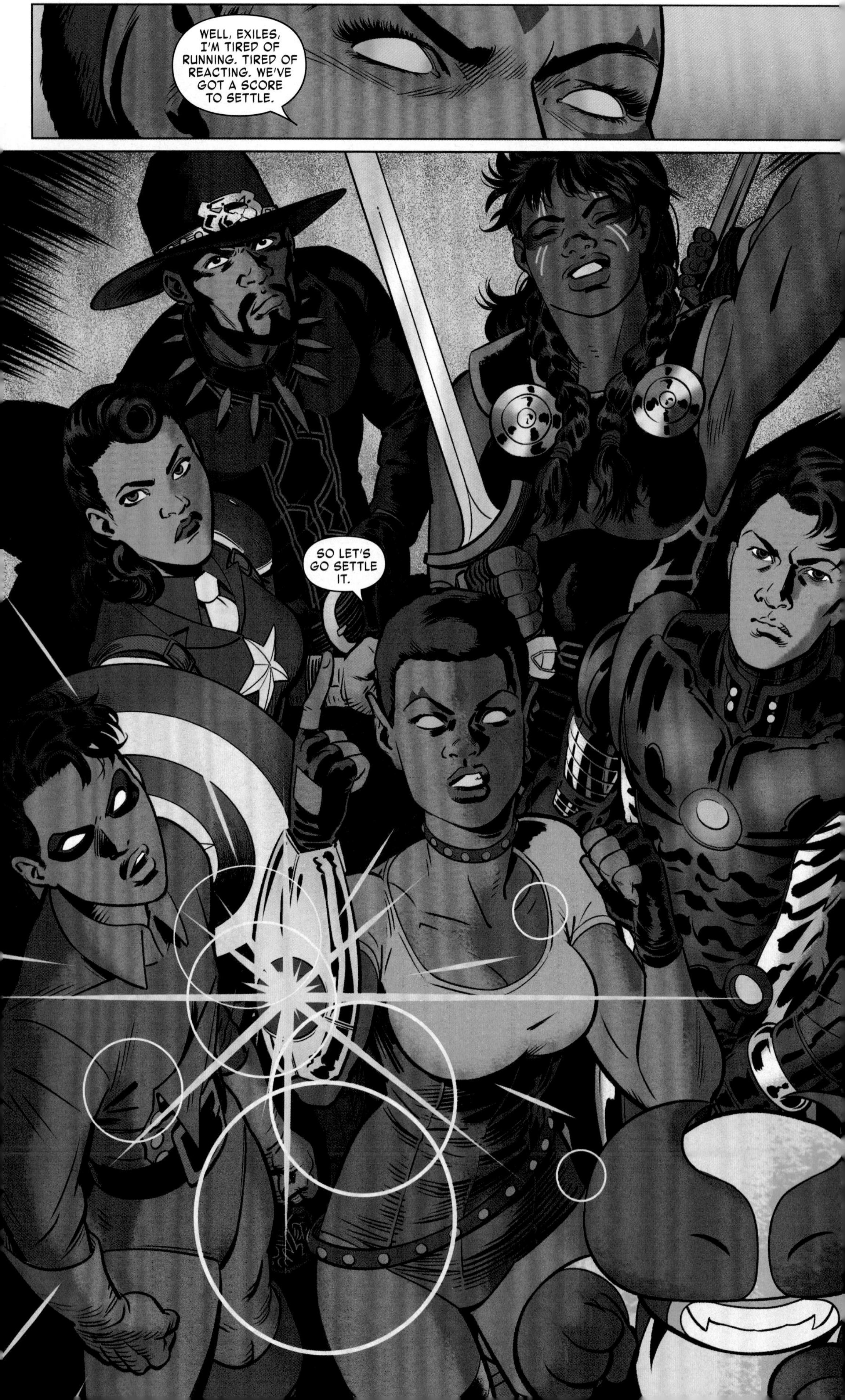
WELL, EXILES, I'M TIRED OF RUNNING. TIRED OF REACTING. WE'VE GOT A SCORE TO SETTLE.
SO LET'S GO SETTLE IT.

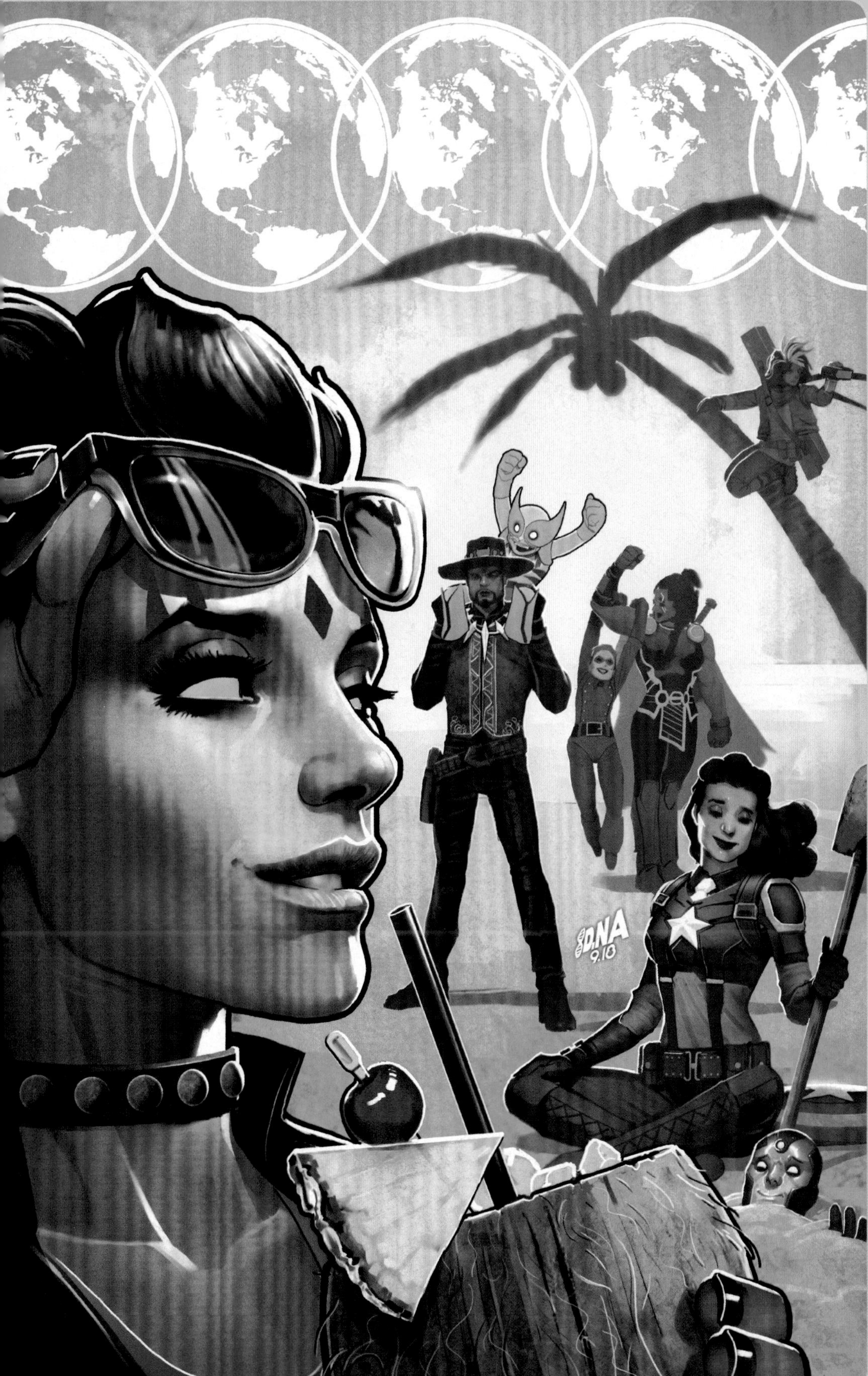
D.NA
9.18

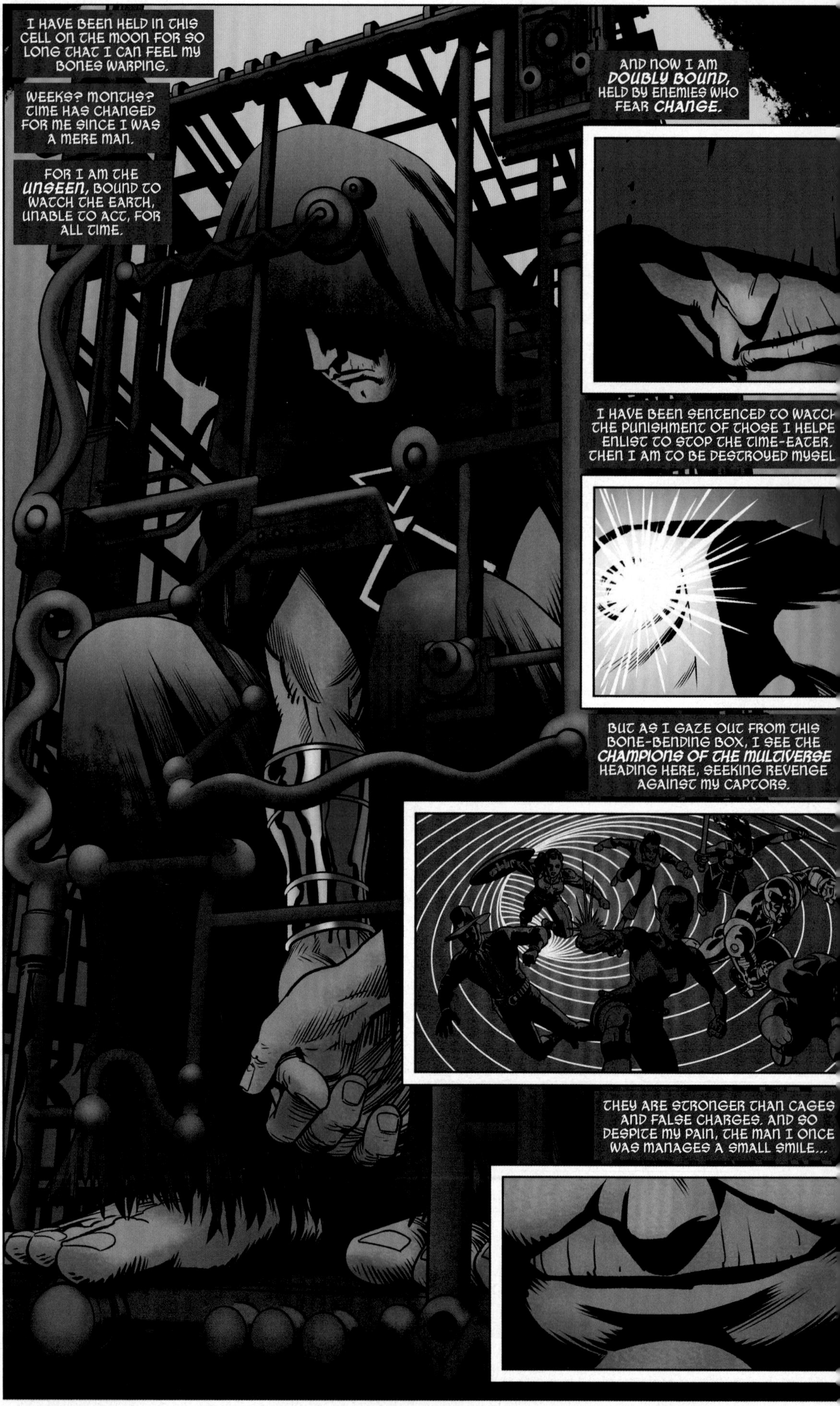

I HAVE BEEN HELD IN THIS CELL ON THE MOON FOR SO LONG THAT I CAN FEEL MY BONES WARPING.
WEEKS? MONTHS? TIME HAS CHANGED FOR ME SINCE I WAS A MERE MAN.
FOR I AM THE UNSEEN, BOUND TO WATCH THE EARTH, UNABLE TO ACT, FOR ALL TIME.
AND NOW I AM DOUBLY BOUND, HELD BY ENEMIES WHO FEAR CHANGE.
I HAVE BEEN SENTENCED TO WATCH THE PUNISHMENT OF THOSE I HELPE ENLIST TO STOP THE TIME-EATER. THEN I AM TO BE DESTROYED MYSEL
BUT AS I GAZE OUT FROM THIS BONE-BENDING BOX, I SEE THE CHAMPIONS OF THE MULTIVERSE HEADING HERE, SEEKING REVENGE AGAINST MY CAPTORS.
THEY ARE STRONGER THAN CAGES AND FALSE CHARGES. AND SO DESPITE MY PAIN, THE MAN I ONCE WAS MANAGES A SMALL SMILE...

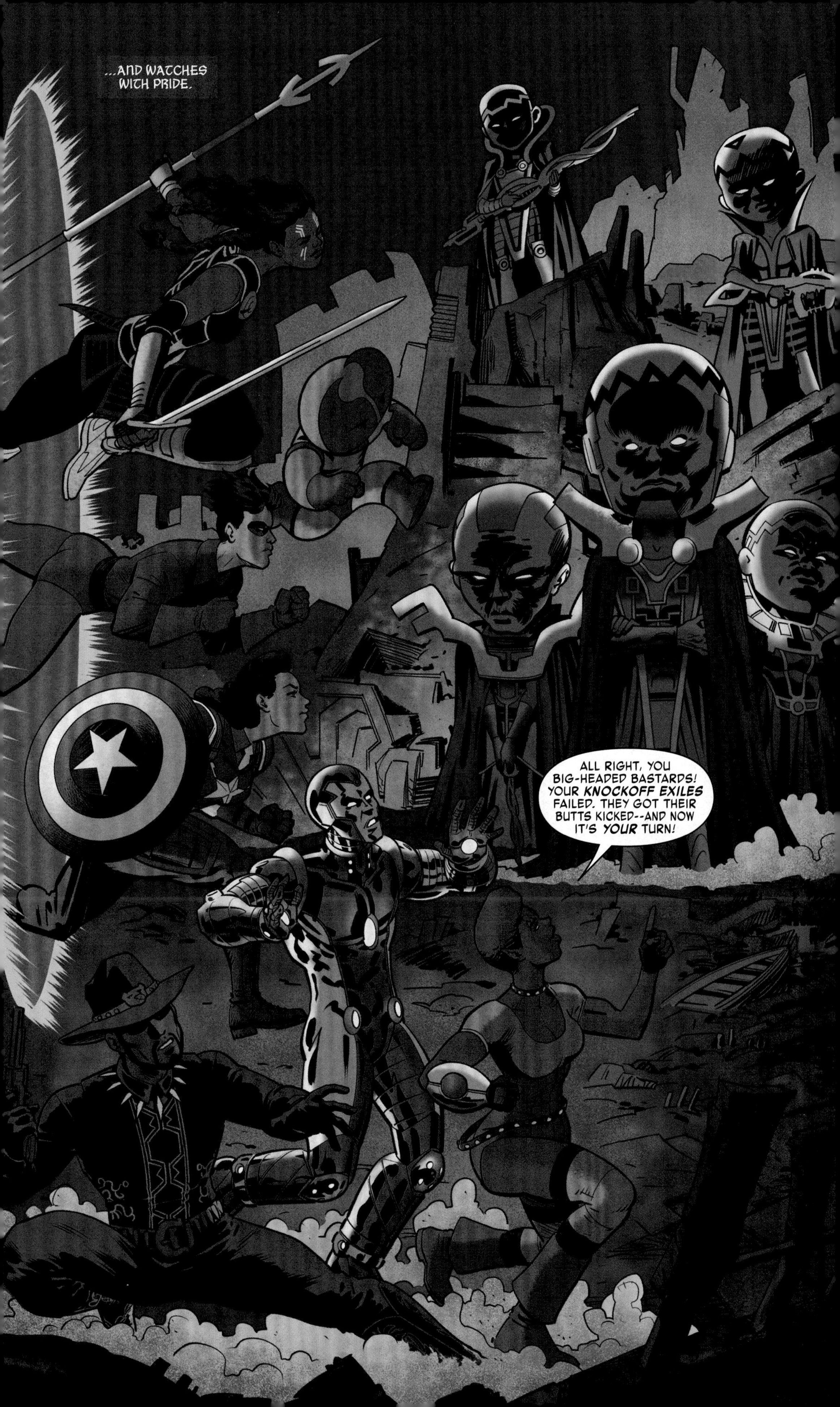
...AND WATCHES WITH PRIDE.
ALL RIGHT, YOU BIG-HEADED BASTARDS! YOUR *KNOCKOFF EXILES* FAILED. THEY GOT THEIR BUTTS KICKED--AND NOW IT'S *YOUR* TURN!

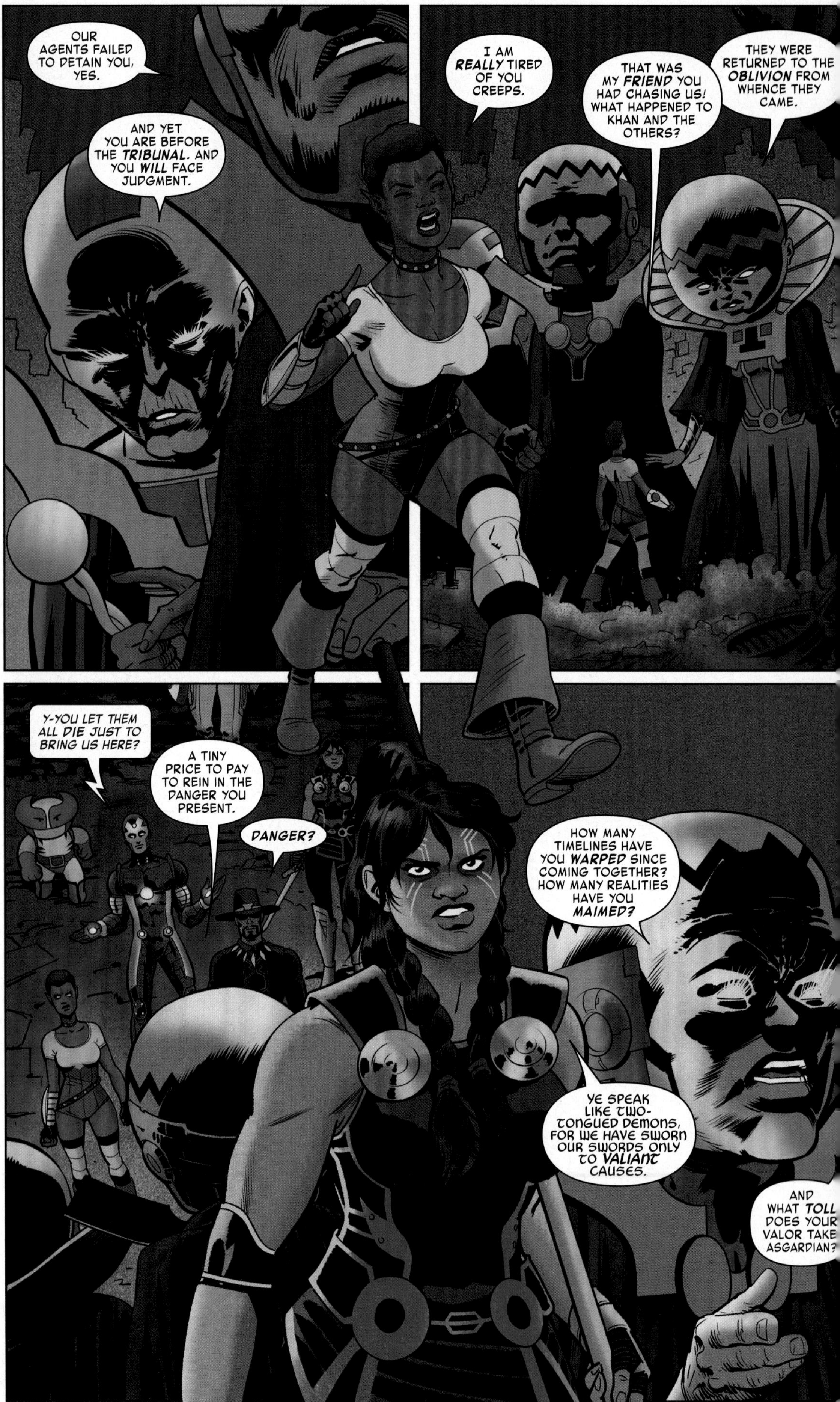
OUR AGENTS FAILED TO DETAIN YOU, YES.
AND YET YOU ARE BEFORE THE TRIBUNAL. AND YOU WILL FACE JUDGMENT.
I AM REALLY TIRED OF YOU CREEPS.
THAT WAS MY FRIEND YOU HAD CHASING US! WHAT HAPPENED TO KHAN AND THE OTHERS?
THEY WERE RETURNED TO THE OBLIVION FROM WHENCE THEY CAME.
Y-YOU LET THEM ALL DIE JUST TO BRING US HERE?
A TINY PRICE TO PAY TO REIN IN THE DANGER YOU PRESENT.
DANGER?
HOW MANY TIMELINES HAVE YOU WARPED SINCE COMING TOGETHER? HOW MANY REALITIES HAVE YOU MAIMED?
YE SPEAK LIKE TWO-TONGUED DEMONS, FOR WE HAVE SWORN OUR SWORDS ONLY TO VALIANT CAUSES.
AND WHAT TOLL DOES YOUR VALOR TAKE ASGARDIAN?

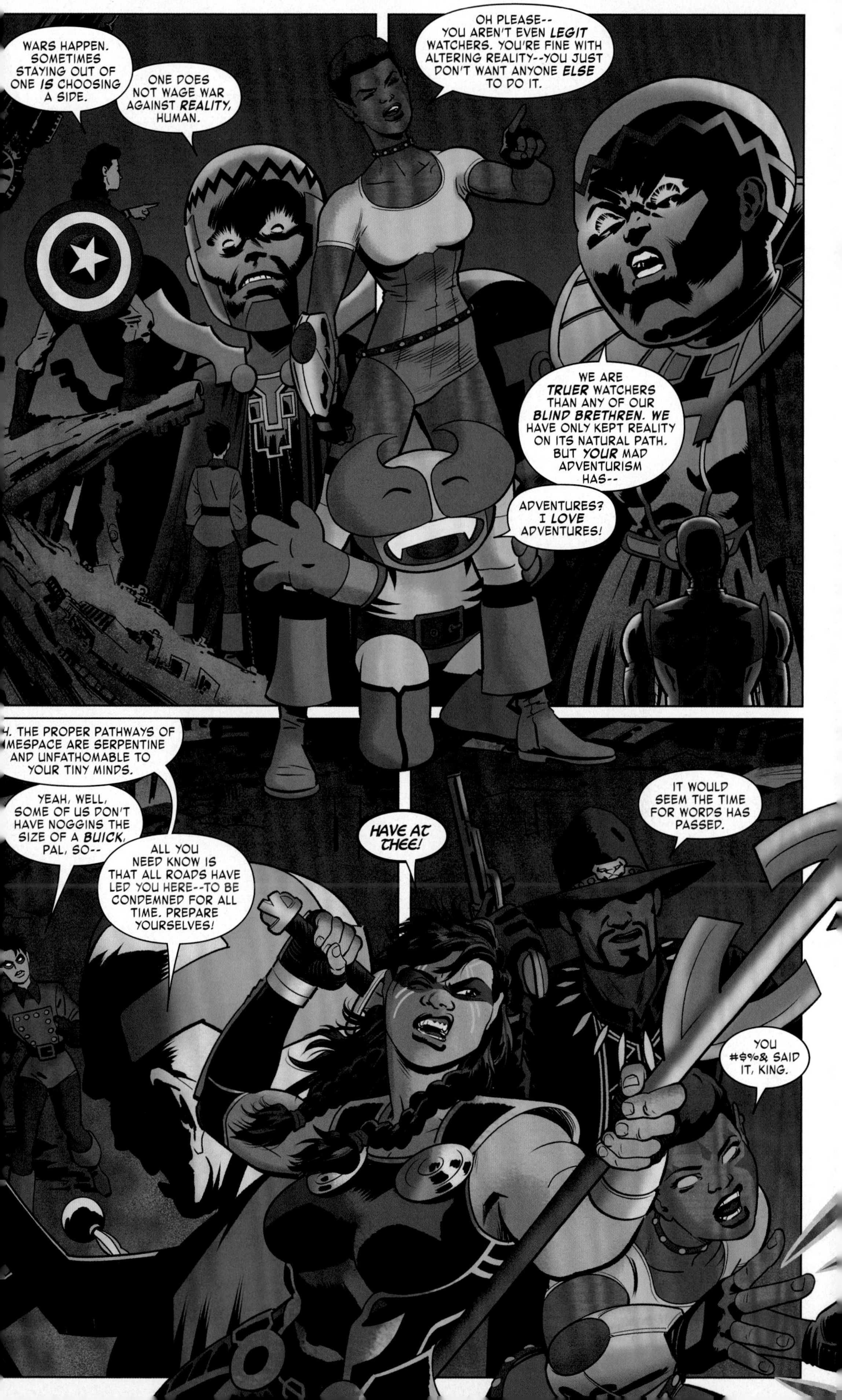
WARS HAPPEN. SOMETIMES STAYING OUT OF ONE IS CHOOSING A SIDE.
ONE DOES NOT WAGE WAR AGAINST REALITY, HUMAN.
OH PLEASE-- YOU AREN'T EVEN LEGIT WATCHERS. YOU'RE FINE WITH ALTERING REALITY--YOU JUST DON'T WANT ANYONE ELSE TO DO IT.
WE ARE TRUER WATCHERS THAN ANY OF OUR BLIND BRETHREN. WE HAVE ONLY KEPT REALITY ON ITS NATURAL PATH. BUT YOUR MAD ADVENTURISM HAS--
ADVENTURES? I LOVE ADVENTURES!
H. THE PROPER PATHWAYS OF MESPACE ARE SERPENTINE AND UNFATHOMABLE TO YOUR TINY MINDS.
YEAH, WELL, SOME OF US DON'T HAVE NOGGINS THE SIZE OF A BUICK, PAL, SO--
ALL YOU NEED KNOW IS THAT ALL ROADS HAVE LED YOU HERE--TO BE CONDEMNED FOR ALL TIME. PREPARE YOURSELVES!
HAVE AT THEE!
IT WOULD SEEM THE TIME FOR WORDS HAS PASSED.
YOU #$%& SAID IT, KING.

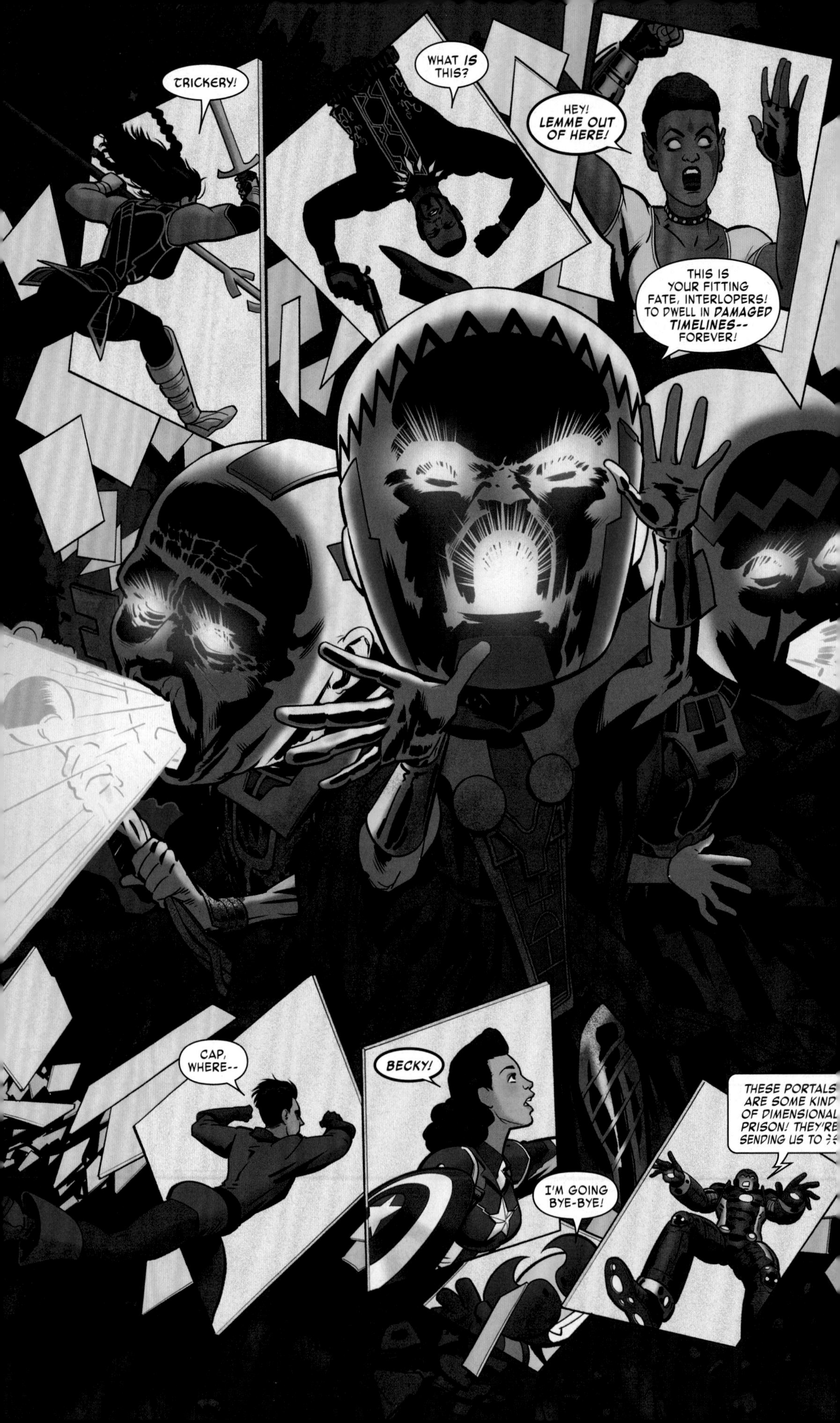
TRICKERY!
WHAT IS THIS?
HEY! LEMME OUT OF HERE!
THIS IS YOUR FITTING FATE, INTERLOPERS! TO DWELL IN DAMAGED TIMELINES-- FOREVER!
CAP, WHERE--
BECKY!
I'M GOING BYE-BYE!
THESE PORTALS ARE SOME KIND OF DIMENSIONAL PRISON! THEY'RE SENDING US TO

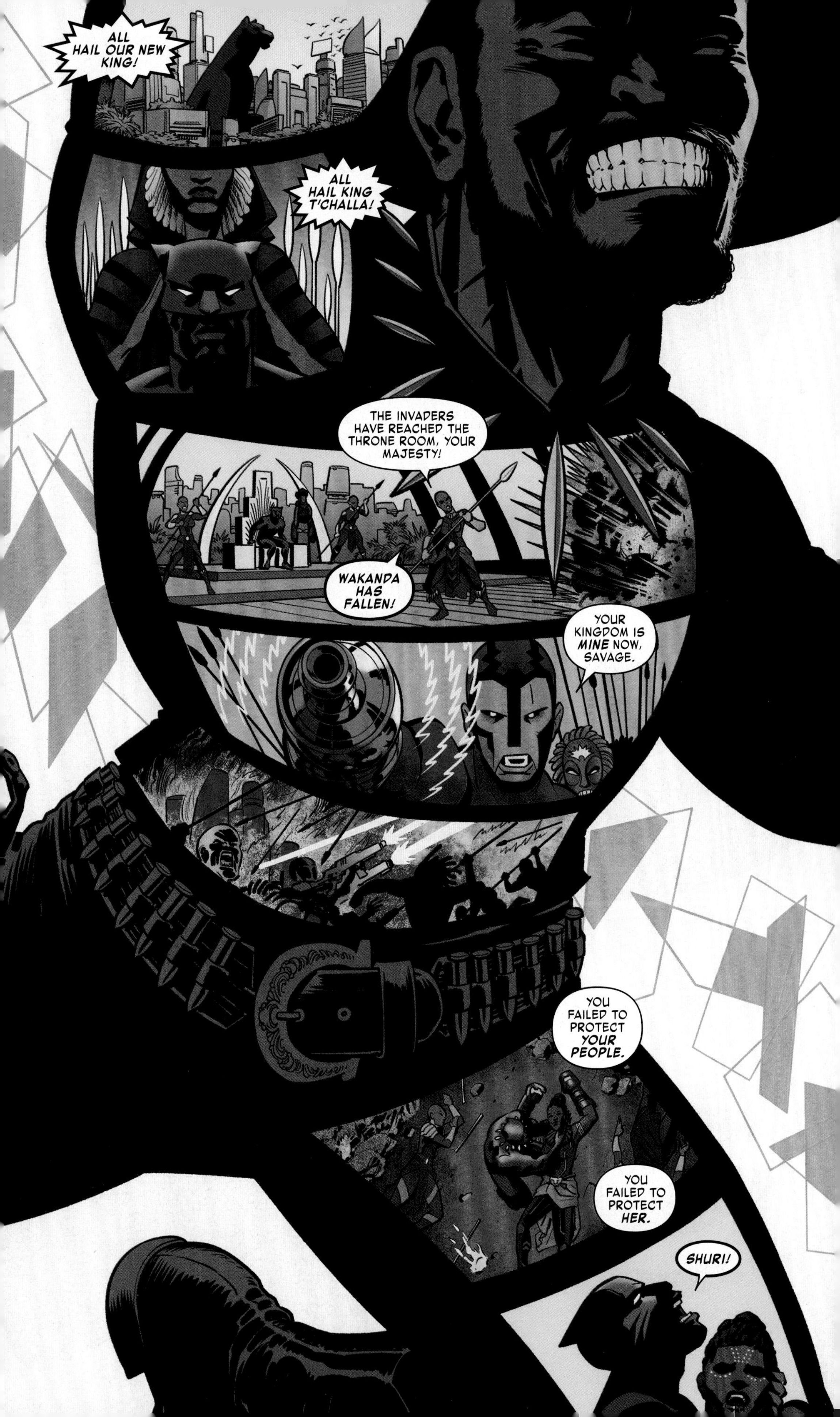
ALL HAIL OUR NEW KING!
ALL HAIL KING T'CHALLA!
THE INVADERS HAVE REACHED THE THRONE ROOM, YOUR MAJESTY!
WAKANDA HAS FALLEN!
YOUR KINGDOM IS MINE NOW, SAVAGE.
YOU FAILED TO PROTECT YOUR PEOPLE.
YOU FAILED TO PROTECT HER.
SHURI!

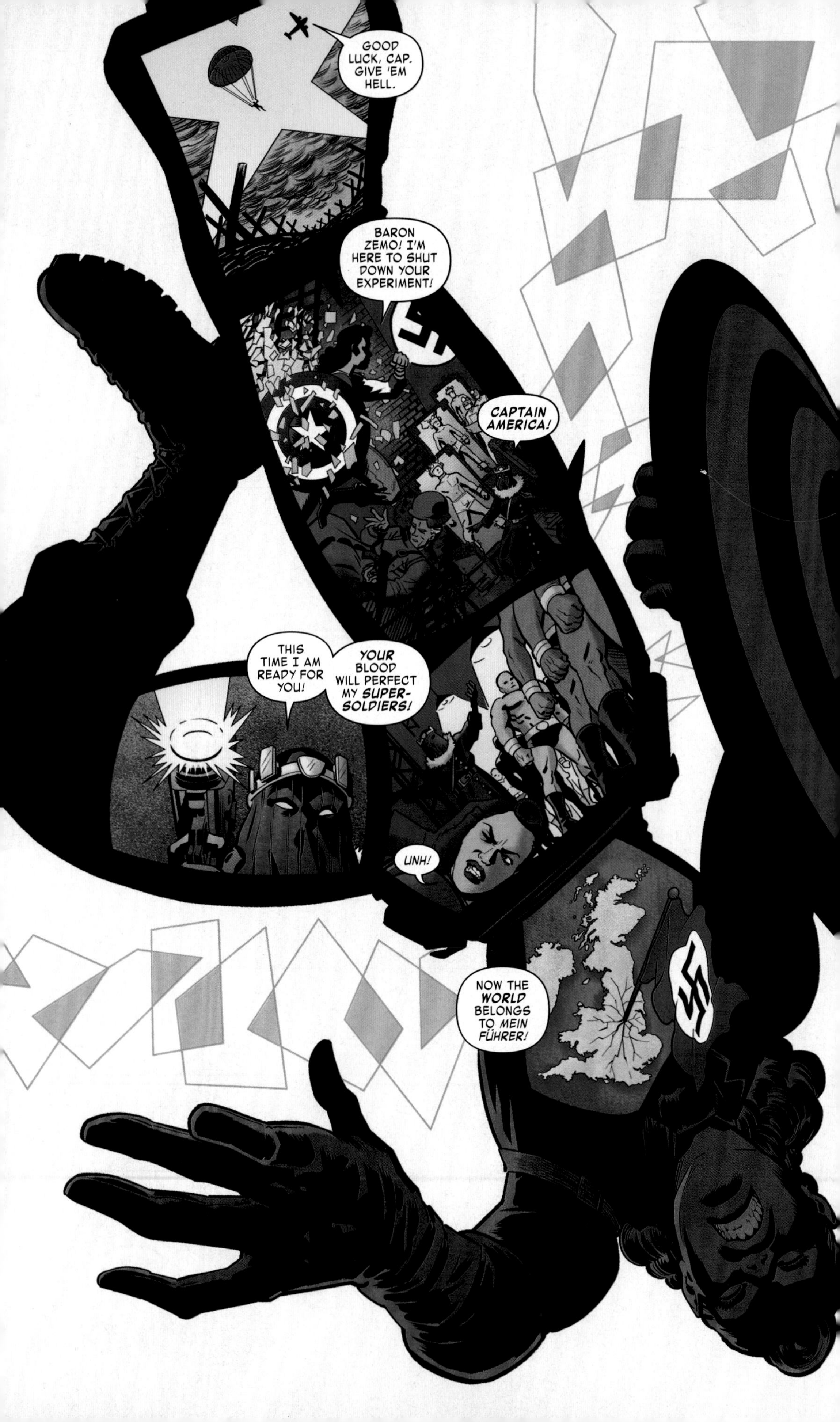
GOOD LUCK, CAP. GIVE 'EM HELL.
BARON ZEMO! I'M HERE TO SHUT DOWN YOUR EXPERIMENT!
CAPTAIN AMERICA!
THIS TIME I AM READY FOR YOU!
YOUR BLOOD WILL PERFECT MY SUPER-SOLDIERS!
UNH!
NOW THE WORLD BELONGS TO MEIN FÜHRER!

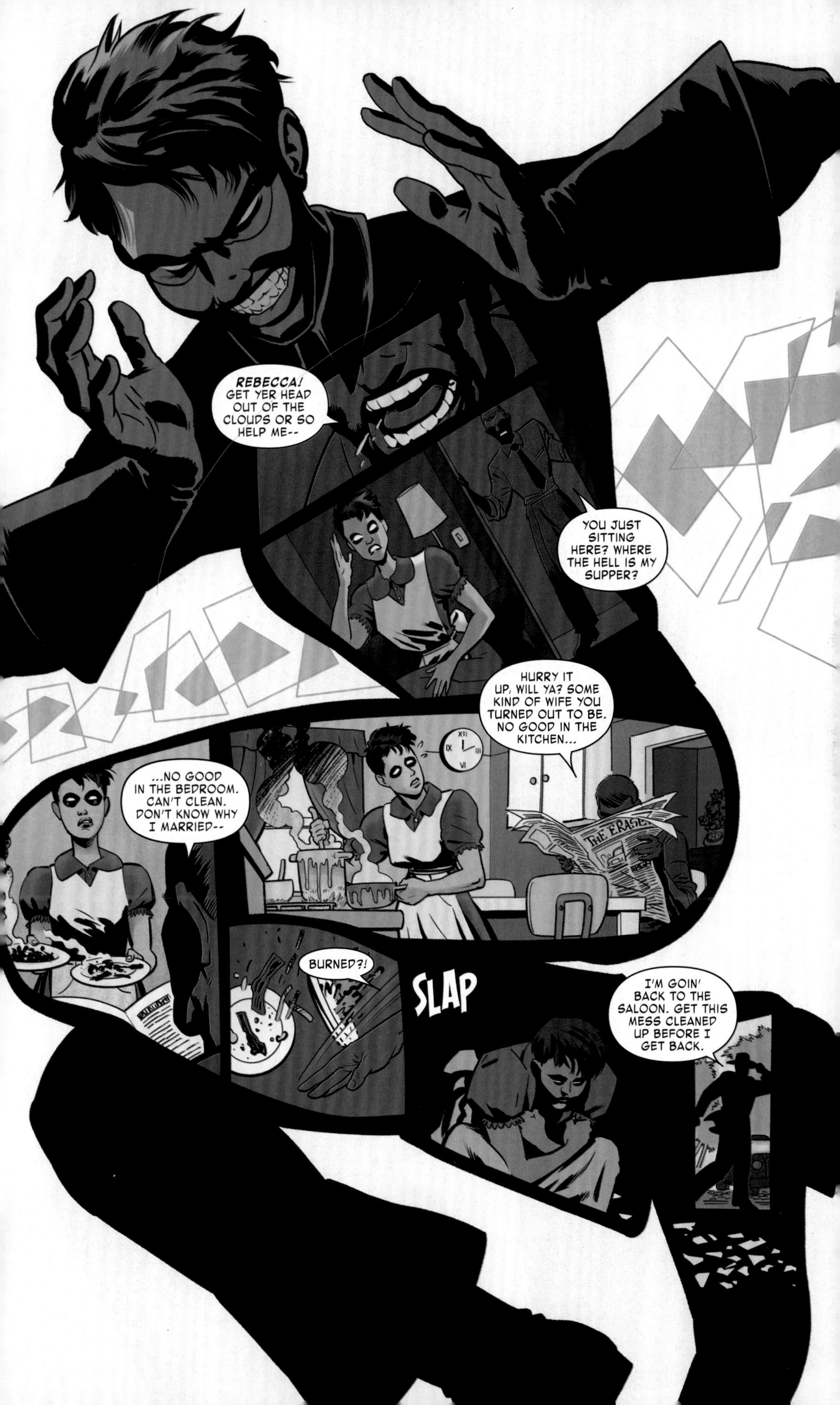
REBECCA! GET YER HEAD OUT OF THE CLOUDS OR SO HELP ME--
YOU JUST SITTING HERE? WHERE THE HELL IS MY SUPPER?
HURRY IT UP, WILL YA? SOME KIND OF WIFE YOU TURNED OUT TO BE. NO GOOD IN THE KITCHEN...
...NO GOOD IN THE BEDROOM. CAN'T CLEAN. DON'T KNOW WHY I MARRIED--
BURNED?!
SLAP
I'M GOIN' BACK TO THE SALOON. GET THIS MESS CLEANED UP BEFORE I GET BACK.

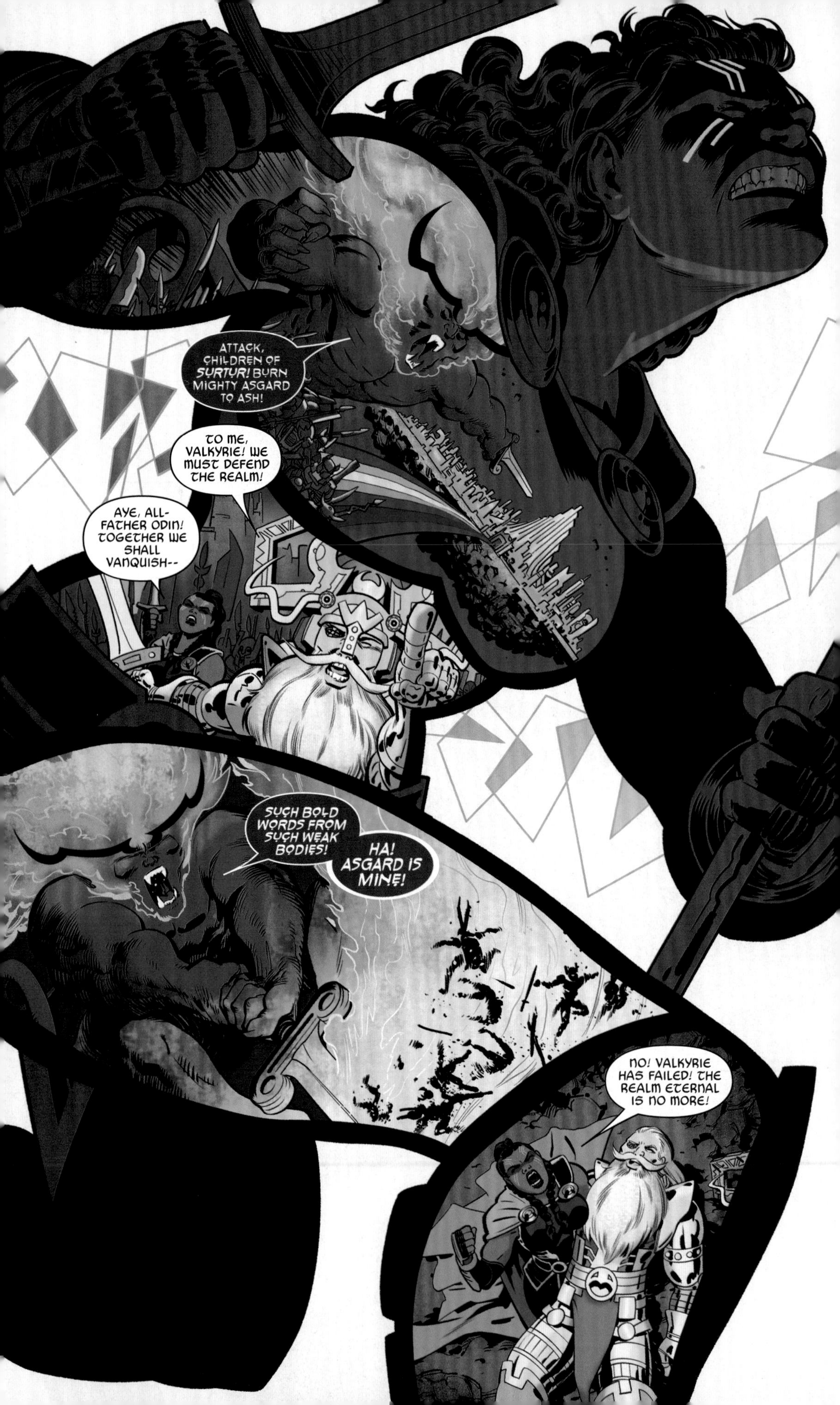

ATTACK, CHILDREN OF SURTUR! BURN MIGHTY ASGARD TO ASH!
TO ME, VALKYRIE! WE MUST DEFEND THE REALM!
AYE, ALL-FATHER ODIN! TOGETHER WE SHALL VANQUISH--
SUCH BOLD WORDS FROM SUCH WEAK BODIES!
HA! ASGARD IS MINE!
NO! VALKYRIE HAS FAILED! THE REALM ETERNAL IS NO MORE!

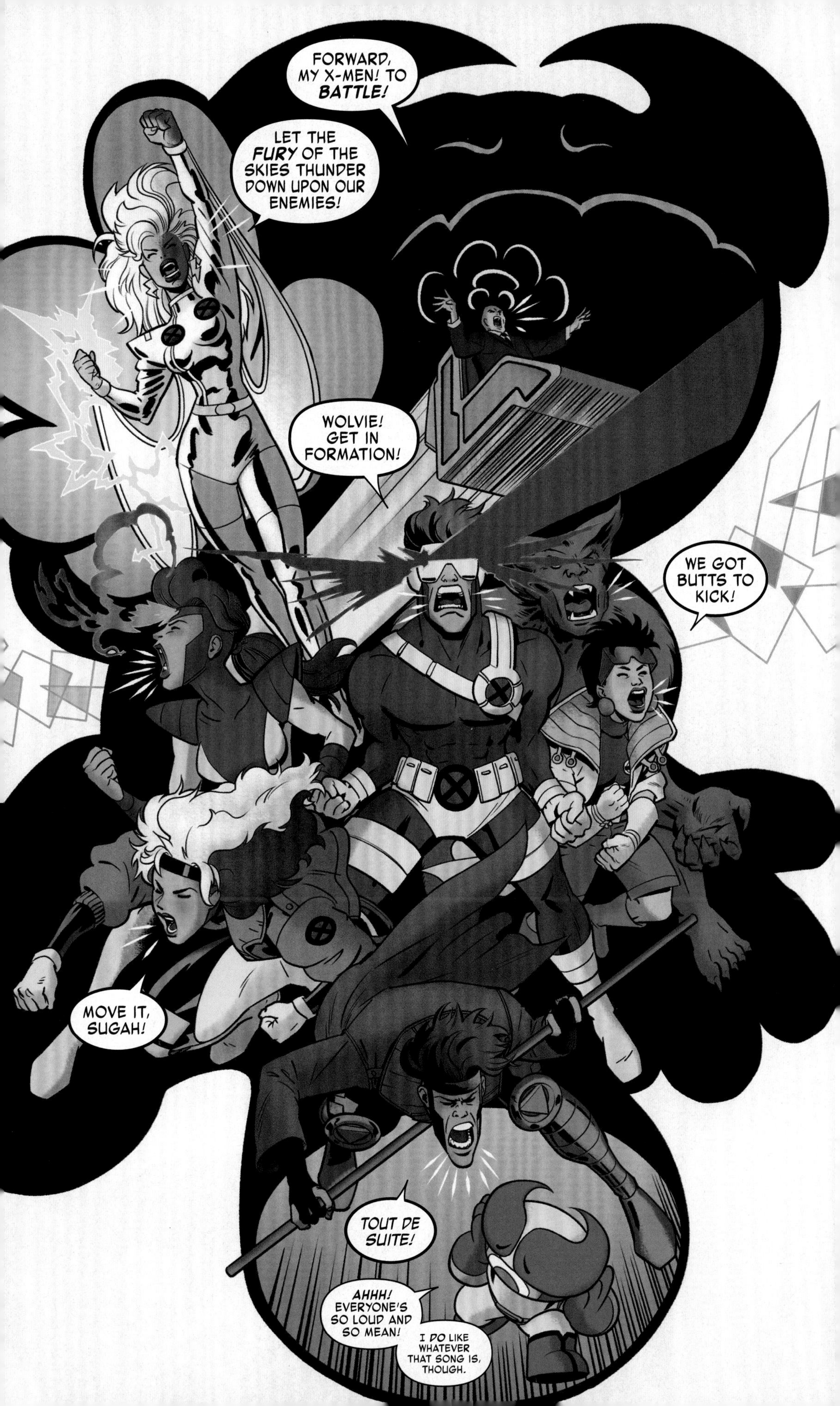
FORWARD, MY X-MEN! TO BATTLE!
LET THE FURY OF THE SKIES THUNDER DOWN UPON OUR ENEMIES!
WOLVIE! GET IN FORMATION!
WE GOT BUTTS TO KICK!
MOVE IT, SUGAH!
TOUT DE SUITE!
AHHH! EVERYONE'S SO LOUD AND SO MEAN!
I DO LIKE WHATEVER THAT SONG IS, THOUGH.

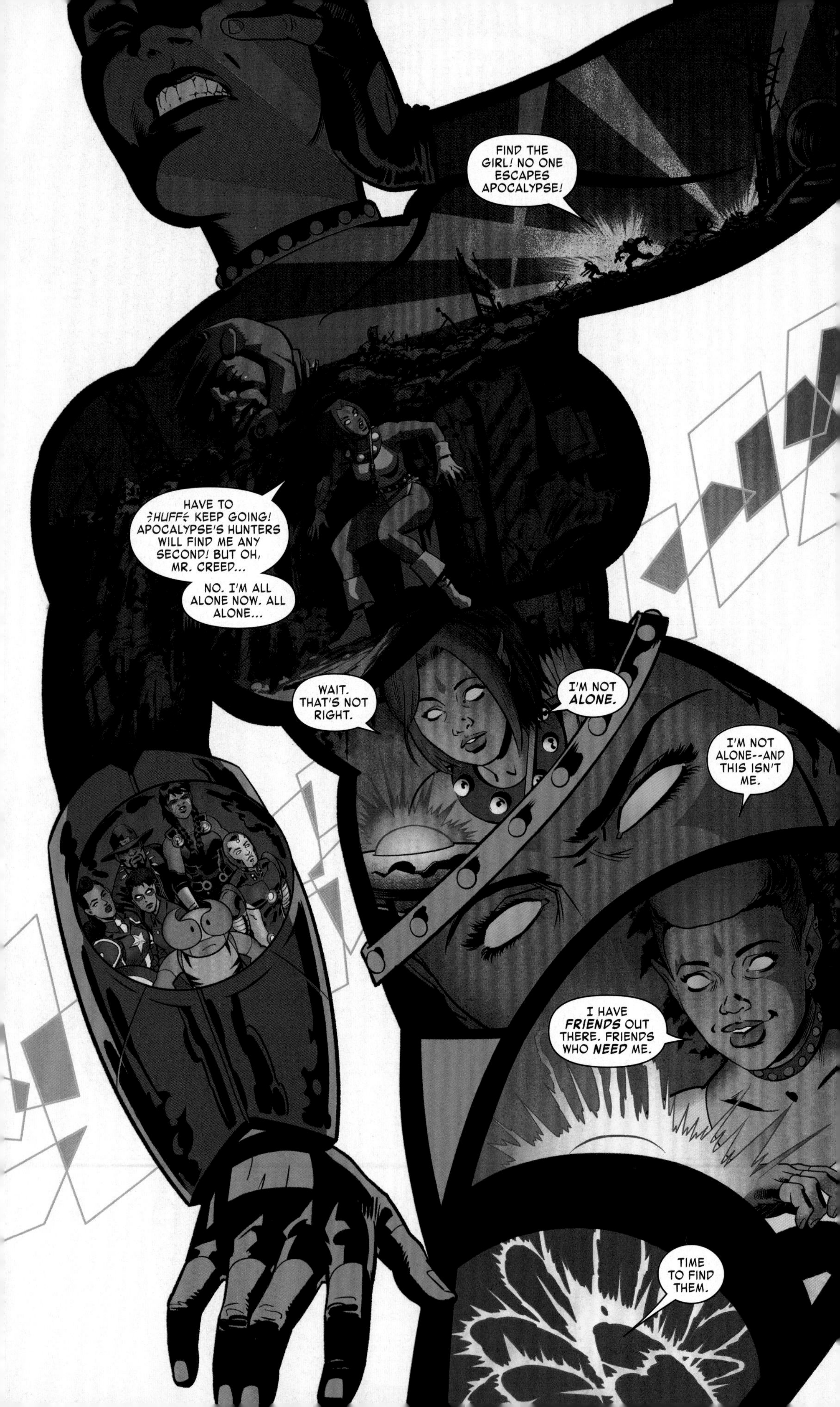
FIND THE GIRL! NO ONE ESCAPES APOCALYPSE!
HAVE TO ≶HUFF≶ KEEP GOING! APOCALYPSE'S HUNTERS WILL FIND ME ANY SECOND! BUT OH, MR. CREED...
NO. I'M ALL ALONE NOW. ALL ALONE...
WAIT. THAT'S NOT RIGHT.
I'M NOT ALONE.
I'M NOT ALONE--AND THIS ISN'T ME.
I HAVE FRIENDS OUT THERE. FRIENDS WHO NEED ME.
TIME TO FIND THEM.

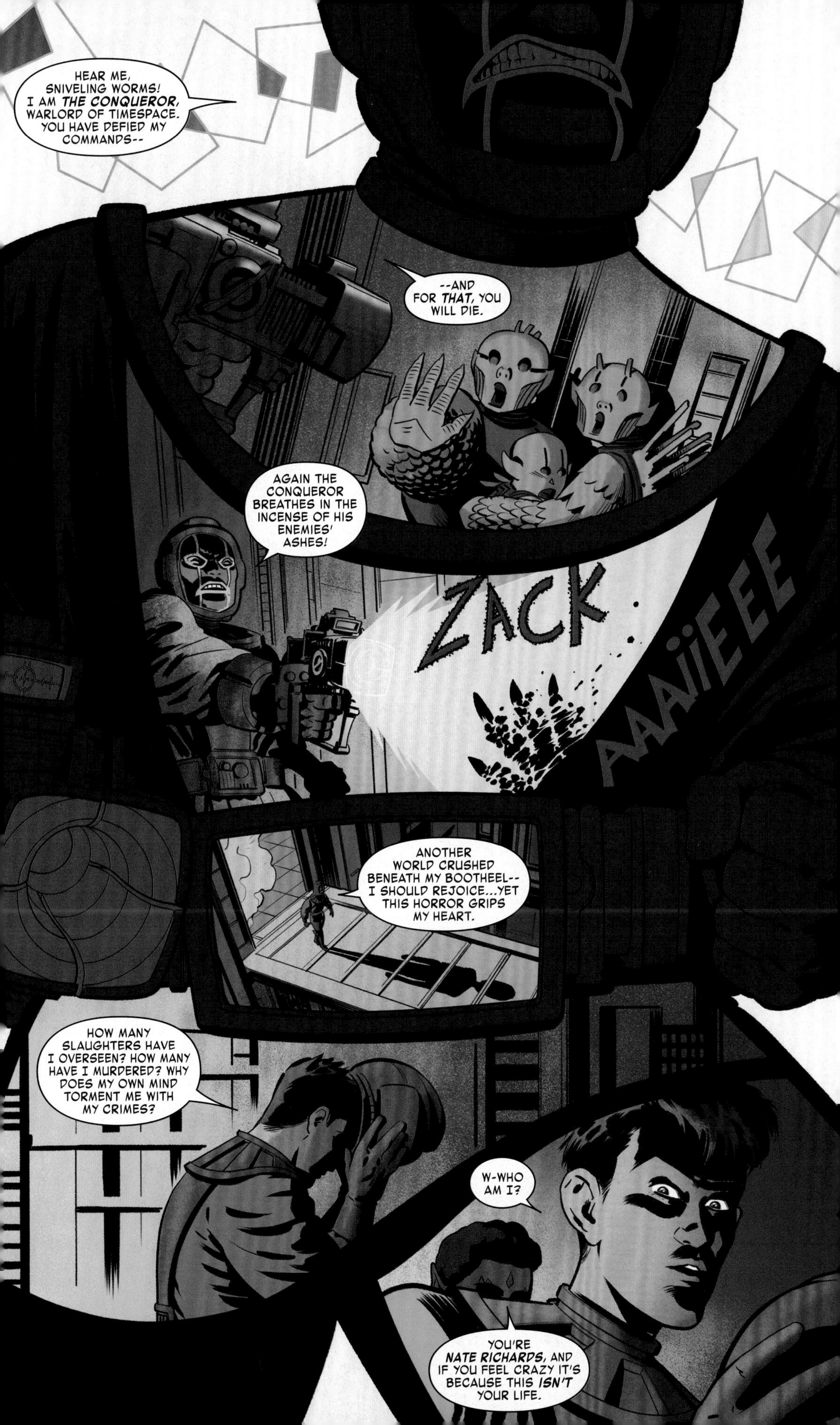
HEAR ME, SNIVELING WORMS! I AM *THE CONQUEROR,* WARLORD OF TIMESPACE. YOU HAVE DEFIED MY COMMANDS--
--AND FOR *THAT,* YOU WILL DIE.
AGAIN THE CONQUEROR BREATHES IN THE INCENSE OF HIS ENEMIES' ASHES!
ZACK
AAAIIEEE
ANOTHER WORLD CRUSHED BENEATH MY BOOTHEEL-- I SHOULD REJOICE...YET THIS HORROR GRIPS MY HEART.
HOW MANY SLAUGHTERS HAVE I OVERSEEN? HOW MANY HAVE I MURDERED? WHY DOES MY OWN MIND TORMENT ME WITH MY CRIMES?
W-WHO AM I?
YOU'RE *NATE RICHARDS,* AND IF YOU FEEL CRAZY IT'S BECAUSE THIS *ISN'T* YOUR LIFE.

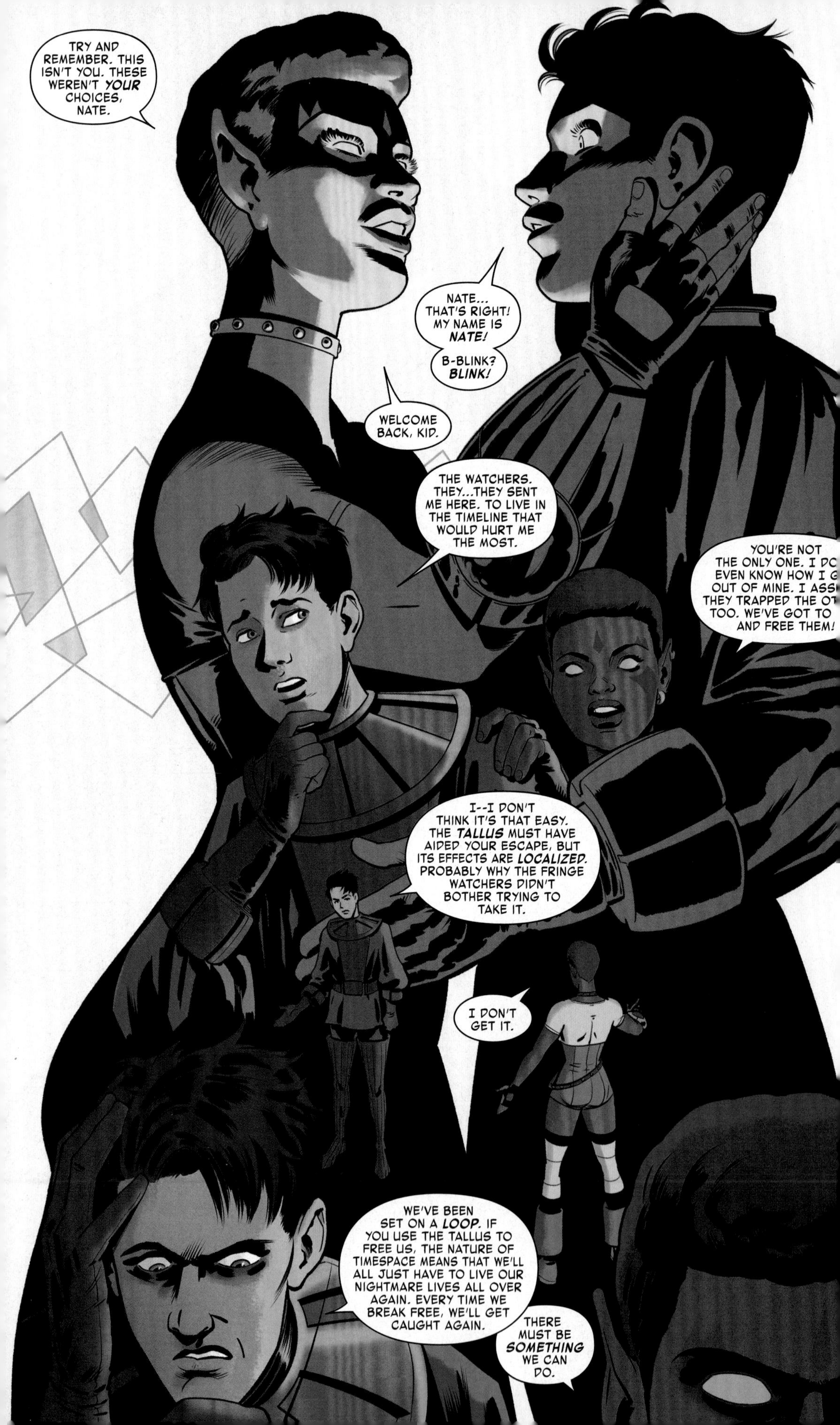
TRY AND REMEMBER. THIS ISN'T YOU. THESE WEREN'T YOUR CHOICES, NATE.
NATE... THAT'S RIGHT! MY NAME IS NATE!
B-BLINK? BLINK!
WELCOME BACK, KID.
THE WATCHERS. THEY...THEY SENT ME HERE. TO LIVE IN THE TIMELINE THAT WOULD HURT ME THE MOST.
YOU'RE NOT THE ONLY ONE. I DO EVEN KNOW HOW I G OUT OF MINE. I ASS THEY TRAPPED THE OT TOO. WE'VE GOT TO AND FREE THEM!
I--I DON'T THINK IT'S THAT EASY. THE TALLUS MUST HAVE AIDED YOUR ESCAPE, BUT ITS EFFECTS ARE LOCALIZED. PROBABLY WHY THE FRINGE WATCHERS DIDN'T BOTHER TRYING TO TAKE IT.
I DON'T GET IT.
WE'VE BEEN SET ON A LOOP. IF YOU USE THE TALLUS TO FREE US, THE NATURE OF TIMESPACE MEANS THAT WE'LL ALL JUST HAVE TO LIVE OUR NIGHTMARE LIVES ALL OVER AGAIN. EVERY TIME WE BREAK FREE, WE'LL GET CAUGHT AGAIN.
THERE MUST BE SOMETHING WE CAN DO.

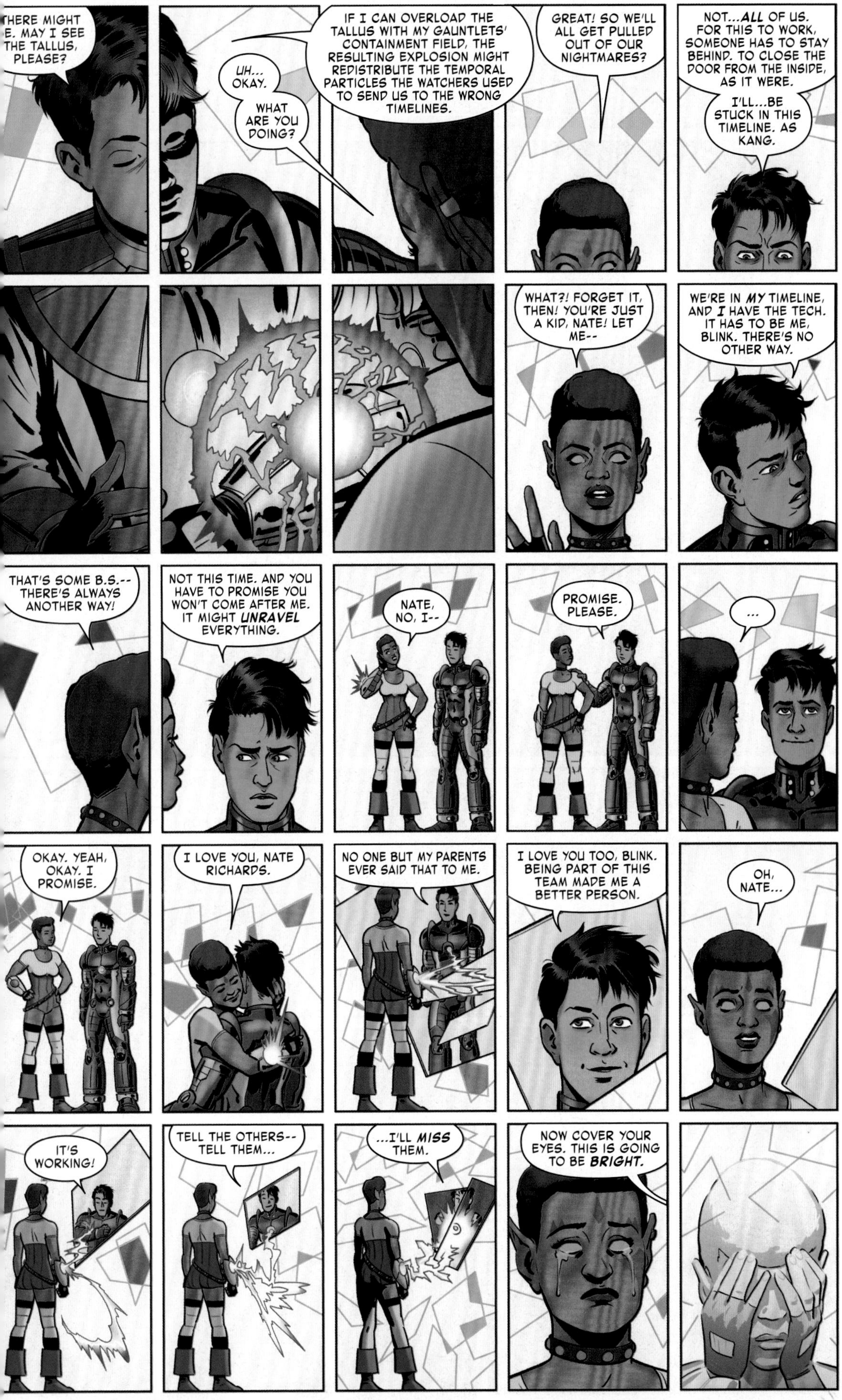
THERE MIGHT E. MAY I SEE THE TALLUS, PLEASE?
UH... OKAY.
WHAT ARE YOU DOING?
IF I CAN OVERLOAD THE TALLUS WITH MY GAUNTLETS' CONTAINMENT FIELD, THE RESULTING EXPLOSION MIGHT REDISTRIBUTE THE TEMPORAL PARTICLES THE WATCHERS USED TO SEND US TO THE WRONG TIMELINES.
GREAT! SO WE'LL ALL GET PULLED OUT OF OUR NIGHTMARES?
NOT...ALL OF US. FOR THIS TO WORK, SOMEONE HAS TO STAY BEHIND. TO CLOSE THE DOOR FROM THE INSIDE, AS IT WERE.
I'LL...BE STUCK IN THIS TIMELINE. AS KANG.
WHAT?! FORGET IT, THEN! YOU'RE JUST A KID, NATE! LET ME--
WE'RE IN MY TIMELINE, AND I HAVE THE TECH. IT HAS TO BE ME, BLINK. THERE'S NO OTHER WAY.
THAT'S SOME B.S.-- THERE'S ALWAYS ANOTHER WAY!
NOT THIS TIME. AND YOU HAVE TO PROMISE YOU WON'T COME AFTER ME. IT MIGHT UNRAVEL EVERYTHING.
NATE, NO, I--
PROMISE. PLEASE.
...
OKAY. YEAH, OKAY. I PROMISE.
I LOVE YOU, NATE RICHARDS.
NO ONE BUT MY PARENTS EVER SAID THAT TO ME.
I LOVE YOU TOO, BLINK. BEING PART OF THIS TEAM MADE ME A BETTER PERSON.
OH, NATE...
IT'S WORKING!
TELL THE OTHERS-- TELL THEM...
...I'LL MISS THEM.
NOW COVER YOUR EYES. THIS IS GOING TO BE BRIGHT.

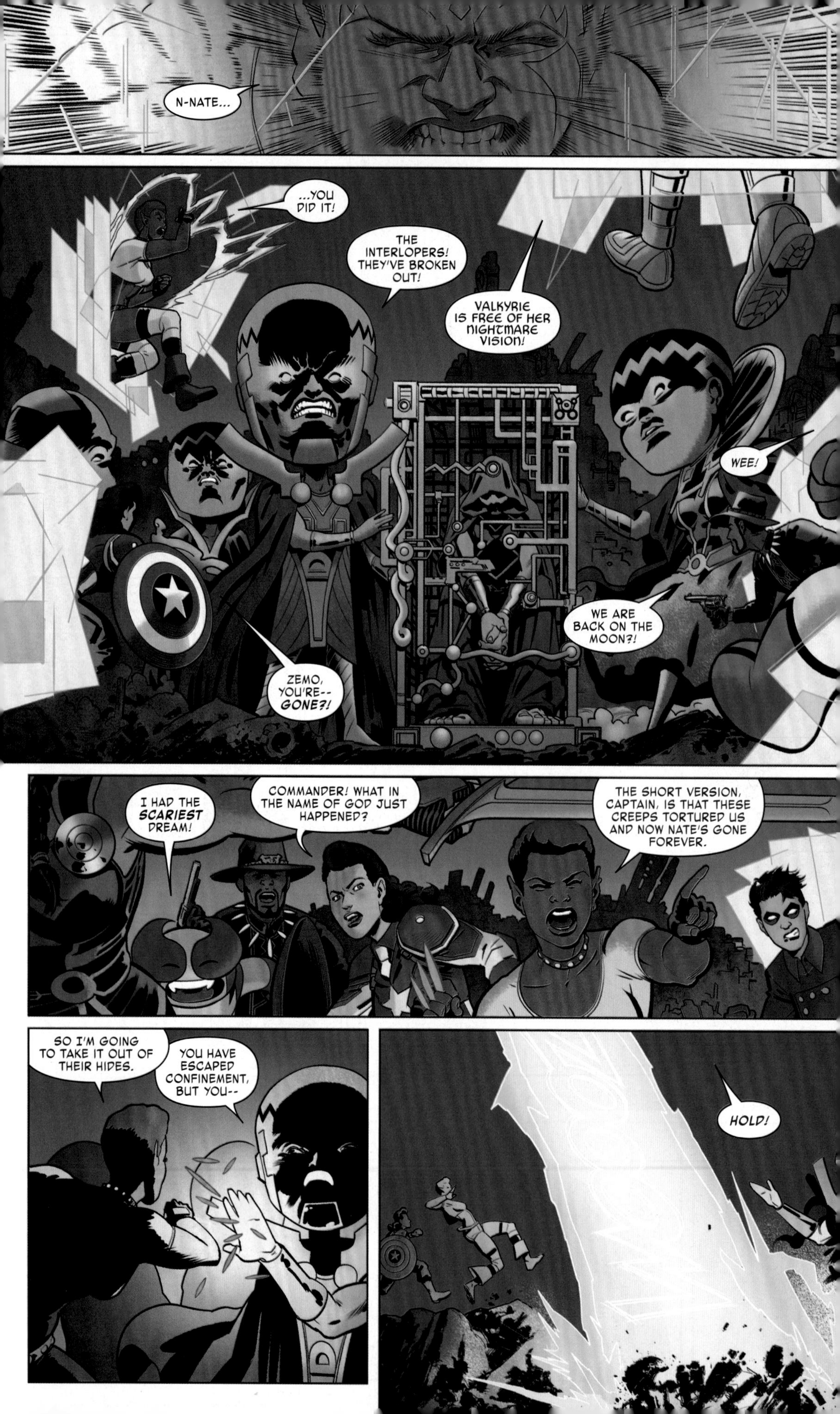
N-NATE...
...YOU DID IT!
THE INTERLOPERS! THEY'VE BROKEN OUT!
VALKYRIE IS FREE OF HER NIGHTMARE VISION!
WEE!
WE ARE BACK ON THE MOON?!
ZEMO, YOU'RE-- GONE?!
I HAD THE SCARIEST DREAM!
COMMANDER! WHAT IN THE NAME OF GOD JUST HAPPENED?
THE SHORT VERSION, CAPTAIN, IS THAT THESE CREEPS TORTURED US AND NOW NATE'S GONE FOREVER.
SO I'M GOING TO TAKE IT OUT OF THEIR HIDES.
YOU HAVE ESCAPED CONFINEMENT, BUT YOU--
HOLD!

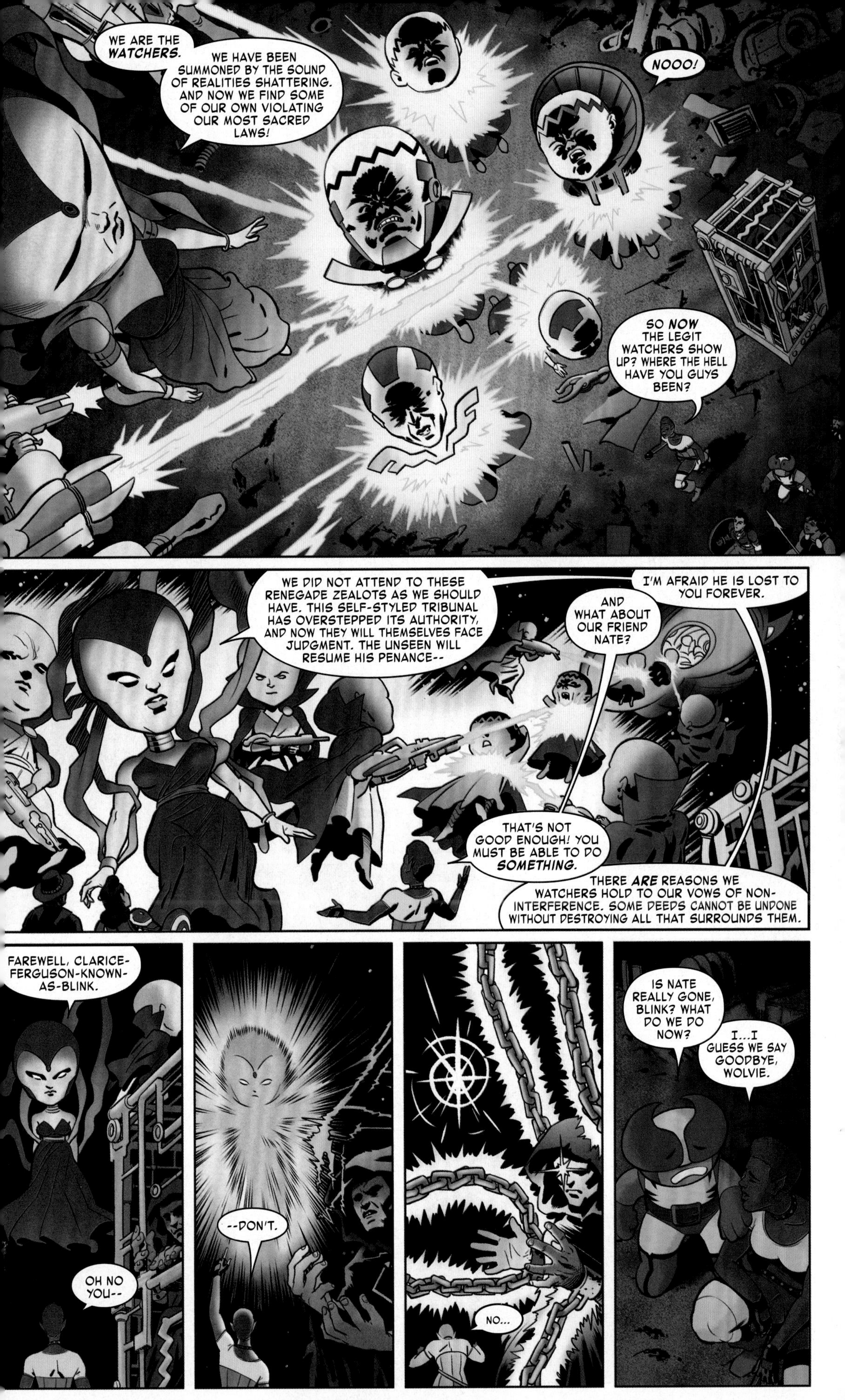
WE ARE THE WATCHERS.
WE HAVE BEEN SUMMONED BY THE SOUND OF REALITIES SHATTERING. AND NOW WE FIND SOME OF OUR OWN VIOLATING OUR MOST SACRED LAWS!
NOOO!
SO NOW THE LEGIT WATCHERS SHOW UP? WHERE THE HELL HAVE YOU GUYS BEEN?
WE DID NOT ATTEND TO THESE RENEGADE ZEALOTS AS WE SHOULD HAVE. THIS SELF-STYLED TRIBUNAL HAS OVERSTEPPED ITS AUTHORITY, AND NOW THEY WILL THEMSELVES FACE JUDGMENT. THE UNSEEN WILL RESUME HIS PENANCE--
AND WHAT ABOUT OUR FRIEND NATE?
I'M AFRAID HE IS LOST TO YOU FOREVER.
THAT'S NOT GOOD ENOUGH! YOU MUST BE ABLE TO DO SOMETHING.
THERE ARE REASONS WE WATCHERS HOLD TO OUR VOWS OF NON-INTERFERENCE. SOME DEEDS CANNOT BE UNDONE WITHOUT DESTROYING ALL THAT SURROUNDS THEM.
FAREWELL, CLARICE-FERGUSON-KNOWN-AS-BLINK.
OH NO YOU--
--DON'T.
NO...
IS NATE REALLY GONE, BLINK? WHAT DO WE DO NOW?
I...I GUESS WE SAY GOODBYE, WOLVIE.

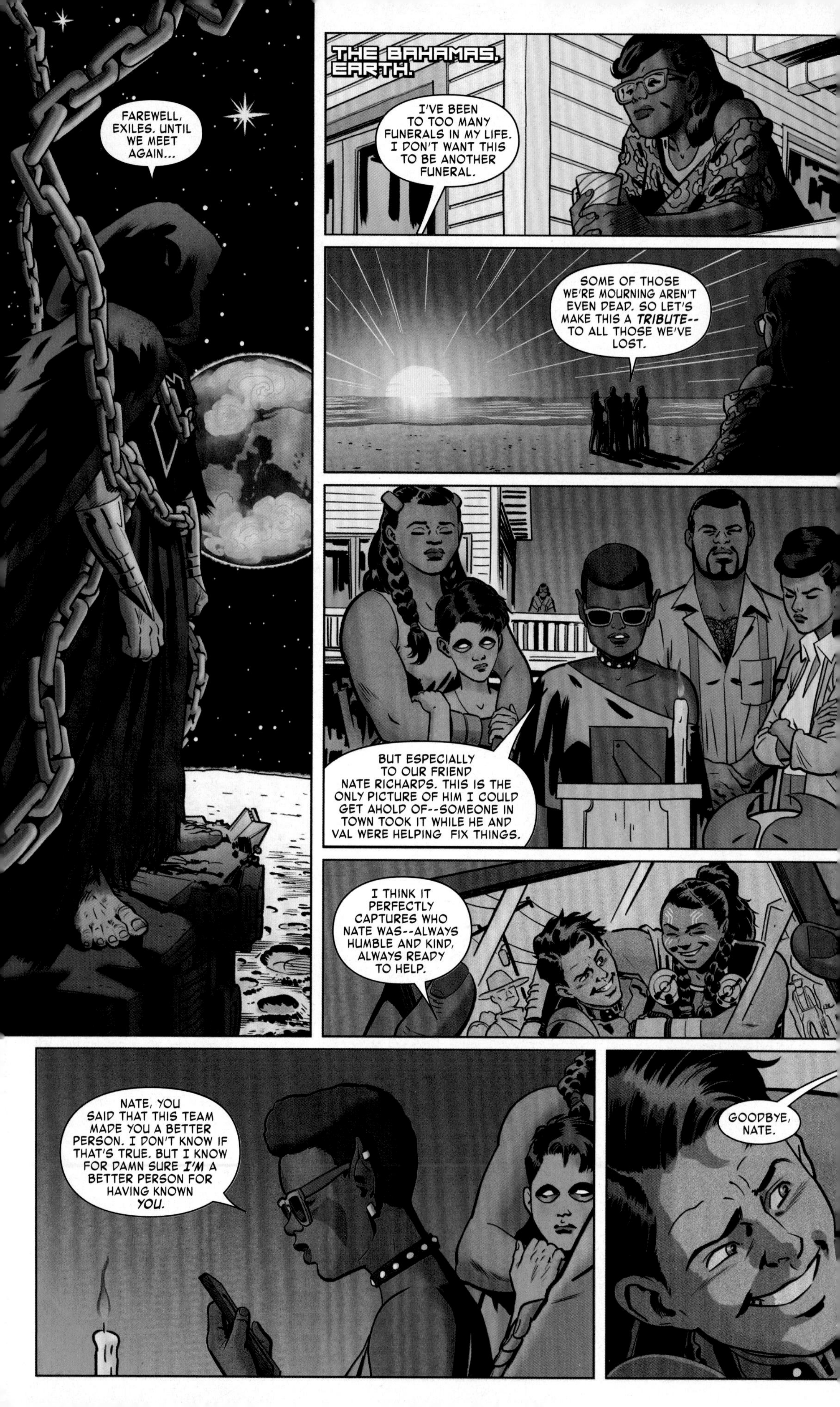

FAREWELL, EXILES. UNTIL WE MEET AGAIN...
THE BAHAMAS, EARTH.
I'VE BEEN TO TOO MANY FUNERALS IN MY LIFE. I DON'T WANT THIS TO BE ANOTHER FUNERAL.
SOME OF THOSE WE'RE MOURNING AREN'T EVEN DEAD. SO LET'S MAKE THIS A TRIBUTE-- TO ALL THOSE WE'VE LOST.
BUT ESPECIALLY TO OUR FRIEND NATE RICHARDS. THIS IS THE ONLY PICTURE OF HIM I COULD GET AHOLD OF--SOMEONE IN TOWN TOOK IT WHILE HE AND VAL WERE HELPING FIX THINGS.
I THINK IT PERFECTLY CAPTURES WHO NATE WAS--ALWAYS HUMBLE AND KIND, ALWAYS READY TO HELP.
NATE, YOU SAID THAT THIS TEAM MADE YOU A BETTER PERSON. I DON'T KNOW IF THAT'S TRUE. BUT I KNOW FOR DAMN SURE I'M A BETTER PERSON FOR HAVING KNOWN YOU.
GOODBYE, NATE.

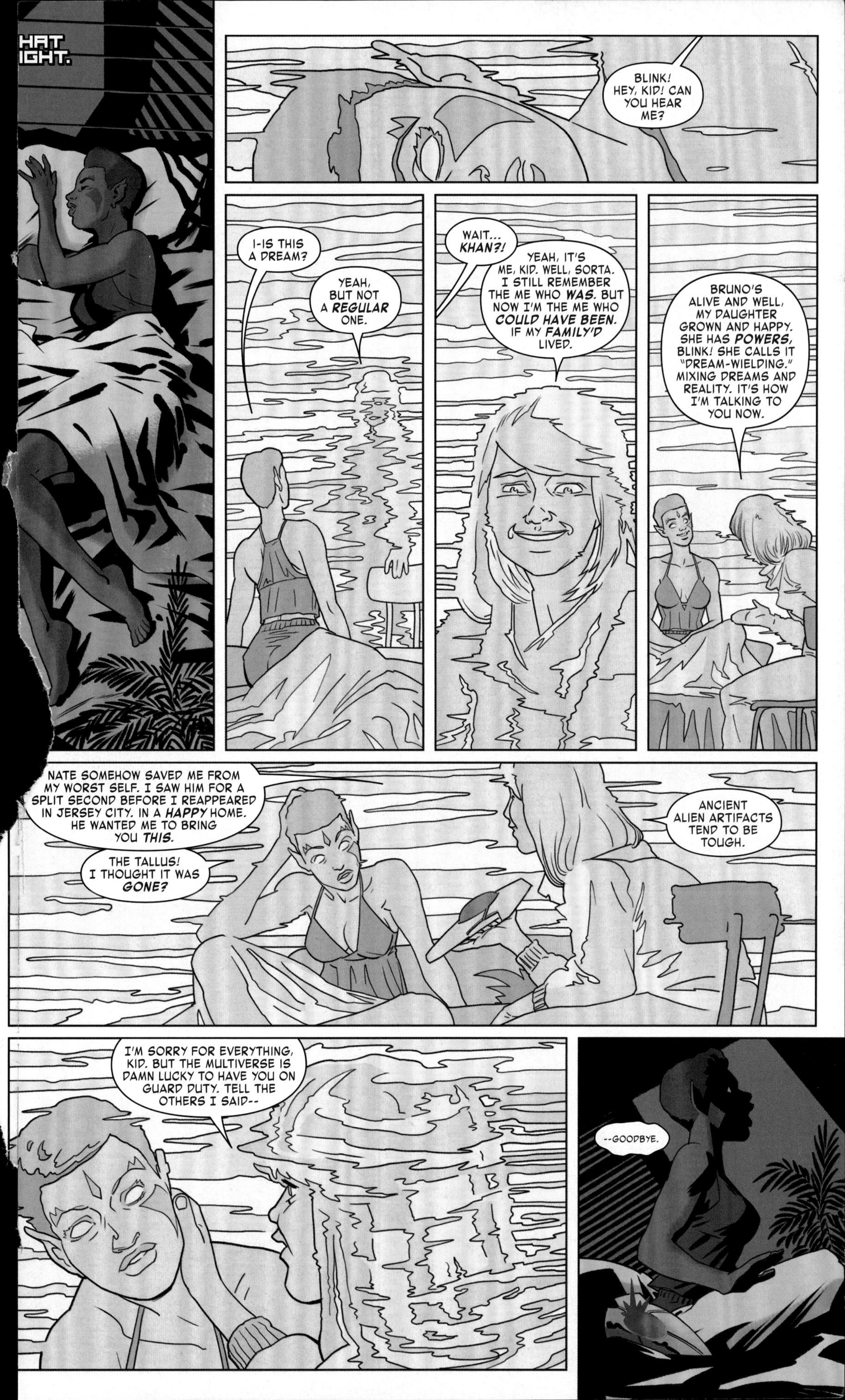
HAT
IGHT.
BLINK! HEY, KID! CAN YOU HEAR ME?
I-IS THIS A DREAM?
YEAH, BUT NOT A REGULAR ONE.
WAIT... KHAN?!
YEAH, IT'S ME, KID. WELL, SORTA. I STILL REMEMBER THE ME WHO WAS. BUT NOW I'M THE ME WHO COULD HAVE BEEN. IF MY FAMILY'D LIVED.
BRUNO'S ALIVE AND WELL, MY DAUGHTER GROWN AND HAPPY. SHE HAS POWERS, BLINK! SHE CALLS IT "DREAM-WIELDING." MIXING DREAMS AND REALITY. IT'S HOW I'M TALKING TO YOU NOW.
NATE SOMEHOW SAVED ME FROM MY WORST SELF. I SAW HIM FOR A SPLIT SECOND BEFORE I REAPPEARED IN JERSEY CITY. IN A HAPPY HOME. HE WANTED ME TO BRING YOU THIS.
THE TALLUS! I THOUGHT IT WAS GONE?
ANCIENT ALIEN ARTIFACTS TEND TO BE TOUGH.
I'M SORRY FOR EVERYTHING, KID. BUT THE MULTIVERSE IS DAMN LUCKY TO HAVE YOU ON GUARD DUTY. TELL THE OTHERS I SAID--
--GOODBYE.

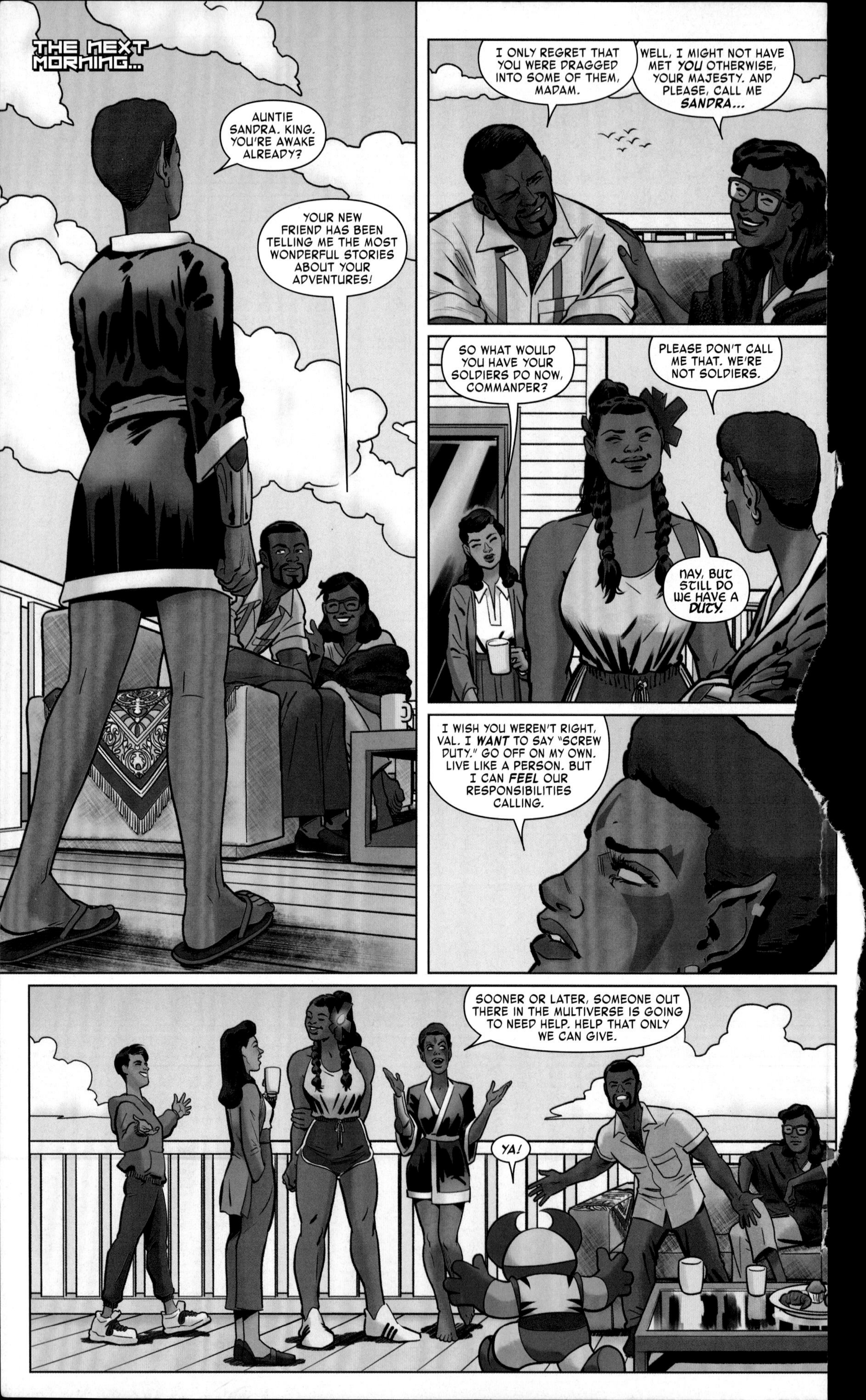
THE NEXT MORNING...
AUNTIE SANDRA. KING. YOU'RE AWAKE ALREADY?
YOUR NEW FRIEND HAS BEEN TELLING ME THE MOST WONDERFUL STORIES ABOUT YOUR ADVENTURES!
I ONLY REGRET THAT YOU WERE DRAGGED INTO SOME OF THEM, MADAM.
WELL, I MIGHT NOT HAVE MET YOU OTHERWISE, YOUR MAJESTY. AND PLEASE, CALL ME SANDRA...
SO WHAT WOULD YOU HAVE YOUR SOLDIERS DO NOW, COMMANDER?
PLEASE DON'T CALL ME THAT. WE'RE NOT SOLDIERS.
NAY, BUT STILL DO WE HAVE A DUTY.
I WISH YOU WEREN'T RIGHT, VAL. I WANT TO SAY "SCREW DUTY." GO OFF ON MY OWN. LIVE LIKE A PERSON. BUT I CAN FEEL OUR RESPONSIBILITIES CALLING.
SOONER OR LATER, SOMEONE OUT THERE IN THE MULTIVERSE IS GOING TO NEED HELP. HELP THAT ONLY WE CAN GIVE.
YA!

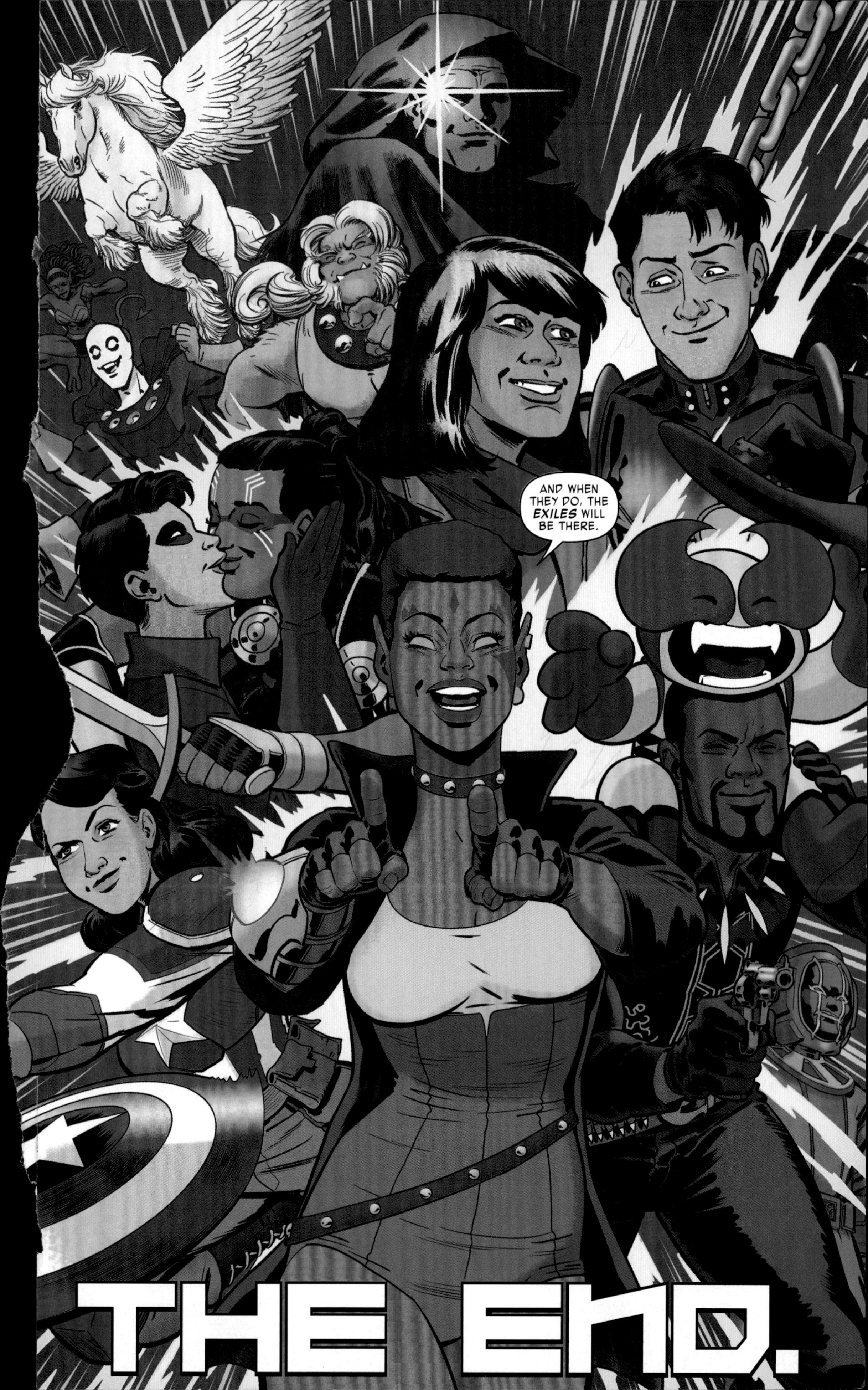
AND WHEN THEY DO, THE EXILES WILL BE THERE.
THE END.

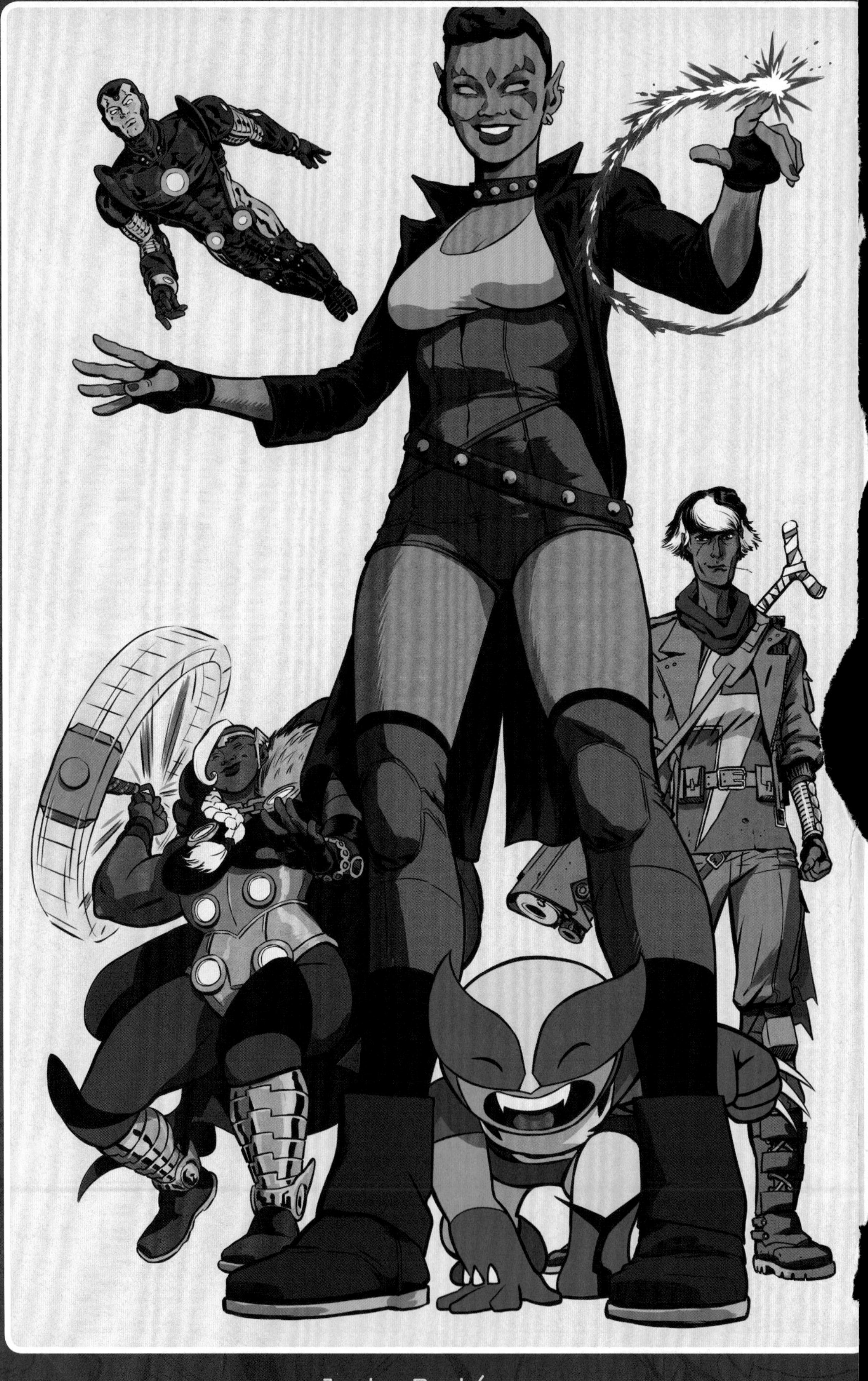

Javier Rodríguez
UNUSED VARIANT COVER

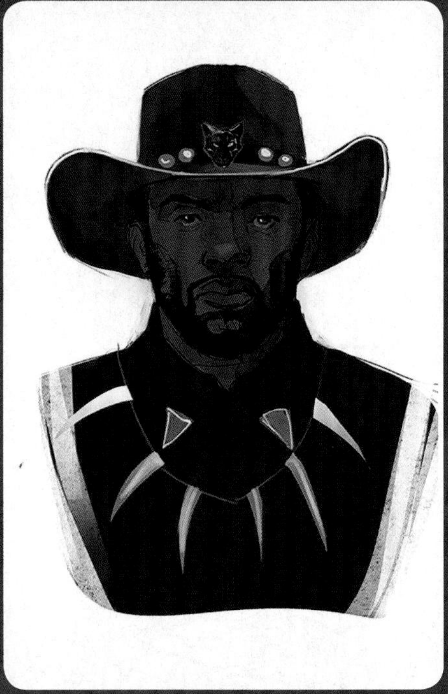

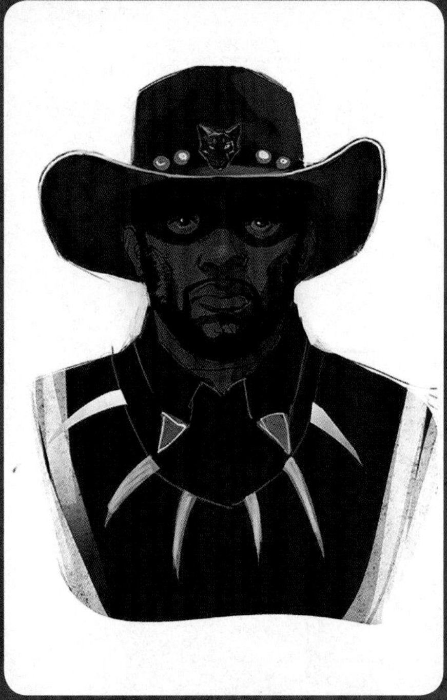

Javier Rodríguez
CALIPH DOOM CHARACTER DESIGN

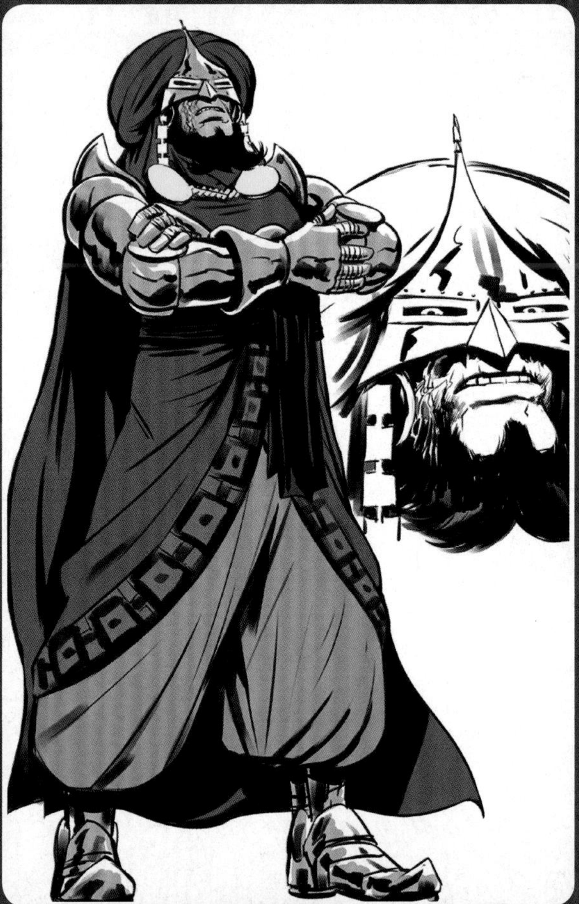

Javier Rodríguez

EXILES #9 LAYOUTS, PAGES 1-4

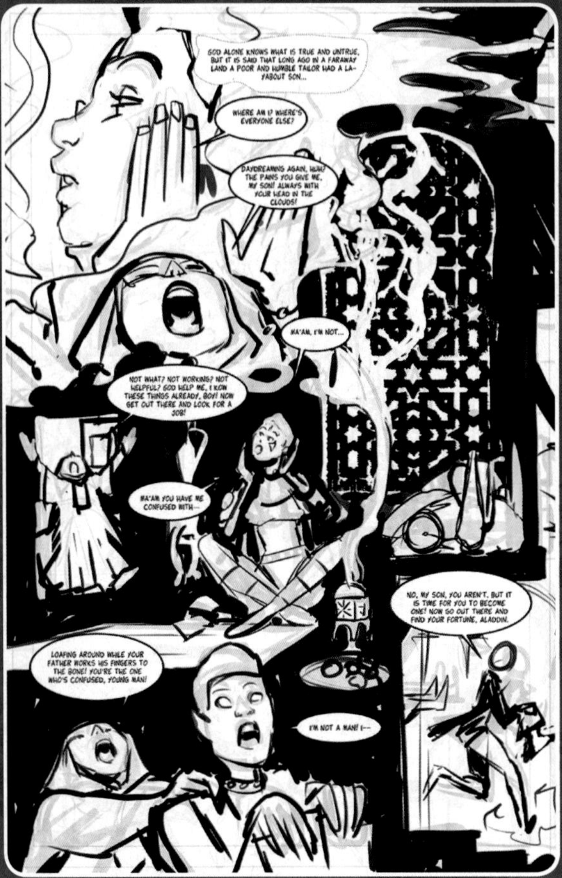
GOD ALONE KNOWS WHAT IS TRUE AND UNTRUE, BUT IT IS SAID THAT LONG AGO IN A FARAWAY LAND A POOR AND HUMBLE TAILOR HAD A LA-YABOUT SON...
WHERE AM I? WHERE'S EVERYONE ELSE?
DAYDREAMING AGAIN, HUH? THE PAINS YOU GIVE ME, MY SON! ALWAYS WITH YOUR HEAD IN THE CLOUDS!
MA'AM, I'M NOT...
NOT WHAT? NOT WORKING? NOT HELPFUL? GOD HELP ME, I KOW THESE THINGS ALREADY, BOY! NOW GET OUT THERE AND LOOK FOR A JOB!
MA'AM YOU HAVE ME CONFUSED WITH--
LOAFING AROUND WHILE YOUR FATHER WORKS HIS FINGERS TO THE BONE! YOU'RE THE ONE WHO'S CONFUSED, YOUNG MAN!
I'M NOT A MAN! I--
NO, MY SON, YOU AREN'T. BUT IT IS TIME FOR YOU TO BECOME ONE! NOW GO OUT THERE AND FIND YOUR FORTUNE, ALADDIN.

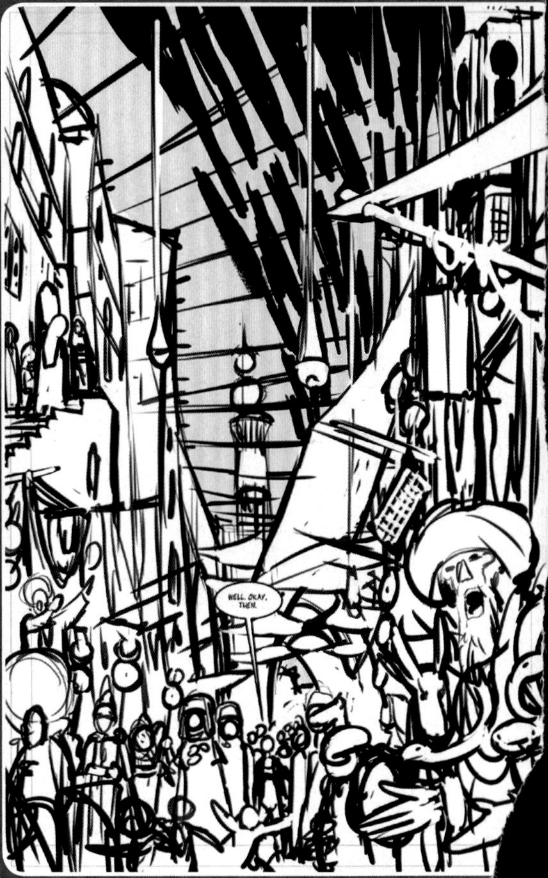
WELL. OKAY, THEN.

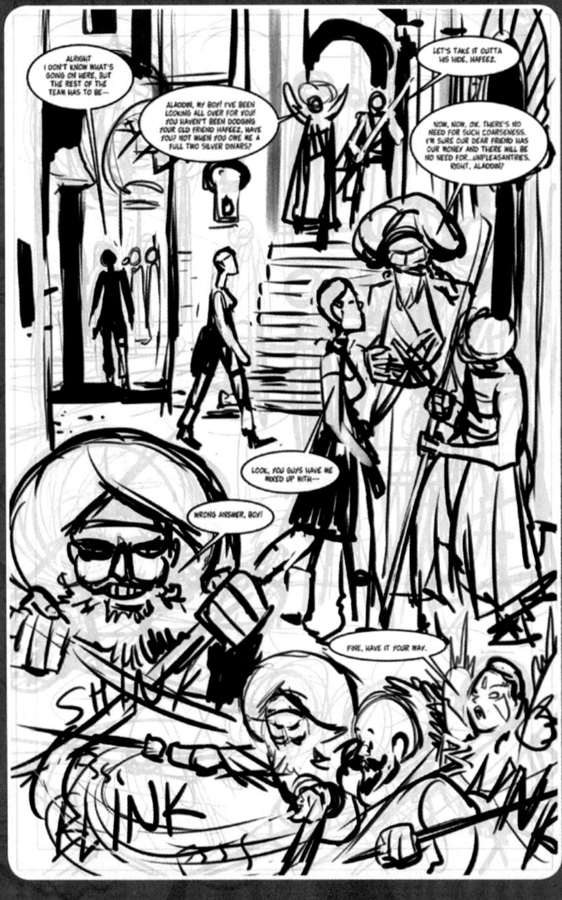
ALRIGHT I DON'T KNOW WHAT'S GOING ON HERE, BUT THE REST OF THE TEAM HAS TO BE--
ALADDIN, MY BOY! I'VE BEEN LOOKING ALL OVER FOR YOU! YOU HAVEN'T BEEN DODGING YOUR OLD FRIEND HAFEEZ, HAVE YOU? NOT WHEN YOU OWE ME A FULL TWO SILVER DINARS?
LET'S TAKE IT OUTTA HIS HIDE, HAFEEZ.
NOW, NOW, OX. THERE'S NO NEED FOR SUCH COARSENESS. I'M SURE OUR DEAR FRIEND HAS OUR MONEY AND THERE WILL BE NO NEED FOR...UNPLEASANTRIES. RIGHT, ALADDIN?
LOOK, YOU GUYS HAVE ME MIXED UP WITH--
WRONG ANSWER, BOY!
FINE, HAVE IT YOUR WAY.
SHUNK
INK

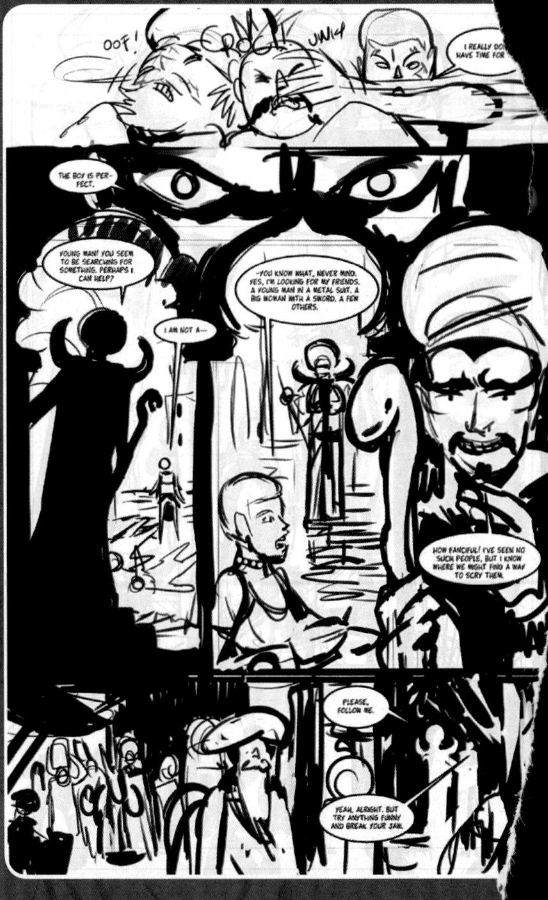
OOF!
CROC
UNK
THE BOY IS PER-FECT.
YOUNG MAN! YOU SEEM TO BE SEARCHING FOR SOMETHING. PERHAPS I CAN HELP?
I AM NOT A--
-YOU KNOW WHAT, NEVER MIND. YES, I'M LOOKING FOR MY FRIENDS. A YOUNG MAN IN A METAL SUIT. A BIG WOMAN WITH A SWORD. A FEW OTHERS.
HOW FANCIFUL! I'VE SEEN NO SUCH PEOPLE, BUT I KNOW WHERE WE MIGHT FIND A WAY TO SCRY THEM.
PLEASE, FOLLOW ME.
YEAH, ALRIGHT. BUT TRY ANYTHING FUNNY AND BREAK YOUR JAW.

Javier Rodríguez

EXILES #9 LAYOUTS, PAGES 5, 8-10

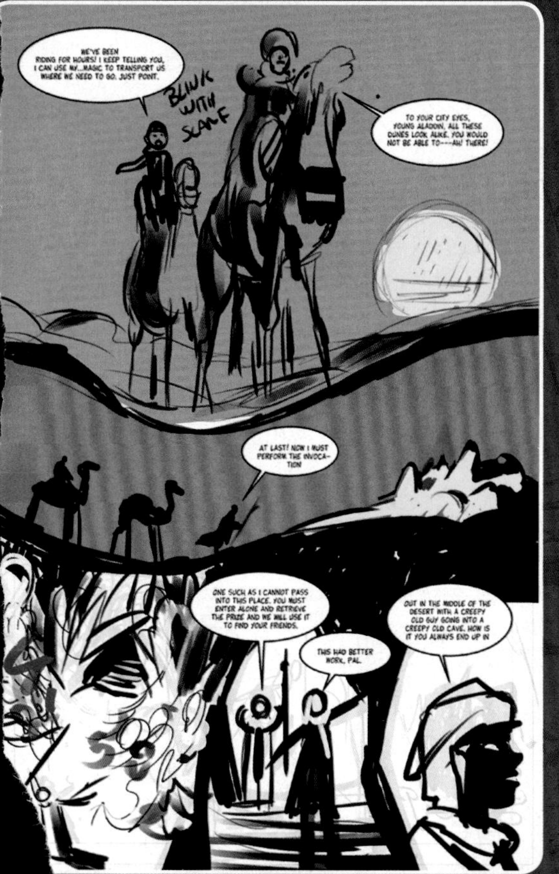

WE'VE BEEN RIDING FOR HOURS! I KEEP TELLING YOU, I CAN USE MY...MAGIC TO TRANSPORT US WHERE WE NEED TO GO. JUST POINT.
BLINK WITH SCARF
TO YOUR CITY EYES, YOUNG ALADDIN, ALL THESE DUNES LOOK ALIKE. YOU WOULD NOT BE ABLE TO---AH! THERE!
AT LAST! NOW I MUST PERFORM THE INVOCATION
ONE SUCH AS I CANNOT PASS INTO THIS PLACE. YOU MUST ENTER ALONE AND RETRIEVE THE PRIZE AND WE WILL USE IT TO FIND YOUR FRIENDS.
THIS HAD BETTER WORK, PAL.
OUT IN THE MIDDLE OF THE DESERT WITH A CREEPY OLD GUY GOING INTO A CREEPY OLD CAVE. HOW IS IT YOU ALWAYS END UP IN

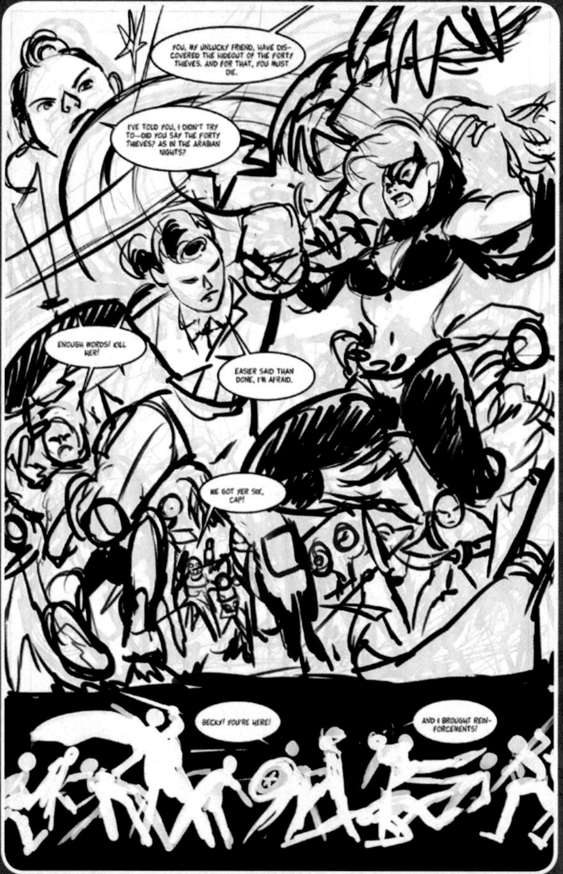

YOU, MY UNLUCKY FRIEND, HAVE DISCOVERED THE HIDEOUT OF THE FORTY THIEVES. AND FOR THAT, YOU MUST DIE.
I'VE TOLD YOU, I DIDN'T TRY TO—DID YOU SAY THE FORTY THIEVES? AS IN THE ARABIAN NIGHTS?
ENOUGH WORDS! KILL HER!
EASIER SAID THAN DONE, I'M AFRAID.
WE GOT YER SIX, CAP!
BECKY! YOU'RE HERE!
AND I BROUGHT REINFORCEMENTS!

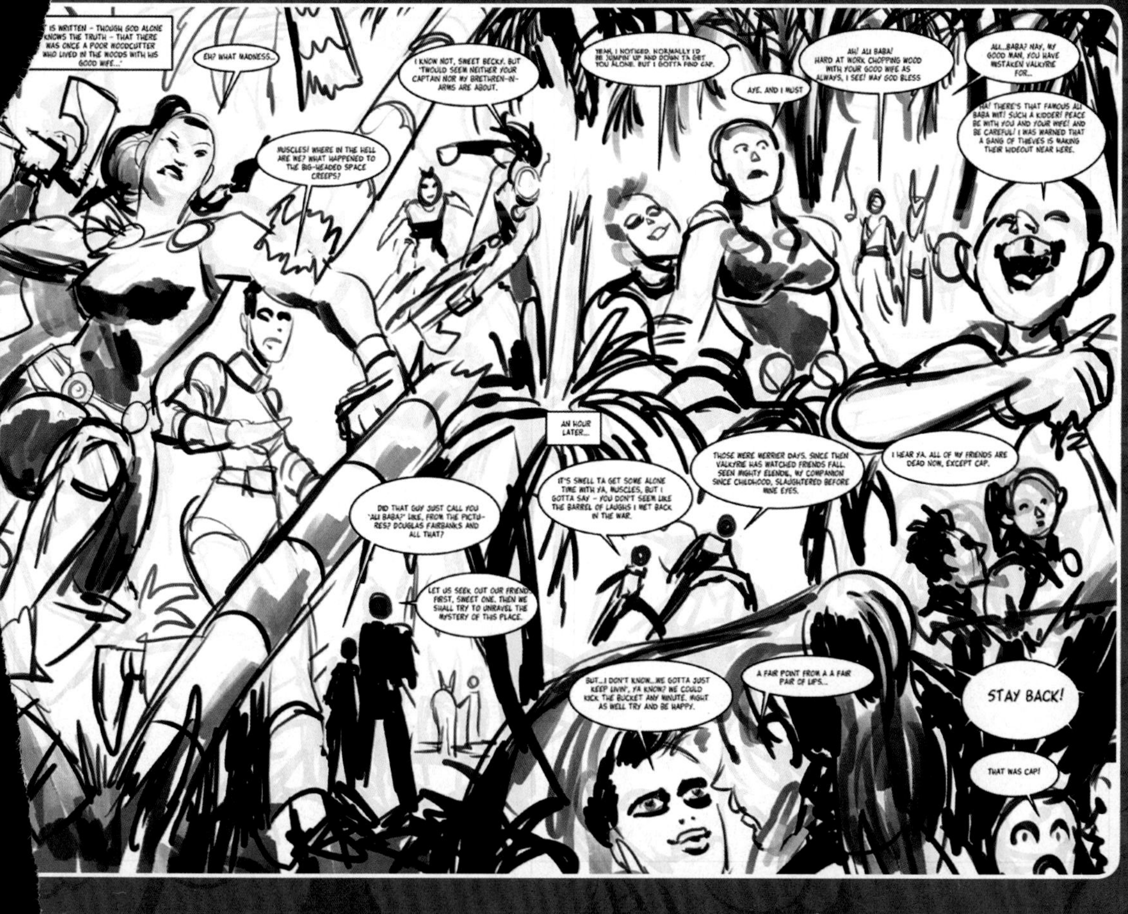

IT IS WRITTEN - THOUGH GOD ALONE KNOWS THE TRUTH - THAT THERE WAS ONCE A POOR WOODCUTTER WHO LIVED IN THE WOODS WITH HIS GOOD WIFE...'
EH? WHAT MADNESS...
I KNOW NOT, SWEET BECKY. BUT 'TWOULD SEEM NEITHER YOUR CAPTAIN NOR MY BRETHREN-IN-ARMS ARE ABOUT.
MUSCLES! WHERE IN THE HELL ARE WE? WHAT HAPPENED TO THE BIG-HEADED SPACE CREEPS?
YEAH, I NOTICED. NORMALLY I'D BE JUMPIN' UP AND DOWN TA GET YOU ALONE. BUT I GOTTA FIND CAP.
AYE. AND I MUST
AH! ALI BABA! HARD AT WORK CHOPPING WOOD WITH YOUR GOOD WIFE AS ALWAYS, I SEE! MAY GOD BLESS
ALI...BABA? NAY, MY GOOD MAN, YOU HAVE MISTAKEN VALKYRIE FOR...
HA! THERE'S THAT FAMOUS ALI BABA WIT! SUCH A KIDDER! PEACE BE WITH YOU AND YOUR WIFE! AND BE CAREFUL! I WAS WARNED THAT A GANG OF THIEVES IS MAKING THEIR HIDEOUT NEAR HERE.
AN HOUR LATER...
DID THAT GUY JUST CALL YOU 'ALI BABA?' LIKE, FROM THE PICTURES? DOUGLAS FAIRBANKS AND ALL THAT?
LET US SEEK OUT OUR FRIENDS FIRST, SWEET ONE. THEN WE SHALL TRY TO UNRAVEL THE MYSTERY OF THIS PLACE.
IT'S SWELL TA GET SOME ALONE TIME WITH YA, MUSCLES, BUT I GOTTA SAY - YOU DON'T SEEM LIKE THE BARREL OF LAUGHS I MET BACK IN THE WAR.
THOSE WERE MERRIER DAYS. SINCE THEN VALKYRIE HAS WATCHED FRIENDS FALL. SEEN MIGHTY ELENDIL, MY COMPANION SINCE CHILDHOOD, SLAUGHTERED BEFORE MINE EYES.
I HEAR YA. ALL OF MY FRIENDS ARE DEAD NOW, EXCEPT CAP.
BUT...I DON'T KNOW...WE GOTTA JUST KEEP LIVIN', YA KNOW? WE COULD KICK THE BUCKET ANY MINUTE. MIGHT AS WELL TRY AND BE HAPPY.
A FAIR POINT FROM A A FAIR PAIR OF LIPS...
STAY BACK!
THAT WAS CAP!

Javier Rodríguez

EXILES #12 PENCILS, PAGES 6-12

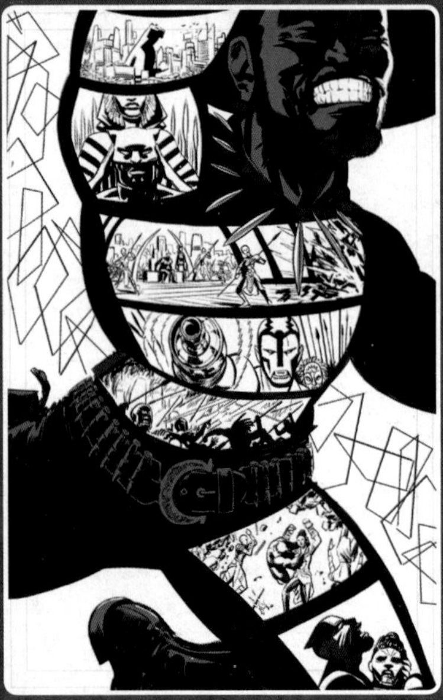

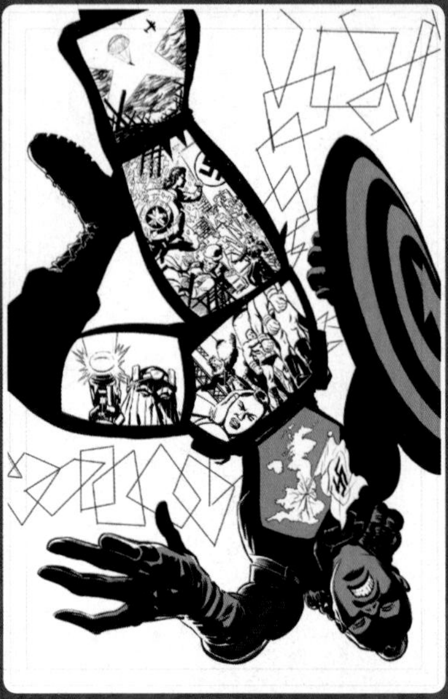

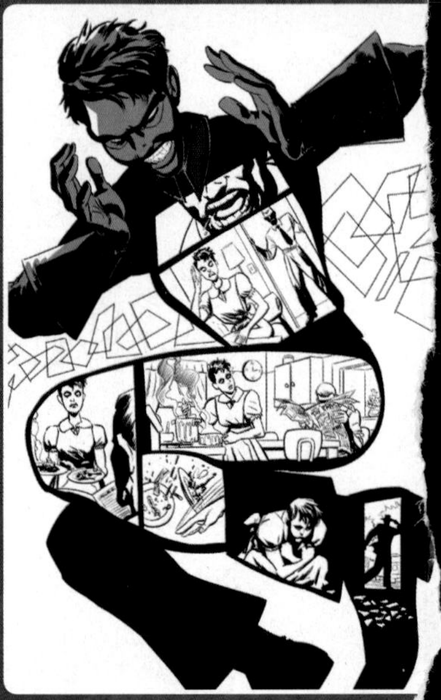

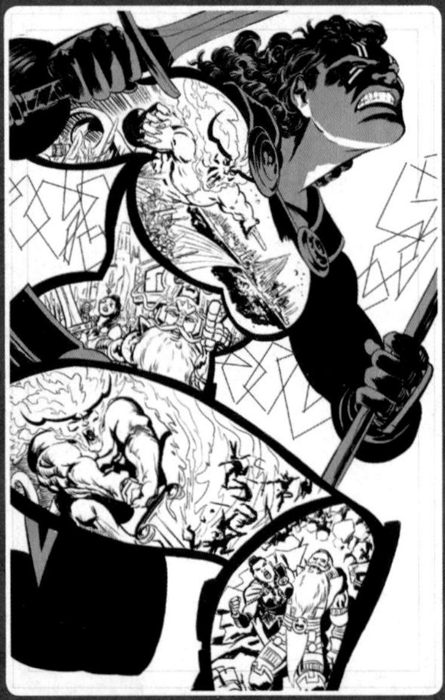

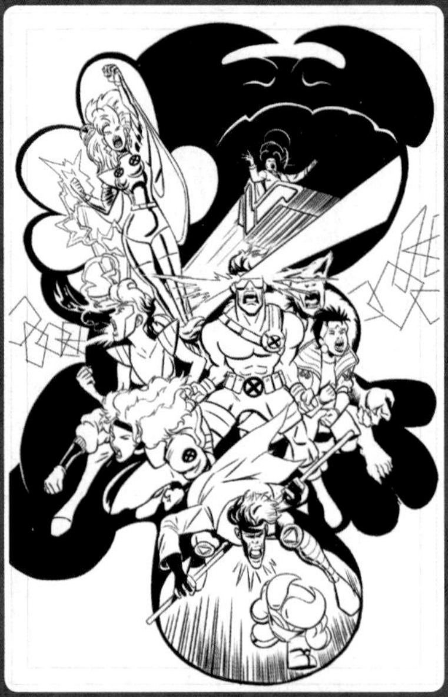

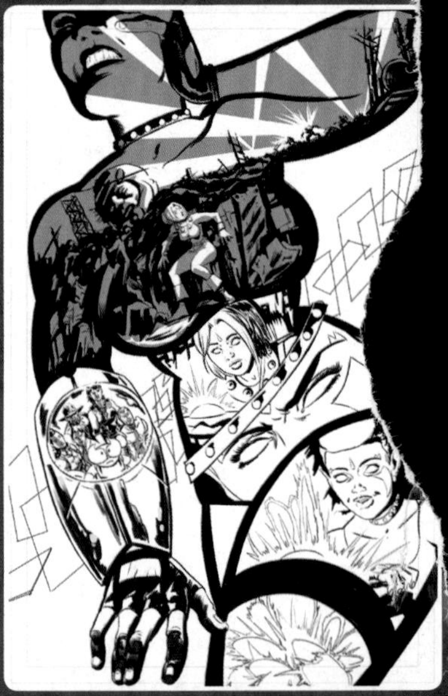

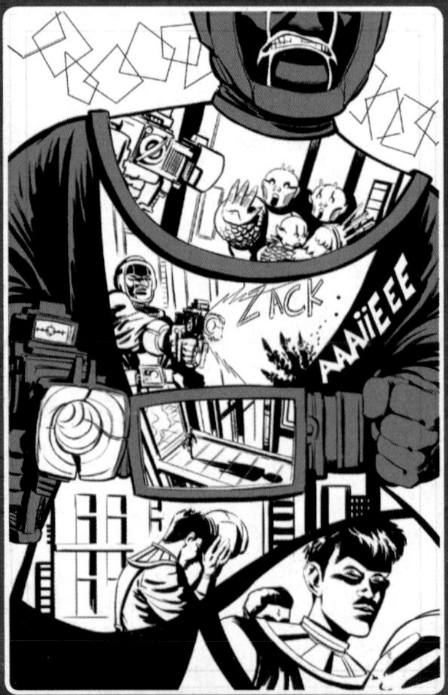
ZACK
AAAiiEEE